"Outstanding memoir . . . as well as closely observed, poignant, and wistful. This is a valuable first-person account of growing up in every way on a property that fewer and fewer of us will see again: the family ranch."

— C. J. Box, #1 *New York Times* bestselling author of *Three-Inch Teeth*

"Magic, understanding, and truth lie within these pages. Mark Miller takes us into the heart of compassion for the people and animals, to tragedy, back-breaking hard work, and the wind-powered love of the land and its creatures. . . . *A Sometimes Paradise* is a masterwork."

— W. Michael Gear and Kathleen O'Neal Gear, *New York Times* bestselling authors

"This fabulous firsthand account about a harsh, unforgiving life is also about a deep love and respect for nature, for animals, and, most importantly, for family and dear friends. A superb story well told."

— David Crow, award-winning author of *The Pale-Faced Lie*

"Mark Miller's tales of the I Lazy D Ranch are as true and strong as the snubbing post his father plants in the center of the corral. *A Sometimes Paradise* is a beautiful book that earns its spurs by reminding us that without the nourishment of care and wisdom, none of our Wests can survive."

— Alyson Hagy, author of *Boleto* and *Ghosts of Wyoming*

"A gritty, poignant account of ranching. . . . The place where he grew up . . . inspired Mark to a career in archaeology, and as a writer who knows how to turn hard ranch work into inspiring stories."

— Candy Moulton, author of the Spur Award–winning biography *Sacajawea*

A
SOMETIMES
PARADISE

Reflections on Life
in a Wyoming Ranch Family

MARK E. MILLER

SANDRA JONAS
PUBLISHING

Sandra Jonas Publishing House
PO Box 20892
Boulder, CO 80308
sandrajonaspublishing.com

Printed in the United States of America
29 28 27 26 25 24   2 3 4 5 6 7 8

Book and cover design by Sandra Jonas

Publisher's Cataloging-in-Publication Data
Names: Miller, Mark E., 1951–, author.
Title: A Sometimes Paradise: Reflections on Life in a Wyoming Ranch Family / Mark E. Miller.
Description: Boulder, CO : Sandra Jonas Publishing, 2024. | Includes bibliographical references.
Identifiers: LCCN 2024935089 ISBN 9781954861152 (hardcover) | ISBN 9781954861169 (paperback)
Subjects: LCSH: Miller, Mark E., 1951– | Ranch life — Wyoming — Carbon County. | Carbon County (Wyo.) — Social life and customs — 20th century. | Carbon County (Wyo.) — Biography. | LCGFT: Autobiographies. | BISAC: BIOGRAPHY & AUTOBIOGRAPHY / Personal Memoirs.
Classification: LCC F567 .C2 .M555 | DDC 978.786
LC record available at http://lccn.loc.gov/2024935089

An earlier version of chapter 10, "Following Frank's Fences," first appeared in *Wyoming Fence Lines: An Anthology of Prose and Poetry*, edited by David Romtvedt and published in 2007 by the Wyoming Humanities Council and Wyoming Arts Council, and is reprinted by permission.

Photography credits: page ix, bottom: Wyoming State Historic Preservation Office; page x: from a base map by ESRI, Digital Globe, GeoEye, Earth Star, Geographics, CNES/Airbus DS, USDA, USGS, AEX, Getmapping, Aerogrid, IGN, IGP, swisstopo, and the GIS user community, courtesy of Wyoming State Historic Preservation Office; page 144: courtesy of Wyoming State Archives. All other photographs are from the author's private collection.

*To my grandparents
Kirk and Marguerite "Peg" Miller,
who introduced me to the cowboy culture
at an early age.*

*And to my parents,
Betty Rose and Frank E. Miller,
who taught me by example how to be
a compassionate person.*

Contents

PEOPLE AND CULTURE

FAMILY ARCHAEOLOGY

I Lazy D Ranch headquarters.

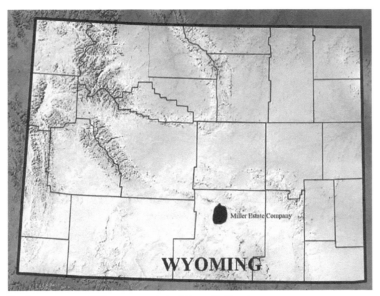

Bird's-eye view of Wyoming and the I Lazy D Ranch.

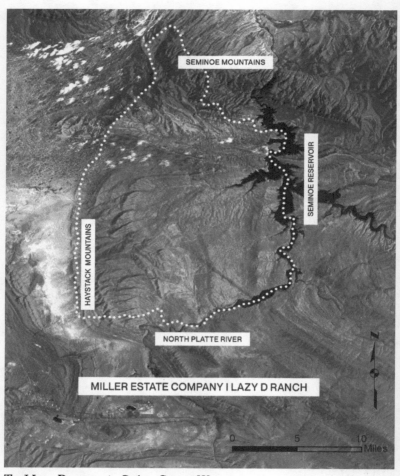

SEMINOE MOUNTAINS

SEMINOE RESERVOIR

HAYSTACK MOUNTAINS

NORTH PLATTE RIVER

MILLER ESTATE COMPANY I LAZY D RANCH

N

0   5   10
Miles

The I Lazy D country in Carbon County, Wyoming.

Miller Family Tree

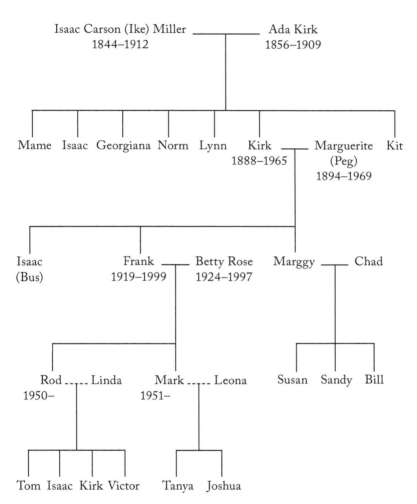

Isaac Carson (Ike) Miller   Ada Kirk
1844–1912   1856–1909

Mame   Isaac   Georgiana   Norm   Lynn   Kirk —— Marguerite   Kit
                                           1888–1965   (Peg)
                                                  1894–1969

Isaac   Frank —— Betty Rose   Marggy —— Chad
(Bus)   1919–1999   1924–1997

Rod ..... Linda   Mark ..... Leona   Susan   Sandy   Bill
1950–   1951–

Tom   Isaac   Kirk   Victor   Tanya   Joshua

Author's Note

This memoir is a work of historical nonfiction. The people, places, and events are real. Most of the scenes and conversations are portrayed as I remember them or as they were related to me by others who were there. In some cases, I consulted outside sources, which are listed in the bibliography. The names of a few individuals have been changed.

A difference exists between actual historical events and those we remember. Sometimes the difference is great, at other times small. Anyone who has researched the human past realizes that most of our history is unrecorded. That deficiency doesn't make spoken stories any less important, but it does encourage authors to document personal experiences and oral traditions as I have attempted here.

PART 1

Family Ranching

Grandpa Kirk and the five grandkids. 1955. *Left to right:* Me, Kirk, Bill, Rod, Susan, and Sandy.

Rod (*left*) and me in our playpen in the front yard at the I Lazy D about 1953. Even kids needed pens until they were old enough to negotiate the rugged country at the ranch.

1.

The I Lazy D

"Be careful, Mark! You can study family history too hard," Aunt Kit told me after finishing one of her stories. "If you dig too deep, you might learn things you wish you hadn't."

I hesitated, my mind filled with questions. Maybe she was right. No, I decided, I wanted to know it all.

I was twenty-eight then, a few months after I had defended my doctoral dissertation in anthropology on prehistoric settlements in northern Colorado. During my research, I kept thinking about the ranch in Carbon County, Wyoming, where I'd grown up. How had my family survived in that rugged country between the Central and Southern Rocky Mountains? Surely, my oldest living relative could give me some clues, so on a bright spring day in 1980, I drove to the Park Manor home for the elderly in Rawlins to see her.

She and I had been talking about her father, Isaac Carson Miller, my great-grandfather Ike, who started the ranch in 1881. Aunt Kit was the youngest daughter of the "old gent," as her brother Kirk called him.

At the time of our conversation—nearly a hundred years after the ranch began—Kit was an octogenarian. Her own adult children had moved her to the facility a couple of months earlier when she became too frail to live unattended. She accepted her exile with dignity, but her ageless, homespun intellect never faltered.

"It doesn't matter, Aunt Kit. I want to know everything about our history, good or bad. And you're the only one left who lived back then."

Wistful tears filled her ancient dark eyes. Closing them, she leaned her frail body back into her floral easy chair and surrendered to the haunting memories of her youth. An easy silence fell between us, and I looked out the window at the budding trees, waiting to continue.

Events and stories from the past preserve the footsteps of our ancestors and the paths they chose, connecting living family members to their heritage and to the routes we follow today. At its basic level, humanity itself is a product of countless, untold family histories.

Suddenly, Aunt Kit opened her eyes wide. "The I Lazy D Ranch is our legacy, Mark," she said, her chin jutting forward with pride. "Papa loved the place, so I loved it too."

For more than a century, Mother Nature fueled a perpetual transformation around the Miller clan, defining the extraordinary artistry in both the landscape and the diverse inhabitants. We successfully evolved in that dynamic setting, its rugged character kindling many family conversations over coffee.

Our large dining room table sat up to a dozen people at a time. The wooden chairs came from an old schoolhouse, originally attached to writing desks that Grandpa Kirk sawed off. One morning when I was eighteen, I joined my father, Frank, at that table with a geologist friend of his, E. A. Merewether.

Dad was a lean, chiseled cowboy who managed the ranch at that time, stoic in demeanor and deliberately inquisitive about every aspect of our country. There was no subject he ignored.

He lit a cigarette. "So where are you headed today?" he asked Merewether.

"Wild Horse Mountain."

Merewether had been doing field work at the ranch during his summer season, investigating past geological events. He hiked across our pastures, carrying plastic tubes full of charts and scribbled notes, and mapped the undulating topography, plotted the configuration of uneven landforms, and described the colorful bedrock.

"Your pastures used to be underwater millions of years ago," he told us.

"No kidding?" Dad said. "How do you know? Show me." He looked over at me. "Want to come?"

I never turned down a chance to explore with him—his unwavering curiosity always kept me excited. The three of us squeezed into Dad's pickup and took off for Wild Horse Mountain. On the way, Merewether told us about the interior seaway that had once divided the continent into two, covering a band of states from Texas to Montana. As we parked, I imagined a vast, turbulent ocean before us.

Facing the distant skyline, Merewether swept his arm in a wide arc. "Water levels here reached depths of more than a thousand feet. Only marine organisms could survive."

He pointed to a large hill near us covered in fractured seashells glistening in the sun. "When the ocean receded, those organisms died, and the sediments containing their remains became the bedrock outcrops we see now."

The new terrestrial landscape, equally vulnerable to Mother Nature's next climatic tantrum, gave rise to new land-adapted plants and animals, occupying what would one day be our family ranch.

I frequently rode horseback across those sedimentary bluffs, abundant in the semiarid western Hanna Basin, an area often receiving less than twelve inches of effective moisture a year. Thirsty cattle wandered the desiccated hills, looking for water and finding none. Ranchers like my father were forced to dig deep wells to reach underground aquifers just so livestock could drink. Water that once was so widespread and abundant had become frustratingly scarce.

The ranch fed my body and soul for the first three decades of my life. During that time, I developed from a young boy just learning about life to an archaeologist studying the way people lived. Scientific methods like those shared by Merewether teach us that all living things exist within parameters measured by horizontal, vertical, and chronological dimensions, including families.

Traditions are reflected in the patterns of intimate stories those families tell, as well as in the forgotten documents, weathered artifacts, and altered landscapes where they once lived. Our ranch is the pattern of existence my family gave to the land, beginning with my great-grandfather Ike and ending with my dad, my brother, and me in 1983. A full four generations.

Our history forms a single layer in the long sequence of stratified events occurring on the same rural terrain. To understand our layer requires a reasonable awareness of others laid down before us, which is how I approached the cultural history of the country. It is how Grandpa Kirk taught me to see the land and its inhabitants.

An immigrant from Denmark, Ike bought his first livestock in 1873, running only cattle on a small scale until he added sheep two years later. After he formed a partnership with Joel J. Hurt in 1881, the two men pooled their resources and built up a large sheep herd on the land adjacent to Hurt's homestead along the North Platte River, just south of the Seminoe Mountains in Carbon County.

Joel had already registered a livestock brand with Wyoming Territory, designed with a capital "I" followed by a capital "D" lying horizontal with its hump side down. It became known as the I Lazy D.

The ranch that later grew from their partnership stretched along the west bank of the river, touching rimrock on top of the Haystack Mountains above Separation Flats, where the Continental Divide splits to form the east rim of the Great Divide Basin. The Seminoe Mountains to the north offered great summer range for sheep and cattle. The ranch headquarters itself sat on a stable dune next to the crumbling ruins of Hurt's old homestead on the south bank of the creek named after him.

The I Lazy D livestock grazed federal, state, and private lands in the western Hanna Basin. Ultimately, close to 160,000 acres.

Our pastures rested beneath the long shadow of Bradley Peak, a rugged mass of iron-rich stone that twirled the compass needle in a plane when it flew overhead. The hardscrabble range suffered the bone-numbing cold from strong north winds but thrived on the steadfast vigor of threadleaf sedge that nourished our cattle during prolonged droughts.

Near the end of Ike's life, his six children started fighting among themselves. A few of them wanted nothing more to do with the ranch, so Ike established a twenty-year trust maturity that postponed any inheritance until the siblings were older and hopefully more responsible. At least one offspring had already built up serious debt with ever-growing bar tabs in town.

"Those were difficult times in the family," Aunt Kit said. She had been a teen in 1912. "Papa died in the spring and missed my high school graduation. But I forgave him."

Ike's youngest son, Kirk, took over management of the ranch. After the trust matured in 1932, the Miller Estate Company was incorporated, and shares were available for sale. In the depths of the Depression, four of Ike's children cashed in on their inheritance.

Sadly, the only people who could afford to purchase anything at the time were nonfamily members—a banker and a lawyer. Kirk and Kit kept their shares, but once their siblings sold out, voting control of the company was no longer in family hands. Even so, the Millers remained in management through hard work and dedication for half a century afterward.

"I couldn't sell my interest," Aunt Kit said. "Kirk wanted to keep the place, and I had to stand with my brother."

"I'm glad you did."

I grew up under this organizational structure, learning the value of proper comportment, personal responsibility, and compassion for all living things, except maybe coyotes. Country life facilitated raising young children like my brother, Rod, a year older, and me, along with my cousins Susan, Sandy, and Bill. I looked forward to raising my own family the same way when I became an adult.

Little did I know how my circumstances would change, or the nature of family ranching itself.

Our folks raised Rod and me in the 1950s and '60s to be good Christian-believing Episcopalians, had us baptized and confirmed. Mom took us to Bible classes every Sunday, in addition to all her other parental chores, encouraging us to serve as acolytes throughout our high school years. Like most teenagers, we both transgressed from regular church attendance, interacting with different peer groups in town. We may have been acolytes, but we were no angels.

I became a lay reader in church when I turned twenty-one, the minimum age for qualification. My scriptural studies stressed one biblical lesson whose lyrical phrases captured my attention. Now, over fifty years later, that Old Testament quote (*Psalms* 103:15–16) returns to mind with surprising regularity:

As for man, his days are like grass; he flourishes like a flower of the field; for the wind blows over it, and it is gone, and its place knows it no more.

King David, the author of that passage, knew life was short and death inevitable. As a boy, he had tended his family's sheep. Their livelihood depended on good water and grass—grass that survived the winds trying to suck the life out of every pasture.

But even the best grass year comes to an end. The forage withers, crumbling in death back into the gritty soil that allowed it to grow in the first place. Its essence transforms into dust clouds that blow free in the powerful clutches of every gale, landing someplace else to deposit new sediment where fresh grass will grow.

We are all part of this earth, I learned early on. Our lives depend on the nurturing environment that first allows our roots to develop, that lets the sprouting leaves of personal experience reach toward the sun, and that accepts us back into her gritty matrix when we fade.

That cycle became a physical reality to me as a young rancher years before my archaeological career. The wind constantly blew, recontouring our landscape, burying the old beneath the new. While the ghosts of our evolving topography may no longer recognize me, I will never forget the ranching heritage my great-grandfather started—or the lineage he bred.

2.

The Ranch Headquarters

According to family tradition, Ike Miller hired a group of skilled Mormon immigrants to build the stone house and barn in 1890, the same year Wyoming earned statehood. He took the men to Stone Quarry Spring on the south flank of the Seminoe Mountains, where they used crowbars and picks to break off large limestone slabs for our foundations and walls.

As young boys, Rod and I found the quarry. The workers had left behind a rusted crowbar leaning against the cliff and a large hole where bedrock had been removed. More than seventy years before, they had hauled the two-foot-thick stones on wagons a tortuous couple of miles through the sand and across Hurt Creek. And then they mortared each one in place, the perfect insulation against heat in the summer and cold in the winter, making the house comfortable in any season.

During part of our youth, my brother and I slept in different bedrooms, but when we were preschoolers, we shared a room with our folks downstairs, warmed by a potbelly stove that burned lumps of Wyoming coal. Bunk beds rested against the far wall, Rod on the top and me on the bottom. After we said our prayers, the two of us would whisper to each other about what we'd do the next day, quieting down once Dad turned off the light and the room grew dark.

"G'night, tweetie," he would say to Mom.

"I love you," she'd say back.

Every evening, a scrape and a sizzle broke the dark silence, just before the scent of burning sulfur reached my nose. Then two beady red orbs glared at me from my folks' bed, like a wide-eyed predator crouched in a dark cave waiting to pounce. With Mom and Dad's every inhale and exhale, those orbs alternately brightened and dimmed, as if the cave dweller were blinking at me. At the end of their smoke, the cave predator closed his eyes, and we all went to sleep, but the pain that creature caused would someday visit my parents.

Years later, I talked with my cousin Sandy about that bedroom. "I wonder what kind of sex life my folks had with Rod and me sleeping at the foot of their bed every night."

"I slept in the lower bunk one night when you and Rod were gone," she said. "I had a nightmare about rattlesnakes and woke up in a cold sweat, screaming at the top of my lungs. Your mom jumped out of bed buck-naked and ran over to ask what was wrong . . . I suspect their sex life was just fine."

When we were in our early teens, Rod and I each got a sheep wagon, decrepit mobile homes dating to the early 1930s, made out of canvas, wood, and iron. Located halfway between the stone house and barn, they held a bed, coal stove, and storage space for clothes.

The wagons' running gear had iron rims supported by wooden wheels and spokes. Those wheels dried over the years, the wood shrinking under each rim until we couldn't tow the wagon ten miles an hour without the wheels falling apart. We'd have to stop periodically to splash water on the spokes until the wood swelled enough against the iron rims to hold them in place. It seemed that even our equipment required water to grow.

When our high school friends helped at the ranch, several of us moved upstairs into the stone house and occupied a long, unfinished barracks. I slept in a tall hospital bed facing a baseboard pocketed with mouse holes along the opposite wall. Tiny claws scraped the tongue-and-groove floor when mice scampered across the room on nocturnal forays, so I gathered some traps from the pantry downstairs and set them beside each hole to capture the four-legged occupants.

One night a loud *snap* woke me from a deep sleep. I heard the sound of wood scraping against wood followed by repetitive thuds. I crept out of bed and spotted a captured mouse trying to climb down its hole, carrying a trap on the end of its tail too large to fit through the opening. Enough with the noisy traps. The next morning, I would replace them with quieter wads of steel wool to plug the holes so mice couldn't chew their way through them.

The pantry held all the supplies we needed for the ranch as well as for the sheep camps, where herders stayed while tending our sheep. The green shelves overflowed with cases of canned soup, condensed milk, tobacco, packaged sugar, sacks of flour, piles of vegetables, beans, and bags of dried fruit.

Mom kept a tall crock on the floor filled with sourdough starter to make pancakes every morning. The pungent odor of the dough hung heavy in the air when I went into the pantry looking for a few pieces of steel wool.

I bagged groceries for Joe Martinez's sheep camp that summer, so after plugging mouse holes, I picked camp supplies from the pantry shelves and marked them off Joe's list.

"We didn't always do it that way," Dad said when he walked in.

"Am I doing something wrong?"

"No. It's just that some sheepherders couldn't read or write English when I was your age, so I never had a complete list."

"How did you know what to pack?"

"They peeled labels from food cans and gave them to me." Dad laughed. "One time a herder pointed to his horse, then grabbed his own shoulder and touched it like it was sore. On my next trip, I brought Absorbine Junior for him to use as liniment on his mare, which made him smile."

Next to the pantry was a walk-in cooler hidden behind a thick, insulated door. Inside, a dozen meat hooks hung on a long pine ceiling beam that stretched from wall to wall, high off the floor. Halves of beef, and sometimes an elk or a deer, were jabbed onto hooks behind their hocks and suspended from the beam.

We used the heavy wooden table in the center as a chopping block, its surface covered in axe cuts and blood stains. Butchering knives of odd shapes and sizes lay scattered, along with a scalloped mallet to tenderize beef, a meat cleaver, and a cylindrical honing stone. Whenever we needed meat for supper, Kirk would walk into the cooler, hack off an armload of steaks, and carry them to Mom in the kitchen.

The oldest standing building on the ranch was our shop, a one-story rectangular structure built of hand-hewn logs notched on each end, locked in place at their corners. It sat only thirty yards from the Supply Ditch flowing out of Hurt Creek.

"That's where Ike and Ada lived before they built the stone house," Aunt Kit told me during our Park Manor visit. "I don't know how old it is."

It was once a blacksmith shop. An old forge stood in the corner next to a brick basin filled with coal and beneath an exhaust hood opening into a chimney pipe through the roof. When the smithy cranked the forge turbine, it blew air that fed the flames, its gears whirring like the wail of a fire alarm, turning coal translucent red as its temperature rose. I played with it as a kid to see how loud I could make the turbine scream.

The smithy would use a pair of long iron tongs to hold an iron horseshoe over the inferno until it turned the same color as the coal and smoke rising in plumes off the metal. Then the smithy laid the shoe on an anvil, pounded the softened iron into the shape he needed for a particular horse, and submerged it in water where it hissed as it cooled. Our horses always wore well-fitted shoes.

When I was a boy, hired hands lived in the old bunkhouse. I stayed there off and on for a couple of summers decades ago. The rough, unsanded floor poked slivers into my feet, and we patched old holes in the wall with cardboard to keep out the wind. No one ever swept the place or washed any windows. Interior light came from kerosene lamps and a forty-watt bulb hanging from the end of a frayed wire at the center of the ceiling. The bunkhouse sat at the far end of the main ranch yard, and we had to walk fifty yards to the nearest outhouse whenever nature called, rain or shine.

Only the musical talent of Dan interrupted the monotonous bunkhouse life. He was one of the young men who contracted fence building with Dad. At dusk, before the mosquitoes came out, he would pull an acoustic guitar from beneath his bed, sit on the porch, and play every country song I knew. His mellow voice smoothed the rough edges on our cowboys, melting in the air like honey poured over hot sourdough.

He even let me play his guitar once until my strumming broke up the crowd.

The Mormon stone masons who built the barn hauled timbers from the Freezeout Mountains across the river for roof joists and for the beams on double horse stalls used by work teams and single stalls for the saddle stock. The timbers have never been replaced, as strong today as when they were installed. One year, I looked closely at the ancient posts and beams and found worn initials carved long ago into the dirty grain.

The barn became the main destination of every mouse we chased from the house. Mice invaded the stalls at the same time bats populated the hayloft. Town friends brought us cats to help us keep the rodents away from the grain. Every tomcat and tabby picked a home in the hayloft or tack room, staking out its turf. The longer they survived, the more independent they became.

Every so often we heard the shrill scream of two cats locked in mortal combat that ended when only one could walk away. After a month on the ranch, no cat survived unscathed, their life expectancy inversely proportional to the distance they wandered beyond the barn. If they stayed close to the ranch buildings, the scent of humans protected them, but if they went too far on their own, the coyotes hunted them down.

Whenever the barn cat population dwindled, we kids mounted an expedition to the dune alongside the meadow in search of bull snakes. They weren't venomous, so we caught them and turned them loose in the barn to live in shaded spaces beneath the floorboards, happily eating the mice.

Opposite the tack room were the milking stalls. Every morning before dawn, Rod, Bill, and I sat on one-legged stools to milk our three dairy cows, balancing with our heads pressed against each cow's belly, our tiny hands gripping the wrinkly pink teats and squeezing until we filled our buckets. The animals were gentle, sometimes swishing their tails at us if we didn't move fast enough to empty their milk.

The barn cats would come up to us, rub against our legs, and look up at the udders. That was our signal to squirt milk into their mouths. Once Rod and I had a "gunfight" with the cow teats, shooting milk at each other, but we didn't want to waste too much.

We usually finished our chore just as the sky started to lighten. After turning the cows back into their own holding corral, we'd carry the milk pails up to Mom in the kitchen, passing the door to the stud stall on the way.

Stallions are strong, aggressive animals, and we needed to keep them separate from the mares when they weren't breeding. In the corner of the barn was a single stall, with a separate, outside entrance all its own. Solid walls isolated it as if it were a prison cell for solitary confinement. The panel door slid on rollers that scraped inside a rusty pipe when it opened. The stoop was chipped by the impact of shod hooves crashing into it when the stallions tried to get free.

The room itself formed a hollow square between two walls of stone and two of thick planks, each plank nailed right on top of another to form walls higher than a horse, closing the view to the rest of the barn. More of a stockade than a stall, it had only a small gap that allowed us to reach in from the outside to feed oats to the stud.

If you stood inside the stall long enough, you could feel what it was really like to be alone.

3.

Life with Horses

When I was young, most of my best friends had four legs. We raised cattle and sheep for market, of course, but horses were the principal tool of our trade, and I loved them. Before I was school age, I knew the names of more horses than I did kids: Midnight, Moody River, Zeke, Tabasco, Ice Cream, Paladin, and so many more.

Aunt Kit's stories invariably mentioned colorful interactions with the horses we kept on the ranch through the years. In the late 1890s, Ike's foreman, Charley Wagers, was a good horseman, but he could be cruel to the horses he rode. One day, he had been fighting with a haltered gelding in the round corral down at the barn when Ike was in town on business.

"Charley yelled at the horse, calling him a son of a bitch," Aunt Kit said. "Then he slapped the animal's nose with his quirt."

Her mother, Ada, had been managing the ranch while her husband was gone and typically gave daily work orders to the hired hands. She had a small build and looked feeble to those unwilling to gaze more deeply, but Ada actually revealed an iron will when it came to managing the ranch—a woman quite capable of handling Charley Wagers.

"When Mama saw him whipping the horse, she ran down from the stone house to the barn, marched right into the corral, and demanded an explanation for what he'd done."

Charley sputtered out a weak excuse, Aunt Kit said, and her mother fired him. Ada ordered him to leave the corral, pack his things, and go to town.

He stood still, his mouth wide open. Charley had worked there for years and had built a solid reputation as foreman. "How will I get to town without a horse?" he managed to say.

Ada looked at him with fire in her eyes. "You may walk, Charley Wagers. You will not use one of my husband's horses again."

Charley left on foot that day to Rawlins, forty miles away.

Ike documented only one or two firsthand experiences about his life on the ranch. In July 1885, he prepared a letter for a biography in the Bancroft Library at UC-Berkeley, admitting that horses captured his heart more than any other livestock he ever owned. He praised the nutritious grass of Carbon County for its quality, declaring the high altitude of south-central Wyoming ideal. "This is the finest country in the land to raise hardy horses," Ike recorded in his scrawling handwriting. It was a country quite different from the Danish island where he had grown up.

Because saddle stock developed larger lung capacity and stronger hooves in the intermountain environment, Ike could ride fifty or sixty miles a day with ease. Good saddle horses were the mainstay of operations on any ranch. We could accomplish little without them, so we cared for each one, never whipping them as Wagers had done.

The ageless cadence of horseback riding connected the country rhythm of my generation to those riders in the saddle of bygone years— the bridge between the past and present that linked us together. The echoes of hoof beats in the mountains made it feel like they were riding with us. Nowadays, the use of four-wheel sport vehicles for herding cattle has erased that intimacy.

My family kept one horse tied in a front stall at the barn so our wrangler could saddle up an hour before daylight each morning and use fading moon glow to ride to the east end of the horse pasture and gather the entire herd to the corral. Thirty-five head of saddle stock grazed that side hill, enough animals for each man to choose a fresh mount for the next cattle drive.

The wrangler's horse would pick his way through the softening dark above and cratered prairie dog towns below, slowly walking to the east end of the pasture, sniffing the air. But the getting back was fast.

As Rod and I got older, Dad expected us to help with the wrangling. I never complained. There was no better way to wake up: riding alone through the horse pasture, smelling the drips of dew on the wheatgrass, and watching the first rays of sun creep over the Freeze-out Mountains.

In the predawn of one morning in early April, I heard a knock on the door of my sheep wagon.

"Your turn to wrangle," Dad hollered.

I was buried under a wool blanket and canvas spread. The comfortable warmth from the small coal stove had vanished. Pushing off the covers, I sat up and dangled my legs over the bed, my socks on all night to ward off the cold. This would be the first wrangle in months. We didn't need to use that many horses when the cattle were still on the winter feed ground.

"Tabasco's in the first stall," Dad said.

I was in high school that spring, excited about raising a young gelding new to the ranch and unacquainted with the rest of the horses in the herd. I named him Tabasco for the ocher hue of his sleek hide and sting of his pepper sauce temper.

Tabasco's shod hooves stomped the wooden barn floor, sending loud echoes through the empty hay loft and stalls. I slid the curb bit over his tongue and led him outside to tighten his cinch under a cloud of moths attacking the overhead light by the door. I smiled. The air had a nice bite to it, a perfect morning.

I lifted my left foot into the stirrup, and Tabasco started walking out of the corral before my right leg swung over the saddle. I grabbed the saddle horn to balance my position while his belly bounced the loose oxbow stirrup back and forth, causing me to stab my right boot at the moving target just to finish my mount. Unhappy with me, Tabasco hunched his back until he felt me settle into the saddle. I worked to even the reins and pulled my hat down over my brow, getting used to Tabasco's nervous energy at the start of our morning ride.

The pasture still slept beyond the yellow arc of barn light, a slumber only slightly disturbed by the chorus of crickets chirping in protest at our intrusion. Tabasco's steps crunched through the thin layer of damp sand capping the top of the dunes. My saddle squeaked when his muscles flexed, pulling my leather cinch strap against D-rings I had neglected to oil. The moonlit silhouette of horse and rider cast a shadowy apparition over the dew-moistened grass of predawn.

Following the night-veiled trail, we reached the east end of the pasture without breaking a sweat and cut in behind the horse herd grazing above Seminoe Reservoir. Before we finished the turn, the herd picked up our scent, whinnied loud complaints, and galloped away in a cloud of dust, charging for the lane two miles away that opened down to our barn.

I rode Tabasco fast but held him back because of his youth and inexperience—his tendency to buck with minor provocation. The herd stretched the distance between us just as the sun painted a golden crescent on the eastern horizon. Easing up on the reins, I let Tabasco run.

He exploded into a gallop, gliding over the dunes, spraying high-arching sand plumes behind us on the trail. We sprinted across a rocky ridge where his metal shoes struck pebbles that sparked when they flew. Beads of sweat erupted on his shoulders, my reins rubbing against them with each stretch of his neck, turning the wet pools into lather. His lungs bellowed every breath. His blond mane sliced through the sky.

Together in that gallop, Tabasco and I shared the perfect freedom of synchronized movement that only horseback riding provides. Earlier cowboys repeated the same scene for a hundred years, and their friendly ghosts loped beside us.

Moody River, the lead mare in the herd, neared the barnyard as Tabasco and I raced to the top of the lane. We galloped toward the gate, but Tabasco suddenly balked and raised his head until his ears twitched in my face, seeking an answer to a question I didn't hear.

"Come on, dammit. We're too far back to do any good, and it's cold out here." I ignored his hesitation, eager now to reach a hot stove and a cup of coffee.

I kicked Tabasco's flanks, loosened my grip, and gave him more rein. He lunged obediently forward, diving headfirst into the stock pond invisible to me in the dark before dawn. The impact propelled me so deep into the chilly water and thick mud I thought I'd drown. Tabasco climbed out the other side alone to finish his own way to the barn.

Dad had often told me, "You need to know where you are all the time, Mark. You and your horse are out there alone, and nobody can help you if you get in a fix."

Dripping wet and caked head to toe with mud, I hurried over to Tabasco, shamed by my inattention. He stood by the barn gate, shivering in nervous tension. I put my arm around his neck and caressed his muzzle to quiet him down, his wide eyes burning into me, his nostrils flaring. Every fiber of his being reiterated Dad's caution about awareness.

"Easy, boy," I choked out, my insides shaking from the cold. I wiped the mud from around my mouth. "My fault. Everything's okay now."

The wrangled horses, once corralled, were skittish that morning. They kicked the sky, nipped each other's ears, bumped into the fence, and churned in the choking dust of the round corral. After a winter of no riding, we had to reacquaint them with the calm acceptance of a saddle and bridle.

The half-dozen cowboys took turns approaching the nervous horses, as tentative as a boy when asking his girlfriend for a first dance, not knowing where the conversation will lead. The ritual dance of a new season is why Ike built the round corral in the first place.

They also needed a snubbing post. Kirk ordered my father, barely sixteen years old in 1935, to set a new post in the center of the round corral. Dad hauled in an eight-foot length of pine, ten inches in diameter, and soaked the bottom half in creosote to preserve it from decay.

After chopping away the sharp edges of the sawed top, he hewed it round so a horse would not cut himself if he bumped against it. Dad carved an inch-deep groove around the post, a couple of feet down from the top, and sanded its cavity smooth.

The round corral sat atop a stabilized sand dune that promised easy digging. Dad quickly finished a hole four feet deep and buried the treated end of the snubbing post in the ground. He tromped the fill dirt with the handle end of his shovel and boot heels to seat the post firmly in the sand, anchoring it into the earth. It stood there solid and alone when he finished, the perfect monument on a trampled plane, so well made that it was the last snubbing post Dad would ever have to build.

For over fifty years, cowboys used that post to not only calm anxious or obstinate horses, especially after the idle winter, but also to break green horses, taming them for the world they would live in as saddle stock on a working ranch.

That morning, one of the horses was more unsettled than the rest, pawing the loose sand and staring at the snubbing post with flared nostrils. When a cowboy approached him with a halter, the animal threw up his head and pulled away. "Steady now," the man said.

The cowboy walked behind the horse and coaxed him into a slow counterclockwise trot around the inside perimeter of the corral while he opened his lariat in a wide loop. Twirling it once clockwise above his shoulders, the cowboy threw it in a gentle glide over the horse's head as he passed by underneath. The loop floated briefly in front of the animal while his own gait propelled him into its grasp. It looked to a young man like me that the horse had roped himself.

After snapping the rope to eliminate slack, the cowboy twisted a quick loop over the top of the snubbing post that pinched tight in the recessed groove. He leaned back into the tail of the rope, stopping the animal with his weight drawn taut against the gripping friction of the loop. The unruly horse pulled in vain against the post, protesting his bond. Relaxed and unhurried, the cowboy drew the rope through the loop, shortening the distance between himself and the horse until he reached the animal's neck. The cowboy patted him and whispered a gentle greeting, calming him down.

Now tied to the snubbing post, the horse was connected to the ranch as if the rope itself were an umbilical cord. Each tethered animal evolved into more than it was before the rope, part of something that had existed for generations, which would survive beyond death.

A similar, durable connection to place permeated every living thing on the ranch, including us grandkids.

4.

Growing Up with Kirk

I stared into a thick morning mist that blanketed the feed ground near the stone house. It dripped cold moisture onto our windshield as Grandpa Kirk and I drove across the frozen meadow grass. I was six then, sitting next to one of my favorite people.

A skiff of light snow crunched beneath our tires while Grandpa's truck heater blew dusty warmth onto my hands. His weather-beaten face beamed with the satisfaction of a lifetime spent around livestock, sculpted by the close relationship he shared with Mother Nature.

A hundred head of lounging cattle scattered to the four corners of the pasture beyond our foggy window that day. Kirk double-clutched his old Chevy pickup, coasting to a stop on a faded two-track road that snaked among the damp stems of redtop and western wheatgrass.

Morning warmth slowly thawed the frost, causing countless seed spikes to stretch impatiently toward the rising sun. I opened my door, intending to run behind the milling cattle and fetch them to the vehicle so we could feed protein cake from the truck bed.

"Whoa! Stay here, Pard," Kirk said, using his nickname for me. "Watch this."

He pulled a T-shaped lever on his dusty console, triggering a loud, seductive tune, "AAUUGGAAHH." Every cow raised her head, looked our way, and trotted across the frozen meadow toward the pickup. Kirk laughed. "Never fails."

We started shoveling the load of protein cake into a long windrow across the meadow behind us, breathing in the heavy scent of molasses rising from it into the mist around the feeding cattle. I grabbed a piece of cow cake, chewed on it, and grinned with pure contentment.

Around me, the I Lazy D sprawled for 250 square miles along the North Platte River. More than anything, I wanted to become a part of this wondrous place, just like my grandfather.

A couple of years later, I was sitting beside Kirk again in his old green pickup, this time with my cousin Bill, the three of us on our way to Rawlins. Bill and I were the youngest of Kirk's five grandkids, so we often rode with him, listening to his stories unfold like pages in a family history book.

"Dad named many landforms when he was out here," Kirk told us that day. "The old gent passed those names on to me."

"Tell us some," I said.

Ike's place-names defined characteristics of my own identity as much as any biological trait inherited from Mom and Dad. Kirk even showed us a couple of places important to Native Americans who had lived in the area before Ike, fueling my early curiosity about the first people who called that country home.

Most of our drives with Kirk began on County Road 351. It snaked south from the Seminoe Mountains through our bull pasture and headed twenty miles to the North Platte River Canyon. No side ditches drained it. No raised ridge helped keep the road free of snow. Sticky spring mud soaked the road one season, and then ice froze it in another. Reaching your destination by driving that dirt road always seemed a dubious proposition.

Kirk rolled up his squeaky cab window to keep the dust out of our vehicle that summer day so long ago. A rising plume draped the country behind us—the cold, lifeless asphalt wouldn't begin for many miles ahead. If Kirk slowed, the cloud engulfed us in a choking haze. If he sped up, our tires slipped in loose sand and gravel until the truck fishtailed. Kirk traveled the perfect speed, creating a symmetry in space between where we were and where we needed to be.

Stepping on the clutch to down shift, he pushed the gear stick into neutral and released the clutch, and then pushed in again, shifting to third gear. Kirk loved to double-clutch, despite a leg crippled by a fallen log. He turned tight to the south when the truck reached the top of ID Ridge, short for I Lazy D.

"The old gent used his other brands to name places too, like the RS Meadow and DO Range," Kirk said. "He called his river house the HO."

We passed Firecracker Hill where our family gathered every Fourth of July to celebrate our nation's birthday.

"Remember the fireworks last year?" I asked.

"You bet. Wouldn't miss 'em."

We drove around the O'Brien Springs fault, passing Seminoe Boat Club on the opposite side of the county road from Cheyenne Ridge. Sportsmen had needed a reservoir shoreline to dock their boats years ago. Kirk and the board of directors sold them a forty-acre parcel for one dollar on a quitclaim deed. Seminoe Boat Club has served the fishing public ever since.

Seminoe Reservoir had inundated much of the valley in 1939, submerging the old river channel that once delineated our southern and eastern ranch boundaries.

"A warm spring was down there when I was a teenager, before the dam flooded it," Dad told me one day. "My brother and I used to ride horseback to the spot and float in the hot pool to loosen our muscles."

Farther south lay Coyote Springs where howling canine predators barked every year. Nearby, Pegleg Butte rose from the plain like a pirate's stump. Kirk, Bill, and I drove past a rugged rock formation townspeople called the Buffalo Pits, but I never saw evidence that it had been used as a bison kill.

The Stone Corral was where our neighbor Jack Tapers once gathered wild horses in the confines of its steep sandstone walls. Gnarly cliffs formed a U-shape opening toward Coal Creek and another toward the valley of Little Shoe. Eagles' nests and pack rat middens crammed into the jagged cracks and crevices among the wind-carved rocks, each filled with the bleached bones of unlucky cottontails and other unfortunate prey.

The turbulent wind carved a twenty-foot vertical hole several feet wide directly into the basement bedrock. The year our family picnicked there, a bobcat and coyote skeleton lay on the pit floor, their bony appendages still locked in the mortal combat they had engaged in when they fell over the lip. Angry momentum pitched them into the cold abyss, ending their argument for good. Anyone witnessing the result of their miscalculation would learn to remain aware of where they were at all times.

Our truck tires bit black asphalt at last, and we rolled down our windows to breathe fresh air, savoring the last moments on the ranch before entering the river canyon on our journey to town. We crossed the iron bars of our last cattle guard stretching horizontal across the road, lying there like a fallen jail door to a prison cell. Like most such doors, freedom lay on one side of the bars and uncertainty on the other. It seemed appropriate to have to drive across it to reach the confines of town.

Kirk steered his truck over the iron bars, wove down the winding road into the river canyon, and passed a two-tiered rock sticking up through the turbulent North Platte current. Kirk's Marker gauged the river depth, telling us of snowmelt in the high country and the promise or threat that defined irrigating season. It was the last-named family place.

"Years ago, we couldn't drive our horse and buggy through this canyon. There was no road. We came around behind the Haystacks and crossed Cheyenne Ridge."

The I Lazy D spread out in all directions behind us. Ahead lay Rawlins, Interstate 80, and the Union Pacific Railroad, a landscape cluttered by a century of settled life, labeled by urban families with names unfamiliar to me. Kirk, Bill, and I left the comfort of our real home and headed toward the land of watered lawns, pruned hedges, and fashionable town gardens.

Every sense in my being pulled me back along the road we had just driven, back to country places where I could still feel the tacky grip of saddle leather, hear branded calves bawling for their moms, smell lathered horse sweat at a gallop, and taste my first bite of sourdough when we woke before the sun every morning.

The moment we entered the river canyon, our ranch faded to a vanishing point inside the frame of Kirk's cracked rearview mirror. I blinked as it disappeared from my sight and prepared myself for the journey into town.

"Set 'em up, frosted root beers all around," Kirk said to the waitress standing by his pickup at the drive-in soda shop in Rawlins.

"I need to wet my whistle," he added.

Kirk, Bill, and I were parched from the dusty truck ride, and we yearned for cold drinks ever since passing the first stop sign on the east edge of town. Five minutes later, a high school girl several years older than me hooked a tray holding three tall cups to the partially opened driver's side window. After handing us our treats, Kirk stirred his ice cream and soda pop with a tall spoon.

"My favorite drink." He bent the big straw to his lips.

I ignored my utensils and gulped messy swigs that left a vanilla mustache under my nose.

Sixty years later, whenever I think of Kirk's drinking, I see that frosted root beer in a tall, wax-coated cup brimming with froth, stabbed by a bent red-and-white-striped straw. But he also drank whiskey, far more than he should, a habit that lured him to town in the fall after shipping our livestock.

Born in 1888, Kirk grew up the son of a wealthy stockman, a circumstance that gave him too much free time to stare at dark colored bottles standing erect in a skirmish line at the back of each bar, ready to do battle with each thirsty patron. Whenever Kirk traveled to town alone, one of his bartender friends gave him the first round for free. He swallowed the bait and was hooked, reeled in, often left hanging for days over a bar stool to dry.

But Kirk also had an inner strength that taught him bad drunks didn't make good grandpas, so he never drank whiskey in front of us grandkids. Ignorant of his addiction then, we became his self-imposed antidote, a gentle therapy that smoothed an uneven path to sobriety. Kirk's time with us was his principal relief to the chronic disease that haunted him—a condition he treated with frosted root beer.

Not until my brother Rod and I were in high school and tempted by weekend keg parties did our folks tell us of the habit Kirk had when we were younger.

"Alcoholism is hereditary. Be careful," Mom said.

Betty Rose McKay, a tall redhead descended from strong Scottish stock, came from a ranching family herself before she married Dad. She had grown up on her mother's family ranch in northwestern Colorado, nestled beside the gentle flow of Talamantes Creek between Diamond Peak and Cold Spring Mountain.

Mom's grandfather, Charlie Sparks, raised sheep on their place and was later joined by his brothers in the enterprise. Charlie's first wife, Rosina, was Mom's grandmother, but she died early in their marriage, shortly after Mom's mother and uncle were born. Charlie and his second wife added two children to the family, so stepsibling dynamics challenged the otherwise tranquil life my grandmother knew as a child.

As a young horsewoman herself, Mom gentled each animal she rode using a calm, compassionate manner. Horses sensed her innate altruism, a personal trait she bestowed on everyone around her. Kindness and motivation led her to complete a quality education, and she became the first family member to earn a college degree.

Charlie's younger brother, Arthur, proved to be one of the best horsemen on the Sparks' ranch. He doted on Mom when she was young. Uncle Arthur and Mom often rode horseback together, and before he died, Arthur gave Mom his favorite brass spurs. She presented them to me when I turned eighteen, knowing my passion for riding and keen interest in family history.

Not surprisingly, Mom had married a successful rancher who also loved good horses. She rode Duchess on the I Lazy D, a bald-faced mare Dad had given to her. It was her favorite mount, and she loved spending hours in the saddle.

Yet Mom also sensed Rod and I needed to broaden our worldview beyond riding, ranching, and helping Dad build miles of fence. She was aware of my limited social skills, of course, because I spent more time with animals than with other kids before I started kindergarten. It was an emotional tight rope she had to negotiate—let us cowboy with Dad and Grandpa Kirk or have us live in Rawlins among our peers.

As much as I protested being away from the ranch, we didn't have a choice. Mom and Dad had asked the county to send a schoolteacher to our ranch to educate Rod and me, but our home was too remote. At least two ranches had to be within reasonable distance of one another to make rural schooling feasible. Since no other families lived for miles around, we had to reside during the school year in Rawlins.

At first we lived in a small house in town behind Dad's parents' home, remodeled from their old garage. Later, my folks built a new home on a lot Dad had earned as a veteran of World War II.

To keep the I Lazy D operation running, Dad had to stay at the ranch for days on end and help Kirk. Mom took care of us in town while we attended school, but she was young and lonely and wanted to see Dad as much as possible. So Dad would come to town periodically during the week, and Mom took us to the ranch nearly every weekend.

Though I moved back and forth between the ranch and Rawlins growing up, my heart was rooted in the land, my thoughts often on Grandpa Kirk. He worked hard on the ranch too, with the eager assistance of his grandkids. We were his crew, and all of us wanted to live out there.

Kirk's wrinkled face and rustic levity masked the chronic symptoms of his alcoholism, his bright eyes glistening with an unbridled energy for life, despite a misspent youth. Still, whenever he was with his grandkids, he always fit in like one of us.

He stooped when he walked, much like the Hollywood star Walter Brennan, whom Rod and I loved to watch in Western movies. In fact, the two men looked a lot alike. Bowed posture teamed with gravity to nudge his work pants below his waist, and if not for a pair of suspenders, Kirk's behind would poke at the sun.

A warped hickory cane helped him walk, a single piece of wood much smaller than the heavy pine log that fell on his leg one day when he and a friend were so drunk that neither one could roll it away. His powerful hands gripped the curved cane handle, wearing it smooth over the years. When one of us kids walked by his chair, he snagged our ankle like he was hooking sheep when we sheared. Kirk smiled at each capture, a bright, captivating grin, safe at the ranch with his grandkids, forty miles from the nearest saloon.

Every few weeks, Rod, Bill, and I went with Kirk to Brownie's Barber Shop on Fourth Street in Rawlins. We'd walk by the Silver Spur, which showcased a wooden bar burned deep with the brands of county ranches, including our I Lazy D. Kirk beamed with pride when he told us about it.

One day, Dad asked me, "Did your grandfather ever tell you about the fight he had at Brownie's?"

"No. What fight?"

"He was sitting in the chair when a drunk stumbled in from the Silver Spur. The guy wanted a haircut, so he slurred an order at Brownie to hurry up with the bald man under the towel."

"What did Grandpa do?"

"Waited until Brownie finished, then walked over to the man, picked him up by the collar, and slugged him in the face."

"Did the drunk fight back?"

"He crashed through the picture window, landed on the concrete walk outside, and fell into an old lady walking by. The collision broke her arm, so she sued Kirk." Dad laughed.

Kirk never got into trouble when he took his three grandsons to the barber for a trim, passing every saloon on the way.

"Need my hair cut, Brownie. Try to get 'em both this time," Kirk would joke when we entered the shop.

Brownie covered all but Kirk's nearly bald head with a white sheet and towel and fussed over combs and clippers since there was so little work to do with his few hairs. The two old-timers always chatted about early Rawlins and the mutual friends they knew.

Then Kirk would turn to me. "Sit down, Pard. You're next."

When Brownie finished, we walked out of his shop and past his barber pole colored like straws in our frosted root beer.

Kirk often drank whiskey with Rex Shirley, a man whose name we attached more to the uniqueness of his appearance than to any other characteristic. His drooping pants always hung loosely and too low on his hips, far lower than Kirk's, barely stabilized by wide suspenders and a knotted rope belt. Rod and I knew to pull up our Wranglers every time Mom said, "You kids look just like Rex Shirley."

One day, Rex drove forty miles to the ranch in a taxicab. We grand-kids were playing on the porch when the cab drove up. Rex walked past us to visit Kirk in the house while the driver parked in front of us to wait with his meter still running.

Wooden chairs slammed against the living room wall. Muffled curses escaped from an angry voice inside as the dinner table slid along the floor. We couldn't hear the topic of conversation, but we knew something bad was happening.

The next moment, Rex came flying out the front door and landed hard against the side of the taxi. Kirk limped from the house with a stick broom in his hand, breathing hard, scraping the porch with his bum leg as he walked.

"Get the hell out of here!" he shouted. "I'm not giving you a job, and you can pay your own damn cab. Don't come around anymore."

I never saw Kirk so mad at anyone. I'm not sure what provoked him, but it probably had something to do with the cost of the taxi. Rex climbed into the cab, drove back to town, and never went drinking with my grandfather again.

Many older men at the ranch in my youth drank too much, except for Dad and his brother-in-law, Uncle Chad. I figure the cause of their plight ultimately derived from the solitude of rural life in the high lonesome, where independence so valued by cowboys inevitably orphaned their soul.

Hired hands lived a life better acquainted with landscape than with people, even if those people were family members. They seldom visited their mothers or other kinfolk, and this absence of hearth and home weighed heavily on the hearts of stoic men.

Whiskey, poured straight and three fingers deep, became a surrogate for the parents they missed in their lives. Something to drink— rather than someone to love—that warmed them inside and drowned the fears they were too proud to claim.

Whatever the reason for their choices, too many country men saw the best years of their lives melt with the ice cubes in the bottom of an empty whiskey glass. Rex may have been one of these loners, and I doubt my parents missed seeing him leave. Small wonder I remember his pants more than the man.

Kirk could be tough when handling ornery men, though he seldom felt the need. It was his legendary humor that always warmed our extended family and circle of friends.

A young Rawlins man named Jerry worked for Kirk one summer before I attended high school. He wore a glass eye due to an injury incurred during a scuffle.

After work, we often drove to a small bay in Seminoe Reservoir below the ranch to swim off the heat of the day, parking on the slope of a stabilized sand dune. Jerry removed his glass eye and laid it with his shirt and pants while we swam in our birthday suits.

"Why do you have to take that out each time?" I asked.

Jerry grinned. "I want to keep an eye on my clothes."

When a friend of Jerry's father died in town, the surviving family members wanted Jerry to be a pallbearer. Kirk gave him a day off for the service and let him drive a company truck to town.

Jerry met his friends after the funeral at a genuine Irish wake that lasted three days. When he sobered up, he noticed multiple parking tickets stuck under the windshield wipers on the borrowed company truck still sitting in front of the bar.

He worried all the way back to the ranch, expecting Kirk to chew him out, maybe even fire him, for being away from work for so long. Kirk looked up from his cup of coffee when Jerry walked in and apologized for being so late.

"Jesus, Jerry!" Kirk said. "How deep did you bury that son of a bitch?"

Whatever I was doing with my grandfather, he had a story to tell. When I was about nine, he wanted to show me how to shoot a rifle, so I suggested we get some tin cans for targets. Kirk wanted to use a pronghorn antelope.

"I feel more comfortable shooting at cans," I said.

"Okay, Pard. That buck over there will live another day." Kirk placed three cans on top of some nearby fence posts. "Did I ever tell you about the time I shot one near Lone Haystack?"

He had been driving back to the ranch that summer, and in his rearview mirror, he could see the lower limbs of a dead pronghorn buck bounce above the sidewalls of his truck bed every time he hit a bump. He had fired his .30-30 carbine straight and true at the animal as it stood by a water hole near the foot of the mountain.

Speeding home with his out-of-season harvest, Kirk passed the game warden driving by in the opposite direction just as his pickup hit another pothole, bouncing the sharp black hooves of the antelope high in the air.

The warden wheeled a U-turn to pull in behind Kirk, flashing his red lights. He had visited our ranch for dinner numerous times and spent hours with Kirk talking about the way ranchers helped save pronghorn when they nearly went extinct from overhunting during the Depression.

Back then, Kirk had prevented hunters from killing animals in his lower meadow, despite aggressive hunting by the hungry homeless after the stock market crash. Unemployed family men often shot game just to keep food on their plates, but Kirk provided one small sanctuary for pronghorn where the public could not hunt.

He refused access to the hay meadows for anyone with a gun. Pronghorn soon recovered from that stressful time and now flourished on the ranch, so Kirk felt freed from his obligation to protect each one.

The game warden walked up to Kirk's window, smiled at his old friend, and then looked in back at the dead buck.

"Damn, Kirk," he said. "Why didn't you pull that tarp over the buck so the legs wouldn't bounce in the air?"

Kirk laughed. "What, and let my beer get warm?"

The warden wrote him a citation and drove off.

The next year, I was hell-bent on becoming a Boy Scout and kept pestering my mom to let me join.

Kirk squinted at me. "Pard, are you sure you're ready for the Scouts?"

"Yes, I'm sure," I said, with as much sincerity as a child could muster.

"Do you know what you need to do to earn the uniform?" Mom asked. "There's more to Boy Scouts than just wearing the shirt."

It wouldn't be easy. I'd have to follow an oath and earn merit badges. But I nagged her anyway. "Please, Mom."

She took a deep breath and blew it out slowly. "Okay, but you have to pass the first test before I'll buy the shirt."

That meant I had to know how to tie knots.

"Sit down, Pard, and I'll show you some," Kirk said.

Knots were a tool of his trade. He used them constantly around livestock. He cut a length of rope from a long roll in the pantry, wrapped it around a table leg, and slid his gnarled fingers up the hempen line, one hand passing over the other, pulling the rope snug, explaining each step to me. His index finger held open the inside of a loop while he threaded the shortest end through. "This is a half hitch. Two half hitches will hold a bull."

Then he showed me the slip knot I needed for tying my horse with a halter rope down at the barn. He tied a granny knot, a square knot, and a clove hitch. "This here is a bowlin'."

"Bowline?"

"Bowlin'."

Kirk wasted no letters at the end of his words.

I liked the sheepshank, a long piece of rope looped into a shorter length and pinched tightly at each end by a half hitch when the slack pulled out. The name reminded me of my stock-growing heritage.

I passed the test after a couple of sessions with Kirk and ordered my new uniform. Several weeks later, shortly after receiving the shirt, I dropped from the group, already tired of the Scouts.

Mom's early caution became clear. I had thought only of the prize at the end of a journey.

"You didn't take your responsibility seriously," she said. "I was worried about that."

"At least now you can tie knots," Kirk said. "Even mistakes can be a good way to learn lessons."

My grandfather always carried his Old Timer pocketknife with him. He used the long, thin blade to castrate bull calves and the short, stubby one for all other tasks. Stockmen took great pride in the sharp hone of their knives, and Kirk mastered the craft.

He would open the castrating blade and spit on the whetstone until it pooled in a shallow basin formed by a hundred earlier sharpenings. With a deliberate grip on the knife, he'd touch the blade tip to the stone, tilting it at a low slant until the metal kissed the grit, a precise angle like a barber maintains while shaving with a straight edge. Kirk pushed the length of the blade smoothly along the coarse surface as though slicing warm butter, rolled the blade over, and pulled it back until his elbow touched his ribs.

"Long strokes, Pard," he'd say. "Keep your angle even all the way through. Don't press too deep."

Kirk never circled a blade around the whetstone face as some of my hunting friends did or dug the blade carelessly into the grain.

"When you castrate, keep it as painless as you can. A clean cut heals fast."

I tried again and again, but I was mediocre at best. Kirk frowned and grumbled, and I was crushed that I disappointed him. It took me years to master the task, and I didn't sharpen nearly as well as Rod when we were preteens, but I never stopped wishing I could.

Everything Kirk taught me related directly to making ranching chores more successful and managing the livestock under his care— valuable skills I would need throughout my life.

5.

The Gang at Play

In the years when we grandkids were too young to perform adult chores, we played with everything we could get our hands on at the ranch. We especially liked the canvas tents used by herders who followed sheep to summer pastures in the Medicine Bow Forest.

We often pitched a tent under the Box Elder tree in the sandy yard at the house, its fading white fabric held in place by two wooden poles bolted together on top, not much taller than Dad when fully erect. We pounded stakes in the loops at each corner and side and then raised the poles until their bases dug in the ground, stretching the canvas into a cone. The front yard resembled an Indian camp.

Streaks of red marker lined our faces like war paint while we sat cross-legged in front of the tent. Our cousins Susan and Sandy would wrap themselves in colorful blankets that covered all but their heads. One day, Kirk drove up alongside us after going to town to buy rubber tomahawks and spears, a couple of bows, and a handful of rubber-tipped arrows.

Rod and I grabbed everything and walked over to the tent just as Mom's camera shutter clicked, preserving another moment of my childhood. She took most of the pictures of our youth, accepting the task as one of her parenting jobs, but as photographer, she appears in so few photos herself. When I look at them sixty years later, I see what Mom saw, the scenes she chose to preserve, transmitting her keen vision of a growing family as a permanent part of every photo.

All my toys reflected an interest in Indians, cowboys, and soldiers. I owned a collection of rubber horses and men that grew in number whenever Kirk took us to Ferguson Mercantile in town.

"You can get anything you want for a buck," he'd say.

Each of us grandkids would run to our favorite part of the store. I always headed to the toy section and grabbed a sack of small figures, building my tiny rubber army one dollar at a time.

I fell in love with a set of Civil War men and horses advertised in a flyer, available through mail order for about twenty dollars. I didn't have enough money, so I worked any job I could on the ranch and saved every nickel, along with my treat dollars from Kirk.

After six weeks, I could afford the set and went with Mom to town to place my order, figuring it wouldn't arrive for months. We walked to the store counter so I could fill out the form.

"Sir—" I began.

"Miller," Mom interrupted.

The clerk nodded. "Here it is, Betty Rose."

He reached beneath the counter and pulled out a blue and gray box loaded with the uniformed soldiers I had dreamed about for weeks.

My mouth dropped.

"I ordered it the day we first saw it in the flyer," Mom said.

"I love the set."

"I knew you would, and unlike the Scout uniform, you have loved little horses and men for years."

"Thanks, Mom. I'll pay you back with my savings."

She always saw past my impulsive nature, into a deeper intellectual curiosity that was rising in me. I will never forget her tender intuition. I don't know how she did it.

"I'm proud of you," she said.

My horses and men disappeared as I grew older, their blue and gray uniforms fading in the sun, buried in the country sand of the ranch yard. Most were gone by the time I started high school.

One of my good friends back then had a brother who wore his own blue uniform as a marine in the mid-1960s. My buddy and I each wanted to wear that uniform too, thinking it was the coolest look around. Then his brother died in the early years of the Vietnam War, and my interest in combat vanished.

All five grandkids followed Kirk everywhere on the ranch. The three of us boys took turns bunking with him at the house. Kirk's wife, Grammy Peg, slept in a sheep wagon out front, where Susan and Sandy took turns sleeping with her. It never occurred to me to ask why Kirk and Peg slept in different beds, but on reflection, it probably had to do with his drinking—or snoring.

Kirk would push himself up each night from his easy chair in the front room and shuffle toward the stairway at the end of the hall. He braced himself with a feeble grip on top of the newel post, slid his hand along the banister, and plodded toward the second floor, pausing on each stair to fill his empty lungs.

"Almost there, Pard," he'd say.

The eighth step always creaked. Our parents heard it from the living room, knowing we had made it halfway.

At the top of the stairway, the worn path on the wooden floor ended beneath a set of elk antlers sawed from the skull of a six-point bull. Their base was wrapped in padded felt tacked to a cedar crest that anchored the heavy rack to the wall. The dust-coated antlers blocked the light from an overhead lantern, casting a tangled web of shadows on Kirk's back when he stooped to open his door.

We would enter the Blue Room, painted the color of the north wind at its core. So dark. No decorative accents to celebrate the colorful life of the stockman who slept between its walls. Pulling off his suspenders, Kirk would sit on the bed, his mattress framed as high as his butt so his tired body could lower and rise with ease.

"Going to be a cool night. Hear the bullfrogs?" Kirk said one night. He leaned over his knees. "Help me with my boots, Pard."

I tugged at the leather heels until his legs straightened and the boots slid off. I set them near a rolltop desk made in 1901 that once held Great-Grandfather Ike's business documents in numerous cubbyholes and bins. Kirk hated paperwork so he threw dirty socks into the drawers.

A potbelly stove in the far corner heated coal to warm the Blue Room. The fuel burned hot and long, so the belly of the stove held a solid grate to keep the coal from touching cast iron sides. I opened the flue to let the outside breeze draw smoke up the chimney and into the night.

"Stoke the fire so it won't go out," Kirk said, making sure I had completed my bedtime chores.

We inhaled the warm musk of ancient, carbonized plants drifting above the bed, the aroma from an earlier time. It was the fragrance of the nights I spent with Kirk.

His only window opened to the east around the corner from our windmill, its sucker rod penetrating deep into the dune in front of the house. When I was a kid, we relied on the ground water pumped up by the windmill into an old well that fed the house.

A soft, nocturnal breeze rotated its rusty vanes, pulling the rod up and pushing it back down, drawing water for the house and a wooden barrel on the porch. Rod and I bathed in a metal tub next to the pantry filled by water from a temperamental electric pump and worn-out pressure tank.

Kirk got up in the middle of the night and peed into an empty Folger's coffee can sitting on his windowsill. The tinny ring woke me up as I lay scrunched against the wind-colored wall. Kirk's flow continued until the final drips matched the tempo with the windmill gears protesting the breeze that pushed metal vanes around. The trapdoor of his long johns fell open when he climbed back into bed.

The Blue Room relaxed once more with the slumber of a nine-year-old cuddled in a wool blanket beneath a creased canvas spread, his gangly body bent in the fetal position, lying next to an old man who had been the child in an earlier century.

"Sleep well, Pard," Kirk said as I squirmed against him.

Everyone slept well in the country, under the shrill whistle of whippoorwills at sundown diving past the window for insects and the songs of meadowlarks nesting in the willows at sunup. Meanwhile, the windmill pumped the most peaceful cadence I knew.

First thing in the morning, I checked beneath Kirk's bed to see if he had dropped any change from his pants when he undressed the night before. I usually found two bits on the floor.

"Must have lost that," Kirk said. "Probably fell through a hole in my pocket. Keep it."

No doubt he saw the huge smile on my face, because mysteriously the coins increased on subsequent mornings, creating an unspoken game. His grandsons would sweep his room, pick up dirty socks, and empty the coffee can in exchange for a share in the wealth beneath his bed. Kirk salted the stash each time with as much change as he thought we deserved. Both generations benefited. Perhaps it hadn't been a game after all.

The summer brought even greater bunking opportunities with Kirk. Once he took all five of us grandkids on a camping trip into the Seminoe Mountains. We loaded his panel truck with thick mattresses, warm blankets, and canned grub.

Unbeknownst to us, Mom and her brother-in-law Chad paced back and forth in the ranch house while we loaded, nervous to let us travel so deep into the country for an overnight trip with a man who battled alcoholism throughout his adult life. But Kirk and his grandkids enjoyed an indestructible bond.

We kids laid on top of blankets and mattresses in the back of the truck while Kirk started the engine and pulled long on his famous horn, "AAUUGGAAHH." We leaned over the raised tailgate, smiled for Mom and her camera, and drove away singing "Banana Manna," happy to spend the night with Grandpa while our parents would be far away.

Kirk turned onto a two-track road twisting up Windy Ridge above Hurt Creek toward the saddle between Bradley Peak and the Seminoe Mountains. We passed several ancient tepee circles on the ridge crest where Indians once camped to avoid flies hovering down by the creek. Almost the entire ranch lay below us to the south.

Our truck stopped at a salt lick between Hurt and Deweese Creeks. Years earlier, Kirk had draped a bisected tire around a fifty-gallon barrel so the barrel stood in the hole where the wheel would have been. He filled the open tire ring with rock salt for the sheep. Salt was a necessary supplement in mountain pastures where salt sage didn't grow.

Cool mountain air filled our lungs, chilling our lips as we drank in the flavor of the high country. Ponderosa pine trees cast a crisp scent from seed-ripening cones, soon to be gathered by the many squirrels scurrying around us.

The shallow ridge of rock and grass formed a saddle connecting the Seminoe Mountains with Bradley Peak, a perfect camping spot with a panoramic view of northern Carbon County. Deweese Creek flowed blue and cold through aspen groves beneath us, cutting across the thick meadows to the north. Mule deer stared at us while grazing along the stream banks, assessing any threat from these two-legged interlopers frolicking on the divide above them.

"This is my favorite spot," Kirk said as he watched us unload.

"We love it too!"

The setting sun brightened the pasture as we set three double mattresses side by side on the hard ground, tucked in cotton sheets, and pushed pillows under heavy blankets. Then it was time to build a campfire for supper.

The five grandkids gathered fist-sized rocks and arranged them into a two-foot circle to support a cooking grate above the kindling. A low blaze soon grew in the central depression, heating the cans we brought from the pantry at the ranch. We huddled together in the fading light and scarfed down hot beanie-weanies and coffee for supper.

Kirk glanced up from his half-empty can, bean juice dripping down the corner of his mouth and coating the gray stubble of his unshaven cheeks. He pointed his gravy-coated fork to the west. "They discovered gold at the foot of Bradley Peak in 1872. Right over that hill. There's an abandoned mining town down in the draw."

We knew about the mine from his earlier stories. Soldiers from Fort Fred Steele escorted a handful of prospectors into the area and named Bradley Peak for the commanding officer at the outpost. Captain Deweese's cavalry troop led the miners across the creek below us, now named after him.

Several Lakota braves rode up Deweese Creek from Indian Territory in 1874 to investigate the new mining settlement. Prospectors saw them approach and set off an alarm before retreating to their piled brush fort on top of a nearby hill. Both sides skirmished most of the day.

Warriors killed a Dutchman who became isolated in an aspen grove south of the brush fort before he could get back to his friends. Mining activity ceased for a time after the battle, but the Lakota never came back.

"Let's camp at the mine beyond Dutchman's Grove next year," Kirk said.

After we cleaned up from supper, I doused the warm embers in the fireplace with leftover coffee. Steam hissed off the circle of rocks as they cooled.

All six of us climbed into bed under a cloudless sky dotted with thousands of stars dazzling in curiously arranged constellations. Pointing and laughing, we called off the ones we knew.

"There's the Big Dipper!" someone shouted.

Off to the east in Sunday Morning Canyon, a pack of coyote pups howled. Loud wails echoed through the long mountain valley, bouncing off rocky cliffs and disguising the den location where the first sounds had come from.

The soft wind gusts whistled through the aspen leaves, rocking the branches of Ponderosa pine. Evening breezes bent the tufted grass until their wiry blades scraped against our mattresses, coaxing nervous grasshoppers onto our bed. The furtive insects hopped around trying to identify the strangers who had invaded their nocturnal stomping ground. One jumped beneath the covers and everyone shrieked. After the wind died down, only Kirk's snoring broke the silence. We grandkids giggled for a few minutes and then fell asleep.

At sunrise, Kirk started the fire while his grandkids stirred beneath their covers. He made coffee, putting eggshells into the pot to sink the grounds to the bottom of the water. We ate some toast warmed over the fire and had just finished loading the truck for the trip home when Mom and Uncle Chad pulled up.

"Is everyone okay?" Mom asked.

Years later, I found out that they had spent a fitful night at the ranch, so worried they couldn't wait for Kirk to bring us safely off the mountain. Grandpa said nothing when they drove up, probably suspecting their ulterior motive but too proud to acknowledge the value of their concern.

Mom and Uncle Chad wore apprehensive smiles as we kids chattered on about the night before, pointing out where we built the fire and laid the mattresses. All the while, they covertly scanned the ground for whiskey bottles. But none existed, so they took off, and Kirk drove us home. Our parents may have never fully realized that, despite his transgressions, Kirk was always just a big kid around us, enjoying every moment we shared.

The salt lick camping trip ended up being our only overnight excursion with Kirk. We never went to the mine. Whenever I poured rock salt in later years, that fifty-gallon barrel and bisected tire reminded me of camping with him. I still imagined those stuffy mattresses, heard clicking grasshoppers' interrupt Kirk's stories of gold, and almost tasted lukewarm beanie-weanies.

The following week, Kirk craned his neck, squinting at the morning sky from the porch door. "It's about ten o'clock. We'll be back long before supper, Betty Rose."

I hovered around Grandpa as he pulled out his watch. Kirk's Hamilton Railway Special pocket watch kept perfect time, though he seldom used it when the sun moved from behind the clouds.

Mom fretted over when to put a roast in the oven so it would be ready to serve when her father-in-law returned from the sand dunes with his grandkids. She prepared meals at the ranch for many summers when Rod and I were young. The task kept her close to Dad for longer periods of time, staving off the loneliness she so often felt in town. She looked up at Kirk from a dishpan full of dirty water. "Please be careful out there."

"Right. Kids, let's go get us some willows."

Kirk drove to Hurt Creek below the ranch, upstream from the Supply Ditch head gate that had irrigated our pastures since 1886. He cut dozens of willows with a quick slice, each branch falling to the ground.

I reached into my jeans, rummaged through dirt clods and empty candy wrappers, and pulled out a pocketknife. Its only blade, seldom sharpened, was stuck inside the handle by a wad of week-old bubble gum. Finally working it open, I sawed back and forth for a couple of minutes, just to sever one branch.

Not long after, Kirk stopped and put his knife in his front pocket. "That ought to do it."

He threw the last armful of willows into the back of the truck and drove to the county road, stopping where the largest dune crept closer to our house every year. We carried cut willows up the leeward slope, crossed over the top of the dune, and picked a flat place to build our fort. Soft morning wind gathered millions of sand grains that scooted past our feet and hopped toward the ranch.

Kirk knelt beside us. "Stick the cut ends into the sand."

He shaped willows into a windward wall and scooped out a floor where we could hide in case of an Indian attack. Then he sat in the near distance with his back to the wind, watching us play.

Small sand particles blew up his back, bounced over his shoulders, and landed on the ground by his feet. Each grain looked identical from my point of view, but they had traveled so far, they surely had changed in different ways during their journey—rather like humans, I suppose.

The active sand dune where we built our fort buried the county road by the time we left the ranch. Highway crews were forced to scrape the route clear of dune sand with heavy equipment every year just to keep it open for traffic.

"We told the county they should build the road behind the dune where the sand had already passed, not in front of it," Dad said one year.

"It would have saved them a lot of work," I said. "That dune will migrate forever."

The county relented long after we left the ranch and detoured the road upwind of the big sand dune. Scientists now say that the dune will bury our headquarters buildings in about two hundred years, considering its current rate of travel.

The wind scoured out long sandy wings along either side of each parabolic dune that stretched back for miles to the southwest, the direction the wind almost always blew from. Sagebrush roots gripped them like twisted vines draped over vertical walls.

The incessant wind carved deeper and deeper troughs between the wings until cold ponds of fresh water bubbled from the ancient water table under the sod. Those ponds grew into long, narrow lakes behind each dune. From the air, this landscape resembled the trail of a giant horse dragging heavy hooves when he walked, forcing underlying moisture to rise in each step.

Emerging dune lakes transformed my childhood world in the early 1960s. Before the lakes formed, mule deer drank each morning from the swift current of Hurt Creek where it snaked through thick willows at the foot of the mountains a mile away. When the ponds rose, the deer abandoned the creek to water in the parabolic troughs. The sand dunes offered less cover than the foothills, but the lakes were more placid, and skittish deer become calm in the open, behaving like the current in the water they drank.

New ponds attracted life to areas once desolate and dry. Cattails grew where only sand once moved, and waterfowl landed on the ponds, leaving shrimp behind that had been embedded in the mud packed around the birds' webbed feet. Tadpoles grew from larvae lying dormant for years in the dry dunes, becoming frogs who croaked at the salamanders when they slithered over our toes as we waded there. No one ever explained where these diverse life forms came from—I only knew they were there.

The largest dune lake grew to a hundred yards long and ten feet deep, shimmering in the sun on quiet days, reflecting the verdant pasture that thrived along its margin. Kirk called it Loch Leven after a Scottish fjord, pleasing Mom because her family, the McKay clan, once lived in the northern Scottish Highlands.

"Let's go to Loch Leven tomorrow," Kirk said when we headed back for dinner after playing at the willow fort. "We'll bring the raft."

He always kept us busy planning new ways to have fun in the country. Earlier that week, we had gathered old bridge timbers and corral planks and then pounded sledgehammers against heavy spikes to build a makeshift raft large enough to hold a handful of kids.

The next morning, Rod, Bill, and I, along with a friend of ours, slid it into the back of Kirk's pickup before climbing in, gripping the truck's side panels so we wouldn't fall out. We parked at the lake and coaxed the heavy raft toward the back of the truck. As we inched it down to the ground, it slipped from everyone's grip and crashed onto the dune, nearly crushing me.

If I hadn't ducked, it would have broken my neck.

"You okay, Pard?" Kirk asked, his face full of concern.

"I'm all right," I said softly.

He squeezed my hand with his barbed-wire-scarred fingers. Fearless himself, Kirk didn't want to bring broken kids back to their parents at the end of the day.

We lashed ropes to the timbers and tugged the raft toward the water's edge, pushing and pulling across warm sand until we reached cool water. We scampered along the shoreline in cutoff jeans and T-shirts, eager to test the seaworthiness of our craft.

Kirk stood on the beach, his rancher's body hidden from the sun beneath a sweat-soaked work shirt and Wrangler jeans. Only his wind-blasted face, red neck, and gnarled hands turned to rawhide under its glare. He never wore a swimsuit or waded in Loch Leven. I think he hated the water.

My bare legs shivered when I stepped past the white foam, and then the underwater sand gave way until I sank ankle deep. If I stood in one place too long, the sand drew me deeper into the dune as if it would never stop. When I pulled my foot out, bubbles gathered on the surface and the gaping suction sounded a loud plop. Knee high in the ripples, I adapted to the cool water alongside the free-floating raft while the sun warmed its unpainted deck.

Ten feet out from the bank, I looked back at Kirk sitting on the dune below the truck, watching us. As we waded thigh high in the lake and began to climb onto the raft, he called out a friendly warning from the beach, "Don't go in over pecker deep!"

The grandkids took raft trips on Loch Leven several times that year, a unique summer with so much water behind the dune. But just as quickly as it rose, the water table receded the following year and Loch Leven evaporated. Mule deer returned to the creek, cattails dried on the bank, freshwater shrimp disappeared, and the salaman-ders wandered away. We never played there again.

A decade after the lake dried up, I was riding Moody River, Dad's favorite mare, through the same pasture while home on break from undergraduate work at the university. Dad sent me to find Adolph, an Angus bull we missed while gathering cattle the day before, but I couldn't concentrate on my task.

I was worried my grades were too low and angry I couldn't com-pete well enough to succeed in freshman football. A steaming pile of bull manure next to a set of fresh tracks caught my eye, refocusing my attention.

Adolph's trail headed straight for the dune that once held the cool waters of Loch Leven. Moody trotted over the grass-covered ridge and into the dry blowout where Kirk's grandkids once swam. The bull's tracks led across the trough past a gray-white object fifty yards away, a sun-bleached pile of desiccated wood and rusty nails resting half buried in the sand. An abandoned raft in a place with no water.

I stepped from the saddle, knelt beside the vessel, and touched the last vestige of one wonderful summer when Kirk's grandkids ruled the Loch Leven Sea. A gentle breeze blew sand across the unpainted deck, burying more of the raft with each gust. Hearing the wind as it passed, I laughed once more at the comical warning Kirk shouted at us when I was a boy.

Moody and I rode to the top of the hill where we saw the bull grazing in the meadow beyond. Adolph and I were old friends. He bucked me off several times in our rodeo arena down by the house, and when he saw me approach, he started off at a leisurely walk toward the next pasture and the rest of the bulls.

I relaxed in my saddle, absorbed by the rhythmic pace of Moody's elegant gait. My concern about college seemed insignificant now, smoothed over by old sentiments I heard in the wind and the synchronized plod of Adolph crossing the dunes.

6.

Grandpa's Final Years

Grandpa Kirk named all his favorite horses after treats. His beloved broodmare, Ice Cream, a strawberry roan, foaled three colts—Cookie, Cracker, and Peanuts.

I knew them all. Cookie was a gentle buckskin ridden by our sheep herders. Cracker was colored like his mom, a handsome horse willing to haul kids around the country. And Peanuts, a shimmering bay and a spirited mount, carried one of our best hands through the pastures.

Cracker lived the longest of the three, into the early 1980s, just before we left the ranch. We gave him to old Jake, a stove-up friend who lived in a cabin on the sunset side of the Seminoe Mountains. I suppose Cracker died up there in some aspen grove below the salt lick campground, the last of Ice Cream's progeny who spanned the years Rod and I grew up on the I Lazy D.

Kirk treated Ice Cream like a member of the family. Her light dappled body and solid dark face were colorful fixtures around the ranch yard. Dad rode her when trailing sheep to the forest every summer before I was born. Well up in years when I was a boy, Ice Cream developed streaks of gray hair in her multi-hued coat and her teeth were nearly gone.

She got sick one summer. Bill and I asked Kirk if we could help care for her.

Kirk turned her loose in the North ID pasture, and the three of us visited her every day in her retirement. She never moved from the spot where we left her, waiting for Kirk to visit each morning.

When she weakened further, we hauled hay and water to her. Kirk curried her sides, combed her tail, and untangled cockleburs from her knotted mane, whispering to her as they relived the many trails they had ridden together.

Then Bill and I started carrying oats to her. Kirk would say, "Don't spill the bucket, boys, she needs 'em all."

He'd rub the top of her nose, murmuring something to her that Bill and I couldn't hear. She eventually got to where she wouldn't even try to eat dry oats, so Kirk mixed them with water to make soft mush she could drink.

Despite our efforts, Ice Cream died next to the county road, just south of a sandstone outcrop called Elephant Rock, where centuries of abrading wind had carved the shape of an elephant's head and trunk at one end. Not everyone who looked at the rock saw the image of an elephant, but Kirk and his grandkids did.

Bill and I sat inside the hollow behind the trunk each time we visited Ice Cream and pretended we were riding a pachyderm across Africa. The county widened the road in later years, knocking the trunk off the elephant's head, but the fractured rock still marks the slope where the bones of Kirk's favorite mare lie.

Ice Cream died about 1962. Her bones weathered and dispersed over the years. Most have long since crumbled into the ground.

Over a decade ago, I gathered her last visible bone and took it to the university where I soaked it in preservative and then returned to bury it under a stone where she died. Now, part of her will always be there.

A strawberry mare who once produced great saddle horses now nurtures the soil that feeds the grass our livestock need to survive. Ice Cream's essence outlives her mortal existence—she is a lasting gift to the ranch. A life in the country should end this way, so others can begin.

"Who knows the answer?" Our fourth-grade teacher quizzed the class by introducing a math term I had not yet learned.

She drew strange chalk lines and numerals on the blackboard, probably wondering if we had studied anything on our own. Silence hovered over the room. Arms folded across the tops of desks, and our little heads burrowed behind bent elbows.

Square root? I'd heard of it before, but what did it mean?

I avoided eye contact with the teacher as she walked in my direction. I couldn't think of numbers when my mind was focused on the .22-caliber Remington semiautomatic rifles Dad had recently bought my brother and me to night-hunt jackrabbits in the hay meadow below the ranch house. Country thoughts. A vicarious safari from the gum-stuck seat of an old school desk. Besides, I rationalized, real cowboys didn't calculate square roots.

Linda sat straight in her chair across the aisle from me and raised her hand like she did every day. The dime-store locket I had given her the week before hung around her neck, its fake pink stone suspended between the subtle contours of her chest. To my relief, the teacher called on her and returned to the blackboard without glancing my way.

"The square root of nine is three," Linda said, and then looked at me with the softest smile I'd ever seen.

For some reason, which I never understood, Linda and I had become great friends. We had gone steady for most of the spring and acted as if we knew what that really meant.

"Mark is a boy, and he is my friend. I guess that makes him my boyfriend," Linda said to a fellow admirer, who liked her smile too.

I had already done my best to convince that classmate of my devotion to Linda by leaning into him against the brick wall during recess and doubling my fist under his nose. I quickly regretted my maneuver, but he understood.

He was a good guy who came from a sheep-raising family like mine. My fist probably bothered him less than when we called each other "Lamb Chops" in front of our friends.

Other boys now out of the picture, Linda and I spent every possible moment together. We talked of things that kids our age are only beginning to understand. She and I did homework at her house where I learned math by trusting her razor-sharp mind.

"Boys develop intelligence slower than girls," I overheard Mom tell a bridge club friend that spring.

"You'll need to study hard so you can go to college," she told me. She wanted her children to get good grades so we could attend a university as she did. But it would be an uphill climb for me. I was pretty ornery as a kid.

According to my folks, they had held me out of school until after I turned six because my birthday missed an enrollment cutoff. But Mom's conversation over a deck of cards that day set me straight. I had actually needed time to mature before entering the brain-teasing world of kindergarten. And she had correctly diagnosed my inability to concentrate on things other than the ranch—that is, until my girlfriend came along.

At nearly eleven, I happily honed my intellect on Linda's whetstone. Not only did she share her mathematical skill with me, but she also conveyed a self-confidence and social maturity far beyond her years. We became inseparable, took turns eating lunch at each other's houses, and walked together from school every day.

We even held hands in public but planned our future in private the way fourth-graders do. Our parents thought we made a cute couple.

"We'll build a house on the river with trees all around," Linda said.

"Trees and sagebrush. I'm not a forest kind of guy."

"It will be a nice home." She smiled.

Linda's father served as a career military officer constantly reassigned to different bases across the country. An only child with few friends, Linda seldom spent two consecutive years attending the same school. She never lived in a house long enough to ever call it a home.

They transferred to Rawlins after I passed the third grade. When they arrived, Linda's parents bought her a dog to give her a greater sense of family, an identity of place. Soldier behaved like a mongrel to me, an abandoned mutt nobody else wanted, but he and Linda were an immediate match.

Her dog became Linda's target when we shot home from school following the afternoon bell. She ran straight and true, and if not for me holding her hand, Linda would sprint the entire way.

Seeing us cross the street, Soldier would jump up from the porch, his tail wagging and his wet tongue hanging out. Linda wrapped her arms around the dog, the most dependable part of her home. He seemed to sense her happiness when we were together, so he tolerated me, letting me pet his head but keeping me at a far greater distance from his heart.

On the last day of school, I walked Linda home, excited about the summer. But when I saw the bags packed in her room, my spirits plummeted. She was moving again. We hugged and cried and fumbled through what both of us hoped was a kiss.

She felt different to my touch. Aloof. As if part of her had already moved away.

"I can't take Soldier with us, Mark. What am I going to do?" The best part of her home would be left behind.

"How about the kennel? Maybe put him up for sale?" I worried more about me at the time and our fantasy house by the cottonwood grove and the sage.

"Do you think your grandfather would let you take Soldier to the ranch?"

"I don't know, maybe."

Linda was the closest thing to love I knew back then, so I asked Kirk.

"He grew up as a town dog, right, Pard?" he said cautiously.

"As far as I know."

"Well, you'll have to take care of him. He's unfamiliar with the country."

I picked up Soldier in early June when I kissed my girlfriend goodbye. All that remained of her now was the dog, a pesky mutt who slobbered on my boots. He whined as we walked to my house, knowing his world had changed.

Our ranch was a foreign land to Soldier. Every new image frightened him. He cowered from his own shadow, so I kept him leashed the first couple of days and walked him around the yard until he grew accustomed to his new surroundings.

Although friendly with my family, Soldier stared in awe at the livestock. Horses, cows, pigs, chickens, and sheep—a place alive with animals that man had tamed, and the dog was his oldest conquest.

Soldier eventually adapted, assuming an air of ascribed nobility at the top of the rangeland hierarchy. His tail began to wag, and his tongue hung out again. At night, Soldier howled in chorus with coyotes on the hill. By day, he ran alone on the rocky slopes of the ranch.

Unlike Soldier, attentive dogs can be trained to work with livestock better than most herders. Such dogs are particularly good around sheep. But the bond is tenuous between man and beast, sustained only by honest loyalty between them.

The dog, the man, and even the sheep occupy a place along an ancient continuum that began in the wild and ended with domestication. The greatest difference among them, it seemed, was the way they ate.

Away from Linda, Soldier walked the narrow path separating a domestic dog from a feral one. As the days passed, that path dimmed. He regressed to the natural state of his wild ancestors, acquiring one fatal flaw that resurrected a vestigial trait of his wolf-pack brethren, a habit inconsistent with the tolerances of ranch life.

Soldier loved the taste of warm blood.

He killed his first ewe after three weeks on the ranch. The carcass lay in the lower meadow where Kirk kept a hospital herd of weak ewes and lambs. Its throat had been torn away, ripped out, leaving a severed trachea dripping in blood, the veins of the sheep's neck exposed. Back at the ranch, Soldier sat on the porch with his hair matted down and bloody wool stuck to his jaw.

"You know what Soldier did, Pard?" Kirk asked.

I nodded but didn't say a word.

"You can't let him do it again." Kirk's abiding love for his grandson spared the dog this time.

That night, I slept in the old stone house and thought of a girl who taught me about square roots. My only comfort lay in knowing that Linda now lived in an unknown place, another house too transient to be home, too far away to learn about Soldier.

Kirk entered my dreams as he often did when I slept in the country. I realized my favorite playmate also managed the ranch that his father, Ike, had started. Kirk bought and sold livestock, balanced the budget books, hired and fired, and fed protein cake to cattle who answered the honk of his horn.

Our sheep were Kirk's responsibility. Without them, we had no income, and without income, we had no ranch. What would my family be if we had no ranch? His responsibility toward livestock had to be shared.

Kirk's early caution about Soldier became clear. My task loomed. But how could I intervene between Soldier and the resolute power of nature that siphoned him back to the wild, away from the tame life he once knew?

I did nothing, as if my head still rested on my desk in fourth grade waiting for Linda to answer the square-root question. I wished Soldier would leave our livestock alone.

But in the morning, the dog killed again. Pumping arteries from a second ewe baptized Soldier into his feral life and banished him from the love I had for Linda. The flavor of domestic blood transformed Soldier from man's best friend into the predator his ancestors were.

"Don't make Mark do it," Mom said to her father-in-law while we all stood on the porch.

"You're right, Betty Rose," Kirk said. "Rod, get your rifle."

Kirk ordered my brother to bring his new .22 semiautomatic Remington to the coal shed in the front yard. I followed with my girlfriend's dog, both of us shivering uncontrollably. Mom and Kirk were close behind.

Mom stared in abject dread while Rod chambered a cartridge in his rifle, aimed the front sight between the dog's eyes, and squeezed the trigger. A loud bang, a wet thud, and Soldier fell to the ground.

No one spoke. Kirk and I stood next to each other under the pall of acrid gun smoke, but our bodies didn't touch. We were miles apart.

Kirk, Mom, and Rod walked to the house while I laid Soldier in a shallow depression on the lee side of a dune next to the chicken coop, covering his limp body with sand. Leaves of rabbitbrush fell from the shrubs blanketing the surface of his grave. I sat alone on the woodpile and thought of Linda for the last time.

Soldier had been my only link to her. Now he was gone, and the place in my heart where she lived was filled with a new apprehension.

I never loved the dog, but I had given Linda my word to care for him. I loved Kirk, but he killed her dog because he killed our sheep.

I began to sense the culture of stock raising, the fragile ecology of the rangeland where I lived, and the vulnerable weave of my family. My apprehension became a penetrating sense of wonder mixed with visceral pain.

At the time, I was hurt and angry that Rod had followed Kirk's orders. But my brother had done only what any grandson of a stockman must do: protect the herd from an imminent threat. Rod did what I couldn't do, and Mom had known it.

An hour after the killing, Kirk sent Rod to the woodpile. "Here, Mark. Grandpa says this is for you."

He held out a five-dollar bill, pensive and alert. He stood in an awkward place, his hands trembling as if the money were harder to grip than a gun trigger, and the outcome of his action less certain.

I swallowed hard. How could Kirk do this? I was his bunkie. He called me Pardner.

After ordering my brother to kill the dog, he sent him to mitigate the pain, a mediator to do his dirty work for him. Rod was only a year older than me, while Kirk was well over seventy.

The difference between his age and mine must have prohibited a mutual expression of remorse. His monetary gesture failed. I closed my mind to his offer.

The fact that Kirk sent Rod to the woodpile instead of coming himself hurt more than the death of the dog. Grandpa and I had things to say to each other that could not be translated by anyone else. But he was stoic and prideful, and he taught me those lessons well.

To my eternal regret, we never spoke of the dog again.

Kirk got sick a couple of years later, and my folks put him in the hospital in Rawlins. His condition worsened while dementia robbed him of his keen intellect and vivid sense of humor. The bright light that lived in those smiling eyes dimmed more every day.

I visited him once in his white hospital room, an antiseptic place so clean and far lonelier than the Blue Room at the ranch. He had been watching television when I arrived, and some network anchorman spoke from behind a news desk. The picture on the old black-and-white portable blurred into snowy and erratic clutter, causing the diffuse image of the man to flip down the screen again and again, exposing a black line between every frame.

"Why does the man keep going to the basement?" Kirk asked.

I walked over to the set and adjusted the vertical control, correcting the picture.

"Thanks, Pard," he said.

I should have told him then that I understood about the dog, but I was afraid to bring it up. Mine had been the healthy mind that day in the hospital. I was in charge of the conversation.

Instead, I froze, unable to apologize to the old man who had graced my life more than any living soul, the man who showed me how to feed protein cake to the cattle. His blood, sweat, and tears taught me the cowboy way. What a coward I was.

"You're welcome, Grandpa." Soon after, I got up and left.

When his health finally failed, Dad's sister, Marggy, moved Kirk to a hospital for mentally challenged patients in Evanston. My parents never took me to visit him there, thinking it was no place for children. Mom and Dad went one last time, only days before he died.

Kirk called out as they were leaving, "Frank, Betty Rose, come over here, please."

They stood beside his bed and leaned down as he weakly whispered the last words he ever spoke to my family. "Tell Mark . . . I hope . . . he forgives me for the dog."

The low drone of our family Oldsmobile echoed off the cut stone wall, drumming a synchronous tune in my brain. It was 1965. We drove past the penitentiary grounds, where Rod and I played baseball one year, and closed the short distance to Walnut Street as our tires crawled through the intersection, crunching the gritty sand that blew across the asphalt.

Dad's white knuckles gripped the steering wheel, cautious of pedestrians crossing the street, deliberate in every motion he made. A tear slid down Mom's cheek as she patted Dad on his thigh. Rod and I sat in the back seat of the station wagon and fiddled with our ties, the smooth cadence of the car's pistons softening an awkward silence in the cab.

We parked, walked through the heavy door at our destination, and stood beside Grandpa Kirk. I had never seen a dead man before.

He lay in an artificial pose fashioned by the undertaker to comfort the mourning audience. His best suit draped over his broad shoulders, dry-cleaned one last time by an old friend on Front Street. The work shirt and jeans he always wore on the ranch were folded at home in his dresser. My grandfather left this earth when I was thirteen and he was seventy-seven.

Kirk once told Bill and me that he wanted his cremated ashes scattered over the ranch by the winds blowing from the top of Bradley Peak. We relayed his request, but our parents didn't take us seriously.

Now his eyelids shrouded the bright light that had animated my youth, closed above the morning stubble someone shaved away. Even his false teeth were in place, but Kirk's lips were silent, inert. He would never smile again. His ears could not hear the weeping whisper from his heartbroken grandson beside him. "I forgive you, Grandpa!"

PART 2

Livestock

Branding time at the Saltiel Corral. 1956.

I have the upper hand this time. June 1956.

Our pet lambs. *Left to right:* Susan, me, and Rod. 1958.

7.

Wintering Sheep

As a young teenager grieving for his grandfather, I relived every memory of him, propelled now to become the best rancher I could be. I began to see the land, the animals, and the work from a different perspective, eager to accomplish what my young mind believed he would have expected of me. With Kirk in my heart, there was nothing I couldn't do.

The last time I helped him work sheep was in 1963, the year he retired. The unspoken words about Soldier hung heavily over us, especially when I spent any time alone with him, but nothing could get in the way of the ranch and the chores we needed to do.

That morning, the sun had just peeked over the crest of Bead Hill when Kirk's truck crushed through the loose gravel and slowed to a stop. "There they are, boys," he said to Bill and me.

Before us, two hundred ewes nuzzled their snouts deep in the spring grass, nibbling on the fresh blades right after the last vestige of snow had melted away. Their thick white wool turned bronze in the early rays of the day. Bill and I hopped out of Kirk's truck, tasked with herding the sheep north on foot into the next pasture.

The flock raised their heads at the sound of our footsteps, pivoted in the direction we wanted them to go, and ran as if they all were glued together, one golden-white flock folding over every hill on the way. Bill and I trotted behind them for a mile and then climbed back into Kirk's truck, happy the two lead animals had bells strapped to their necks that all the others would follow.

"That was easy," Bill and I said together, smiling at Kirk.

"Good job!" He turned the truck back onto the road. "The lead will reach the gate in a few minutes. Let's beat 'em there."

Back then, we raised both cattle and sheep, but I much preferred working with sheep. They were less harmful to the stream banks than cattle when they grazed, and they were easier to winter, without requiring so much supplemental feed. Plus, they gave us two paychecks a year, one for wool shipments and another when we sold some of the older animals.

Most importantly, though, being around sheep reminded me of Kirk, and I owed it to him to never let another animal die on my watch.

By the time I was born, the Miller sheep knew our pastures well, having grazed there for seventy years. They thrived on the best winter range in the country thanks to Joel Hurt's research back in the 1870s. Joel had interviewed old hunters and learned where the pronghorn wintered. He chose the same range to start his sheep ranch, knowing pronghorn and sheep had similar habitat and food preferences.

The sagebrush steppe of the western Hanna Basin supported many tall shrubs that could survive with limited rainfall, providing nutritious feed for our flocks. North-trending hogback ridges trapped snow in deep drifts against the steep windward side of several uplifted escarpments. Prevailing southwesterly wind skipped over the rocks, passing above their lee side on its way to the river.

Livestock hunkered down in these windless oases between hogbacks, protected from the frigid bite of harsh winter storms. Few animals could survive our blizzards without this crenulated landscape to protect them.

One Saturday morning during high school, I was sitting at the dining room table with my folks having breakfast when Dad pushed back his chair and rose to his feet. He swallowed the last of the coffee in his cup. "Finish up, Mark. I'm heading to the Upper Coal Creek pasture to repair the windmill, and I need you to spot me while I climb the tower."

"I'd like to go too," Mom said, clearing the table. "It's been years since I visited that country."

"Then load up, you two. We're burning daylight." Dad smiled. "We'll go right past Sefarino Gonzales's old sheep camp, Betty Rose. You remember him."

We piled into the pickup and took off, the dust kicking up behind us. When we reached the main road, my folks both lit up cigarettes and cracked their windows as I sat between them playing with the radio dials.

"Sefarino was from old Mexico," Dad said. "A dedicated tender, for sure, but I always thought he was kind of a renegade."

We needed good herders to tend the sheep, no matter where they came from or how quirky they were. Dad point to the tableland where Gonzales's camp once sat north of Coal Creek beyond the crest of a steep canyon. The spot was next to the windmill we needed to repair.

"Your mom liked Sefarino, so she always rode with me when I brought groceries to resupply his sheep wagon." Dad chuckled. "He had a fiddle. Couldn't play very well, but he liked to serenade your mom."

We drove through a gate near Sefarino's old, abandoned sheep camp and checked the condition of the pasture on the way to the troublesome windmill, "tucking in the edges," as Dad would say.

"Sefarino wasn't that bad," Mom said.

"He herded a band of two thousand ewes, but he didn't like to ride horseback," Dad said. "I don't think he trusted them. He kept a walking stick instead and stayed behind the herd on foot when he brought them back to the bed ground after their evening feeding."

One night, an early-season snowstorm blew in from the north

while Gonzales and his herd were still half a mile from camp. Visibility dropped to a couple of feet in front of the man's face in a matter of seconds. Bone-numbing cold bit into his limbs.

The sheep drifted toward the familiar bed ground with their heads bent down as the entire pasture turned white. Blinding snow stung Sefarino's face until he lost sight of the landscape and the animals. Howling wind drowned out any herd noise.

Sefarino had stumbled through the blizzard looking for the sheep in the direction he hoped was the evening bed ground and the safety of his camp. He stepped into the swirling whiteout and disappeared in the tempest.

"I found his body the next morning when I checked on all my herders," Dad said. "I figure Sefarino walked right past his sheep wagon camp in the storm and stepped off a cliff into the blowing snow."

When Dad found him, his body lay stretched out in the bottom of a dry stream channel as if he had just gone to sleep. He had only a little scratch and discoloration on his side. No blood stains, no contorted face, no twisted limb. Just a dead fiddle-playing sheep herder who never rode horses. "He must have injured himself when he fell."

"I sure missed him," Mom said softly. "It just wasn't the same without him."

Sefarino had collided head-on with the unpredictable caprice of Mother Nature. A man can become so familiar with his landscape, crisscrossing it on a regular basis for years, until suddenly the volatile balance of nature turns against him and creates a world of uncompromising terror.

One minute you're in the middle of a typical workday, and the next minute you're dead. We could never take the landscape or the weather for granted. Familiarity can be a tenuous thing.

Buck sheep (rams) were more difficult for herders to handle than ewes. The outfit hired Jim Jensen as a buck herder before World War II, a prudent man who steadied unruly animals under his charge. If the bucks were stubborn, Jim became determined. When they were sullen, he offered more care.

"Jim lived life like the bucks, dividing his day into four separate parts," Dad told me during another of our drives in the country. "He would get up at three every morning to follow two hundred rams to their predawn feeding. They would eat until eight, and then lethargy set in when the day started to warm. After Jim herded them back to the bed ground, he'd shade up in his wagon and go back to sleep."

Jim moved the rams out to graze again when the sun dipped low on the western skyline and evening breezes cooled the pasture once more. Five hours later, following their supper of sagebrush leaves, rabbitbrush, and sedge, Jim brought the rams back to camp for the rest of the night. The first phase in the cycle repeated before dawn.

Good buck herders kept rams away from the ewes until breeding season. Before we put the males in with the females, we powdered the rams' backs with Rawlins Red ocher, so they would stand out when we flew a helicopter over each herd. A painted back in with the ewes at the wrong time of year signaled a death warrant for the buck. It was critical that ewes not get pregnant too early or they might drop lambs while the temperatures were still freezing, endangering them. And if a ram mixed with a neighbor's ewes, only his quick demise might prevent a lawsuit. A negligent buck herder could cost lives and money.

"Jim had the best damn bucks in the country," Dad said. "And he was the best buck herder in the country. He also liked to drink, but only when he wasn't working. After we put the bucks in with the ewes, he would go to town and get drunk—and stay drunk. When breeding season ended six weeks later, Jim came back out, sobered up, and was ready to herd again."

During Dad's time, the ranch shifted breeds from the Merino herds my great-grandfather ran to Rambouillets. They were gregarious and had tight wool, but it grew over their eyes and blinded them. Wool-blind bucks moved in a tight herd since they couldn't see well, needing security in the company of others.

Early in December we would gather them at the Halfway Corral to shear the thick wool from their faces. Eventually, we shifted breeds. Columbia sheep, an American variety, produced heavier, coarser wool that didn't cover the animals' faces.

At our peak, we herded six thousand ewes in three equal bands separate from the rams, a herd size calculated to provide thirty females for each buck during breeding season. Cool nights of late autumn triggered untapped passion in the bucks, but if their sexual aggression peaked too soon, we had to lock them in corrals. Toward the middle of December, we would divide the bucks into three bunches to mix with ewes, Jim herding one, Dad the second, and another man the third. Herders needed only to point the rams in the general direction of females. Each knew where to go and what to do when he got there. Even a fast herder could hardly keep up.

Hired hands encouraged more successful breeding by riding through pastures searching for ewes without bucks, gathering them together, and mixing them in a band already with bucks on the bed ground. Good bucks worked hard at sex, each servicing multiple females a day, so they didn't have much strength left to walk around searching for more ewes on their own.

Looking back on my young life around livestock, I was surrounded by sex and death. I had to learn about both.

Shorty was one of our best ranch foremen, starting with us a year after my grandfather died. It was a mystery how the man got his name—he wasn't short at all. A tough ex-marine, he was a lean, muscular cowboy who knew livestock better than anyone, except Dad.

Shorty had ridden for only a few different outfits before he came to us, like the Pine Grove, working so hard every owner was happy to keep him on their payroll. He earned the admiration and respect from every rancher simply by riding for their brand. But his passion for perfection could be hard on teenagers, like the time eight of us rode Indian Creek looking for cattle.

"You didn't clean the pasture," Shorty barked at the riding crew.

"I saw half a dozen cows over on the divide." He nodded to the west and spat out a wet wad of chewed tobacco.

"We can never clean a pasture with only one ride," Dad said to us kids, trying to ease our minds. "Our pastures are just too large."

Shorty grunted. "Maybe so, but we still missed 'em. We'll have to ride it again tomorrow."

As demanding as Shorty was, no one showed more compassion for young men on the ranch. He and Rob, an experienced hand, were riding back from a cattle drive one day when Rob's horse tumbled down a frozen dune and rolled over him. He got hung up in the saddle and hit his head on the frozen ground. His back snapped under the horse's weight.

Shorty galloped Zeke into the ranch yard and yelled for Dad. Zeke's hooves slid on loose gravel and he fell too, throwing Shorty from the saddle. He landed face down on the ground, crushed his glasses, and poked a jagged shard into the skin next to his eye. Blood poured from the open wound as Dad rushed over.

"Hurry, Frank," Shorty said. "Rob had a wreck. We need to help him and catch his horse."

Dad doctored Shorty's eye first and then loaded a wooden door into the back of his truck to lift Rob and drove them both to the hospital in Rawlins. A man like Shorty who put others first, over his own safety, was the kind of man we kids felt comfortable with in the country.

Early one February after breeding season, he took me along to trail the bucks to their pasture at Big Spring. Most of them were worn out and ready to rest. Older rams plodded beneath the sun's growing warmth.

One indolent buck lagged fifty yards behind the rest, his painted red body heaving up and down with each labored breath. He stopped to watch as we shrank in the distance with the rest of the herd, beyond the focus of his sad, jaded eyes.

Shorty turned in his saddle. "Better go back and kill that one, Mark. He can't make it the rest of the way."

The buck, too weak to live another season, stood panting on the hill. I loped toward him pondering the drastic tasks I sometimes performed in my ranching life. Stay healthy, have sex, get old, then die. Simple. One way or another, we all got our turn at the back of the herd.

The buck's head drooped. Green snot dripped from his nose. He didn't even fight when I pulled up his snout to cut a gash in his throat from one ear to the next.

Blood oozed out, coaxed by the heart-pumping stress of a long trail. He dropped to the ground, and I rode back to Shorty with a pounding headache, wondering how the other bucks felt after witnessing my deed.

Shorty peered over his shoulder a few minutes later. "What's that on the hill behind us?"

I looked back and the "dead" buck was standing stiff-legged on the slope staring at me through half-murdered eyes, his life's blood drying in red streaks stuck to the wool under his chin. The knife I never kept sharp couldn't even kill an animal too weak to live on his own. My shallow cut had missed his jugular vein.

I didn't answer Shorty's question, my face hot with shame and embarrassment. I turned silently to the herd, letting the old ram behind me choose for himself when he wanted to die.

Shorty loped back on his own, almost severed the buck's head, and reined in beside me when he returned. "Want a chew?" He took a pinch of Copenhagen and handed me the open can.

"Thanks, Shorty." I studied his weathered face and the narrow grin beneath the brim of his sweat-soaked Stetson. Would he tell Dad of my failure? For sure, Kirk would have been disappointed in me. But Shorty looked relaxed, unperturbed, as he had the whole day.

He slapped his reins against the stovepipe chaps that covered his thighs. "Let's get the rest of the bucks to Big Spring."

No mention of the ram at all. I knew then that he would keep it between us.

Back at the ranch, he and I sat down for a hot cup of coffee, always available from a pot sitting on a warm burner of the stove. I laughed to myself while I drank. For Shorty, every workday had to begin at five in the morning with him getting up and starting the coffee. It was his way of taking control of the day.

A top hand with a sense of humor like mine once decided to tease Shorty by getting up at four thirty and starting the coffee himself. When Shorty came down the stairs, he glowered at the already hot coffee pot, poured a cup, and sat down at the table, but said nothing to any of us. Next morning Shorty was up at four to make the coffee. We got the message and didn't fool with him any longer.

I learned early on that sheep have a herd mentality, even more so than cattle. They do the same thing others around them are doing, with no regard for consequences. I can forgive them their ignorance and lack of invention. After all, they are a product of having been tamed.

Sheep have lost most of the wild in them, their will to fight back, like the ewe we called Mary at the ranch. We grandkids tried all one summer to teach her how to smoke cigarettes, but she would only eat the tobacco and spit out the filters. She never learned the skills we tried to teach, and we never learned not to try, but we loved playing with her.

Later, as a teenager, I trailed three ewes across Coal Creek below the shearing pens, scatter riding the pasture for stray animals. The tributary channel was caked with dry mud on top, while a bentonite gumbo lingered soft, sticky, and moist just beneath the surface.

The lead ewe walked into the middle of the creek bed, broke through the crust, and sank belly deep in gray mud that coated her fleece as thick as molasses. The other two ewes followed head to tail behind her, stepped into the channel, and got stuck there too. Looking down at them from a hill above, the small group resembled the numeral "1" scribbled in white on a dirty chalkboard.

Riding downstream below the bog, I circled back to the far side of the creek before dismounting and wrapping my reins around a tall greasewood. I stepped gingerly into the mire surrounding the three sheep until I reached the lead ewe, her head barely above the surface, choking for air as the grip of soggy clay sucked her deeper into the bog.

Her eyes pleaded for rescue behind rolls of muddy gray wool twice its normal weight. She lunged forward, again and again. The more she fought the deeper she sank, and the ewes behind her cowered in fear.

I eased my rope under her belly and snaked it up behind her forelegs. Then I tied a clove hitch with the other end of the rope around the saddle horn and led my horse up the slope, pulling the first ewe from her muddy tomb onto dry ground. The bog gurgled when she broke free, causing a huge bubble of mud to burst in her wake. The next animals were easier to save now that they could follow the wide trough she had plowed.

When I got back to the ranch, I threw away my ruined Wrangler jeans and cowboy boots, an expensive lesson learned. Many years later, when I was an archaeologist traveling across the state, I saw another man's ewe stuck in his bog. Unable to ignore her fate by driving away, at least this time I stripped off my boots, socks, and Wranglers before walking in.

The rancher drove up right after I pushed his ewe in front of me onto dry ground. He waited while I stood embarrassed in mud-soaked underwear and tried to explain what I had been doing behind his ewe.

Fortunately, he believed me, admitting he had watched me with binoculars from a nearby hill. We laughed together, marveling at how ranchers could keep sheep alive long enough to shear them and sell off their wool.

8.

Adventures with Woollies

On a warm afternoon in April, a high school friend and I drove across a side hill pasture looking for sheep we missed the day before. Every year at this time, we gathered sheep at the shearing pens to cut off their wool, bag it, and send it to the warehouse in Rawlins, where it was stored until sold. That particular day, my buddy and I spotted two pregnant, unshorn ewes lying down on a hot slope where shade had long since vanished. What was wrong with them? Why hadn't they moved to a cooler spot?

A bald eagle hovered above the farthest prostrate ewe, circled overhead, and then perched on the ewe's front shoulder. The sheep kicked dirt into a cloud and raised her head in a feeble flinch to frighten the big bird away. Heedless of the movement, the eagle pecked at the ewe's bobbing head, feeding on prey before it was dead.

"Get the hell outta here!" I yelled.

I honked the horn while my partner pounded the outside of his hollow door until the eagle flew away.

Approaching the ewes, we could see what had happened. Both had bedded for the night on a gradual slope with their feet pointing downhill. A year's growth of heavy wool and near-term fetuses weighted their bodies flat against the slope overnight. They woke paralyzed, unable to get their feet beneath them to stand. Shallow trenches, plowed under their hooves, traced the path of their futile struggle to rise.

My friend and I lifted each ewe, held her steady on her feet, and released our grips. Both slumped to the ground. We pulled them forward a few steps, forcing them to walk, yet they fell once more when we stopped.

Finally, we loaded them into the pickup bed and drove two miles to where Dad waited at the north end of the pasture. Our tires bounced over bumps and ruts, the transmission lunging when we knocked down thick brush, stimulating every nerve in the numb limbs of the sheep. We parked next to Dad, opened the tailgate, and the ewes jumped to their freedom, running away as if nothing was wrong.

I admire eagles despite what happened to that wounded ewe, but I resent some of their dietary choices. I always scared them away rather than killing them when they confronted our stock.

Coyotes were a different matter.

Bitches slaughtered young lambs just to show their pups how to kill, sometimes leaving the small woolly carcasses to rot. Coyotes are so well adapted to their environment—their size reflects the latitude where they live, and their color blends in with the range. As they roamed all over the ranch, their howls broke the silence of dusk and dawn as if they never slept.

A couple of days after my friend and I scared off that eagle, Dad and I were in his truck checking for more stray livestock. As we neared the Stone Fence landscape, he stopped and leaned forward. "There they are." He looked through his binoculars and pointed to a small band of sheep that should have been miles away at the shearing pens. "But a coyote is stalking them."

I squinted at the brushy slope below the Stone Fence rock formation. A coyote disappeared into a draw behind the sheep and then emerged at the foot of the hill just below where they grazed, his sleek brown and gray profile bouncing. Soon his silhouette blurred behind tall sagebrush.

Dad pushed his truck into gear. "We better hurry."

"I'll get him."

I pulled the .30-30 Winchester carbine from the gun rack behind the seat while Dad raced through the brush toward the sheep. It had been several years since I forgave Kirk for killing my girlfriend's dog. By then I was nearly an adult and eagerly sought vengeance against any predatory canine lusting after our sheep.

Five minutes later, Dad and I crossed the dry arroyo and drove up the slope where the sheep had been when their position passed from our view. The herd was gone except for one bloody ewe sprawled beside the coyote's big paw tracks in the dirt. The cold-blooded killer scampered away before I could take a clean shot, his back legs passing his front as he ran, his head stretching back over his shoulder to watch us during his cowardly escape.

A jumble of tracks told the story. Charging the herd from the draw, the coyote isolated the slowest animal and ran alongside until his sharp teeth ripped a hole in her from belly to brisket. The unlucky ewe lay at the end of her tracks, steaming viscera rolling from her gaping wound, dripping into the turbid sand beneath her.

Pungent vapors still rose from under her ribs when we arrived. Her eyes blinked with resignation as shattered breaths escaped her lips. I raised my rifle and put a bullet in her brain, though she was not the target I had originally intended. The rest of the herd made it back to the shearing pens unmolested.

Sheep shearing required plenty of preparation and labor. Kirk had built multitiered shearing pens at O'Brien Spring in the center of the I Lazy D, an architectural design promoted as part of a wool reform movement around World War I. The elaborate trilevel affair boasted corrugated walls and a tin roof, full-sized holding pens, long alleys, and sloping chutes to maneuver our sheep. A concrete base around a vertical post had been engraved with a record of its completion on May 20, 1918.

Dad sheared at these pens every April. He had to finish thousands of sheep before lambing in late May, or the little ones might get trampled in the crowded pens. Contract shearers arrived from Texas and New Mexico to schedule their work among several neighboring ranches, a tight window with little wiggle room. If their travel was delayed or Mother Nature rebelled, the sheep might suffer at a time they were most vulnerable.

In 1965, when Bill and I were thirteen and Rod fourteen, Dad decided we were old enough—and strong enough—to handle more shearing responsibilities. That year our job was to keep the sheep moving through the system of corrals, holding pens, and alleys. The pressure was on us to make sure the shearers always had plenty of animals within easy reach.

The three of us coaxed them up a wooden ramp to a heavy door hanging on iron rollers at the entrance to a large pen on the top tier of the complex. Inside, old canvas strips covered the windows and shut out the blazing sun. High paneled walls, made from inch-thick boards, were nailed to smooth posts that reached up to our chests and separated the pens from the alleys.

Hundreds of sheep crowded together, their bleats and baas bouncing off the tin walls and echoing through the stifling shed. Thousands of hooves beat the floor suspended four feet off the ground on strong wooden supports. Pushing the last animals through, we closed the heavy door behind them.

As I walked among the sheep, my legs rubbed against thick wool, lanolin grease soaking into my jeans from packed bodies that reached up to my thighs. Busy filling alleys and pens, I would have to check later for sheep ticks that hitched a ride on my legs. If one bit into my flesh, I'd burn it off with the wooden matches I kept in my shirt, hoping to avoid tick fever.

My knees pushed a cluster of sheep away from a panel gate I opened between the holding pen and a narrow alley spanning the length of the building against the west wall. Two hundred animals ran through the gate thinking they had found an escape, but I closed it behind them before they discovered the truth.

A dozen smaller gates hinged along the east alley panels, each leading to a small holding pen in front of a long strip of dirty canvas dangling from an overhead beam. Beyond the canvas was a low drop-off to the next tier. We filled each small pen with a dozen sheep from the alley and then waited while the shearing began behind the canvas.

The stale air in the cloistered corral tasted thick on my dry lips, nearly too heavy to breathe. It hung in my nostrils and coated my mouth. The back room between tin walls became a sauna fueled by body heat rising in clouds off the thick wool of unshorn sheep. Sweat flowed over caked dust on my cheeks, dripping onto my tongue with the sting of wet salt. All three of us boys longed for diversion as we waited to fill the pens, hidden from the eyes of our parents who stood beyond the moldy canvas drapes.

"Hand me a chew," Bill whispered.

I reached into my back pocket for a half-empty can of Skoal. "Take a pinch."

The second tier on the other side of the canvas skirts lay below the drop-off along the east end of the small holding pens. These skirts were stained brown and greasy on the side facing us, but they shone white like an artist's canvas on the side facing out to the second floor.

Each shearer stood on a raised platform, positioned beneath electric clippers suspended from a jointed metal arm attached to the wall next to the white canvas skirt behind him. Waiting for more sheep, a shearer often grabbed a waxy marking pen and drew images on his canvas, usually naked women embracing well-endowed men in a variety of intimate positions. Sometimes he would sign his name, write down the date, or carve initials in weathered wooden planks with his knife. The artwork usually outlived every artist.

Reaching up under the canvas skirt, the shearer would leg out another ewe, and slide her down until she stopped on his platform. Then he'd tie the back feet to a front foot with a length of pigging string. His clippers cut the fleece from one side of the animal to the other, and he gathered the wool in a roll between his knees before tying it off. When the shearer cut dirty wool from under the sheep's tail, he piled it separately in a brown mass we called tags.

Tags, or dags, still contained fecal residue from the shorn animal, so they would need to be extensively cleaned or "skirted" before anyone was likely to pay much for it. We left that process up to the purchaser. Even then, tags would not generate as good a quality product as the premium wool.

Good shearers finished a hundred ewes a day without wounding a single animal. Careless workers did far less and spent too much time suturing cuts inflicted by haste.

Shorn animals slid down a slip chute leading to the ground-level tier beneath the small holding pens. Vertical posts supported the structure above them. Sheep rested there until the top tier was empty, waiting for freedom beneath the dust and urine that dripped through the cracks overhead.

When we finished our duties in the upper pens, we turned the sheep out to get dusted for ticks and parasites and then branded with paint. Afterward, we walked outside smelling like old sheep and sweating from the heat radiating off the tin walls. It felt good to finally escape the cloistered holding pens beneath the floor.

"Man, I sure could use a shower," I said.

"Me too, but Dad wants us to tromp the tags this year," Rod said.

I groaned. I'd forgotten.

Smiling, Bill took off to help brand the ewes. "Have fun, you guys!" he called out over his shoulder.

Rod and I trudged to the tier level where the shearers worked, a wide-open area with a broad wooden floor holding dozens of fleece piles from recently shorn sheep. At the hydraulic wool-tromping machine, bolted to a single axle frame with a red trailer tongue, a shearer would insert an eight-foot hemp sack into the tube before closing the iron lid around it. Then he'd toss in several clean fleeces, power the plunger to pack the wool tight, and sew each full sack shut.

It was up to Rod, Bill, and me to roll the heavy sacks onto the stock truck when the main floor was filled, so they could be hauled to the warehouse in Rawlins. There, the bagged wool would be stored, and a middleman would buy it at an agreed-upon price. He'd then sell the fleeces to a reputable woolen mill, which in turn washed out the lanolin and spun them into high-quality wool fiber for a variety of clothing options or other products.

As for tromping the tags, Dad wouldn't use a hydraulic press—not when he had people to do the job. That year he had teenage boys around. Decades before, he had built a ten-foot-tall wooden frame made from pine boards, standing it on the tromping deck against the opposite wall from the wool press. A slivery platform sat on top of the rectangular structure, with a circular sawed hole that opened down to the floor. Dad nailed a creaking ladder to one end of the frame leading up to the deck. The structure resembled an unfinished, one-hole outhouse with no walls, for a giant with long legs.

I grabbed an empty wool sack and walked over to the ladder, impatient to get the whole thing over with. "I'll do the first one."

"Fine by me. I can wait," Rod said.

We had watched the process for several years by then and knew what to do. I lowered the sack through the sawed hole and lipped its open end around a three-foot diameter iron ring resting on the deck around the perimeter of the hole. The sack's own weight pulled the ring tight to the deck, holding the bag open and suspended above the floor.

Rod threw me an armful of tag wool, followed by two more. I dropped them into the sack before lowering myself in on top of them, sinking until my head dropped below the sack mouth.

My boots pressed the brown tags, still moist with bodily fluids and lumpy from sheep feces. Rod tossed more tags into the sack like a basketball free throw now that I was unable to catch them from the platform. New loads landed on my head before sliding down my shoulders to the pile at my feet, leaving greasy streaks on my long sleeve shirt and blue jeans.

I tromped hard on the tags, building height in the pile so I could reach the opening again and escape the sour air inside. Four more tags and I touched the iron ring, another load and my head topped the platform. A few more and I stood above the sack, gripping ceiling rafters for balance as I tromped the bag full.

After I climbed down the ladder, I drank deep from a plastic Clorox bottle full of ice water. My throat burned from breathing the dank air, and the cold water washed it clean.

Dad sewed the finished tag sack shut and labeled it with a black marker. "We tromped all the wool this way before we had hydraulic machines. You boys are lucky just to tromp tags." He grinned at us. "Okay, now back to work."

Rod reached for a new sack. "My turn."

Just as we started the next load, the shearer closest to me hollered in Spanish to the man working the hydraulic tromper twenty feet away, "*Necesito un cuchillo.*" (I need a knife.)

The tromper stopped his plunger, smiled at the shearer, and reached into his pocket for a switch blade. He tripped the latch, and a double-edged, six-inch fang of cold steel shot from the handle like the strike of a snake. Bending his elbow, he threw the knife across the room toward the tag sack frame.

Thud. The blade stuck into an upright post three feet from my face. I rocked the knife back and forth until it exited the wood and offered it handle first to the shearer who had asked for it. "Next time, I'll loan you mine." I knew he could speak English.

The shearer poked the knife into the exposed tag sack, probing the area where my brother stood in a pile of dirty wool, and laughed. The two men, older than Rod and me by a decade, played with our innocence, trying to scare us.

But after tromping tags at the shearing pens, we were seldom intimidated.

The shearers taught me the value of hard labor—and respect. They were always polite to my family and expressed their gratitude for giving them work. As a boy who had never lived outside Wyoming,

I loved their stories of trips up north and the ethnic dishes they prepared occasionally for the crew.

But as hard as they worked—and they were jaw-dropping to behold—the shearers in my great-grandfather's time outmatched them.

When I was in college, I was nosing through the drawers of an engraved oak sideboard that stood in a corner of the living room at the ranch. It had a cut marble top and a wooden front permanently scarred by linear scratches left behind by a century of cowboys striking matches to light morning smokes.

In one of the drawers was a brown ledger book. On the front cloth cover, printed in bold black letters, it read, "I. C. Miller Shearing Pens." Ike had signed the inside cover and added, "1903 Shearing Book, Shearing Accounts."

A decade before, we kids had played with that book but never paid attention to the writing on the opening pages. We just scribbled on the blank pages in the back, using it as a faux register when pretending the ranch was a rural motel for travelers. We wrote down our names and added room numbers with imaginary fees to customers. But the first half of the ledger contained valuable historic information about my great-grandfather's time on the ranch.

Ike Miller had recorded sheep-shearing activity in it for the spring of 1903, conducted at his pens north of Rawlins, years before Kirk built the facility at O'Brien Spring. Kirk and his brother, Norm, were teenagers working for their dad at the time, hauling sheep carcasses from the corrals by the wagonload, victims of scabies, a contagious itch contracted from parasitic mites that ran rampant through western herds at the turn of the century.

The ledger detailed shearing data from April 17 to May 12, including records for 89,213 sheep trailed to Ike's facility from sixteen separate herds owned by area stockmen. Each man had contracted with Ike to shear their sheep at his pens.

Fifty shearers cut wool for over three weeks, finishing nearly 3,900 animals daily for an average of 78 head per person each day, an amazing feat for laborers using the standard $1.35 handheld shears of the time, not the electric-powered clippers we used when I was a boy.

Frank Saglor sheared 2,823 sheep that season, far more than any other crew member, yielding a daily average of 123. Saglor sheared more sheep in that amount of time than most men could do today with modern equipment. His achievement is worthy of inclusion in any serious historical account of the Wyoming sheep industry.

Ike paid Frank Saglor and the rest of the crew the same way we paid them in my time. When a man finished an animal, the floor boss handed him a washer the size of a quarter, called a chit. Shearers gathered at the end of the day, emptied their pockets on a piece of canvas laid over the floor, and knelt behind their pile of chits so the floor boss could count them and pay out for each washer.

Wages weren't extravagant, but hard workers made a decent living. Ike charged the sheep outfits twelve and a half cents per head for shearing their ewes and yearlings, and twenty-five cents per head for shearing the more obstinate bucks. He paid salaries from this income, and a hard worker like Saglor earned a few dollars a day for shearing ewes.

Every June, following the shearing and lambing, we amputated, or docked, the lambs' tails. For practical reasons, this process protects the health of the animal by reducing fecal contamination. When I was a boy, we docked the lambs' tails, along with castrating the bucks and branding and earmarking each lamb, at the Saltiel Corral. It was named after the Saltiel family who had once lived along the nearby creek below the south face of Bradley Peak.

Annie Saltiel, widowed around the end of the nineteenth century, remained on her homestead after her husband died. Decades later, her buildings lay in ruins a couple of hundred yards upslope from our sheep corral. Vandals had broken the windows and crushed the wooden door. The stone walls sagged to the ground. What remained of her trash pile was loaded with bent food cans, broken liquor bottles, and cut-glass perfume stoppers, clues to her lonely life so far from others.

One summer, my brother and I cleaned out the Saltiel irrigation ditch to flood the side hill and grow more feed near our pens. Rod reopened the channel with the tilted blade on the back of our John Deere tractor until the rear end jerked and the blade bounced out of the ground.

"What's that?" he yelled.

"I have no idea. Check it out," I said, standing a safe distance from the action.

He jumped from the tractor and pulled on a long metal object sticking out from the side of the ditch. "It's an old rifle."

Rod had discovered the rusted skeleton of a model 1894 Winchester lever action rifle that somebody, perhaps Annie, had tossed into her ditch. A circular groove sawed below an old bend in the barrel testified to a failed effort to salvage the weapon for further use. Its serial number indicated the rifle sold about the time Annie lived there. She probably bought it after her husband died to keep intruders away.

The townspeople called her place the Elkhorn Stage Station, since it might have been used as a mail stop on the way to the Seminoe Mining District in the late 1800s, but it was Annie's home to me. The stage station name robbed Annie of her identity. Besides, elk have antlers not horns.

Kirk had designed the Saltiel Corral to maneuver sheep through a series of small pens to a docking table. Split pine boards, still covered in bark, were nailed vertically side by side to shut off the view between adjacent pens. Reinforced walls also supported canvas panels so the animals couldn't see one another when we took the lambs away from the ewes.

During docking season, we anchored a long wooden table to the vertical corral panels separating the holding pen from the release pen. Splotches of dried red paint caked on its weathered surface, the color we used before switching to black. Dried blood and desiccated membrane clung to cracked grains in the wood, residues from earlier dockings.

When we docked the lambs in June 1966, Shorty had just started as ranch foreman and would be in charge of the entire docking crew. Dad was there, too, but he spent most of his time away from the hired hands, tucking in the edges, and keeping a quiet eye on Shorty's people skills. Dad was hoping Shorty was the man for the job. After all, he came with excellent references, unlike his predecessor.

A year or so earlier, Dad had brought in a fellow from Rawlins who talked a good show. But Dad became suspicious of Ed's self-professed talents when he saw how unsure he was around both the livestock and the crew, making numerous mistakes. Dad didn't have much of a choice, though. He had been elevated from foreman to ranch manager after Kirk retired and needed someone to direct the hired hands.

Then Ed did the unthinkable: he took off to get married and left the outfit to high school kids to manage. Dad was not around at the time. When Ed came back, he stopped at the house to introduce his new bride, and Dad fired him on the spot.

At the docking table, Shorty worked with some of the older men and my cousin Susan, tending to the needs of each lamb as it passed. Rod and I had been helping for a few years by then, so we knew the ropes. We walked through the holding pen, looking for lambs in the herd. Nearly every ewe birthed at least one lamb each year, many had twins, and a few triplets. Our range favored sheep over cattle, so mothers delivered plenty of offspring.

We forced the milling ewes in the pen to move about, revealing the hiding places of lambs tucked in beside them. When I found a buck lamb, I lifted the twenty pounds of wagging fluff and fidgeting tail and held him tight against my chest. I gripped a fore limb and a hind limb with each hand, crossed the legs over, and squeezed the joints, clasping the lamb into my palms. Then I spread the left limbs from the right to expose his belly and genitals to the operators at the docking station.

Shorty had just finished docking a ewe lamb and was now available. Standing at the table, he wore a canvas bib with two large pockets sewn into the garment at waist level to hold his tools. Shorty bent the left ear on my lamb, snipping off the tip with razor-sharp clippers, and then switched to a set of tension pliers with four dull prongs projecting an inch from the end of the instrument, called an elastrator.

He rolled a tight rubber band over the prongs, pulled the lamb's tail straight, and squeezed the plier grips open to spread the rubber band as wide as a half dollar. After threading the lamb's tail through the open rubber band, he released his grip. When he yanked the prongs away, the rubber band closed over the tail, shutting off circulation so the tail would fall off a week later in a bloodless amputation.

Shorty snipped the end of the buck's scrotum with sharp scissors. "I won't use a rubber band on testicles. It's too hard on the lambs."

No one ever showed more compassion for the animals under his care.

I gripped the legs tighter as Shorty poked fingers at the lamb's belly, drawing its nuts into the sack until they peeked through the surgical cut. He squeezed the base of the scrotum between thumb and forefinger and then grasped the nuts between the plier teeth on the end of the clippers and pulled.

The lamb cried and his belly constricted. Shorty tossed the nuts into a water bucket so we could cook them later for supper. I slid the new wether's butt along the docking table to the next station, where a hired hand dabbed ink on the inside of the unmarked ear and squeezed a needled stamp into the skin, its pattern of pinpoints arranged like a double-ended wrench, one of our registered brands—an ear tattoo as an ownership mark.

At the final stop, Susan dipped a wooden-handled brand into black paint and pressed it against the lamb's left side. Her deliberate touch always produced excellent brands. The double wrench soaked into the wool and dried in the stifling heat.

The docked wether, now free in the release pen, ignored his castration but kicked sky high trying to dislodge the tight band squeezing the base of his tail. Lost circulation soon killed all feeling in his appendage, and the animal settled down to recover.

The fading sun had dipped low behind Bradley Peak by the time we finished working the herd and started heading back to the ranch. Docked lambs would ship in the fall, and then we'd start the breeding cycle all over again the following winter.

As Dad drove away from Saltiel Creek, I sat in back with a bum lamb in my lap. The poor fellow didn't have a mother to care for him, but Mom would gladly feed him from a bottle at the ranch.

I glanced over at Annie's old home. The shadow of her crumbling house stretched a long black hand over our corral, as if Annie were waving goodbye to the crew.

9.

The End of an Era

April 1973 marked the hundredth anniversary of our family's role in Wyoming's range livestock industry. I came home from college that spring eager to help Dad and Shorty with shearing. Dad hoped for a good lamb crop in a few weeks. Coyotes and harsh weather had killed over twelve percent of the previous year's herd—several hundred ewes and lambs—our worst loss in many years.

We sheared the sheep and turned them loose with fresh painted brands drying on their sides. Small bracelets of uncut wool dangled above their hooves, and their ears flapped when they raced into the holding pasture naked from their shearing ordeal.

The last group bent their heads to graze north of the shearing pens and outbuildings. They were clean, a bit nervous, and plenty hungry. More than that, they looked so vulnerable without their wool.

After we finished at the pens, we set out for town, the sky darker than usual. Southwesterly breezes had shifted to a steady north wind, blowing in clouds that blocked out the stars after dusk. Heavy moisture gathered overhead until the clouds grew into grotesque shapes floating over the range, like hideous banshees ready to spread chaos and destruction on the ranch.

By the time we reached the outskirts of Rawlins, hard rain was pelting the windshield. Dad started the wipers low, but soon cranked them full blast to push driving sleet from his view. Pulling into the muddy lot beside our house, he turned off the engine and looked at the tormented sky. "If it freezes tonight, this will turn into snow."

"What about the sheep?"

He shook his head and sighed. "They're on their own."

We woke the next morning to cold, wet snow covering everything. Gray clouds smothered the skyline out toward the ranch. The icy rain had come hard, soaking everything it touched, and during the night, the water froze from the bone-chilling wind.

As soon as the dirt roads on the ranch were passable, we drove to the shearing pens pasture to check on the recently shorn sheep. I walked to some rocks on the south face of the ridge above O'Brien Spring where animals would have been protected from north winds and saw several freshly shorn sheep packed inside the dark hole of a rock shelter, motionless.

The early spring storm struck so fast the very first night after they had lost their warm wool, it caught them helpless against the cold. Sick ewes weakened by the storm sought any cover they could find, climbing deep into rock shelters facing the southern sun.

They piled by the score beneath half a dozen overhangs, three animals deep from top to bottom, huddled together to escape the storm. Animals on top of each pile died from exposure to the bitter cold. Those at the bottom suffocated from the crowded flesh heaped on top of them. Herd behavior so common in that species had created the ambient environment of their death.

Early-season grasses lay broken by the weight of the storm outside the shelters. The plants along O'Brien Spring itself had become invisible next to the stream, buried beneath the rotting carcasses of two hundred more sheep. I could walk across the meadow on top of their backs and my feet would never touch grass. Silent white corpses lay side by side in the pasture, as if heaps of early spring snow still covered the ground.

Crippled animals wandered aimlessly, sluggish from the recent ordeal, their backs bent, and nerves weakened from fighting the pain in frostbitten bones and torn muscle. The whole herd was dying this time.

"I'm selling them all this fall," Dad said, standing over the carnage. "We'll raise only cattle from now on."

Domestication had made sheep too vulnerable to nature's volatility. That's why they became so dependent on the families who raised them and they were a threat to no one. The catastrophic mortality at O'Brien Spring made me realize how fragile life was for livestock—and for the humans who nurtured them.

I felt as helpless as I did the day Kirk sentenced my girlfriend's dog to death for killing just two sheep. Mother Nature was the culprit this time, though, and she couldn't be eliminated by a bullet. We lived in an unpredictable—and frequently unjust—world.

Would I survive?

Tom Taylor fostered the sheep we kept near the ranch house, a kind old gentleman who lived there during my youth. Tom loved our family. He gave Mom a Wyoming jade ring one day just to convey his honest affection. He taught me how to butcher a sheep and prepare the carcass, and always kept our heavy equipment running.

When I was about eleven and Rod twelve, Mom sent us with Tom to the meadow behind the house to kill and butcher a wether for the walk-in cooler. We found the lone sheep standing in a low spot in the pasture, a remnant of the Garden Ditch Joel Hurt had dug in the 1870s to irrigate his six-acre vegetable patch.

Rod shot the wether, the gunfire echoing off the dune and surrounding the ranch yard.

"Go raise the shed door so we can hang him up to skin," Tom told me.

While he and Rod bled the animal out, I ran toward the tin shed, excited to help with the butchering. The enormous building loomed up ahead, its massive wooden door penetrated by huge bolts and rusty hooks. From it, we would hang a singletree rigging to spread the animal's hind legs apart for skinning.

I reached the building just minutes after Rod shot the wether. In a hurry to finish my task before they arrived with the animal, I started turning the handle on the gear crank, gathering slack from the cable attached to the large door to pull it open. Two revolutions, then three. The rigid cable, now tight enough to strum, would not move the door.

Puzzled, I locked the crank teeth, walked through the narrow door behind the shed, and noticed the big door latched inside by two hooks. I couldn't budge them loose because I had recklessly wound the cable too tight.

Returning to the crank, I pulled the lever down to ease pressure off the door, but the lock plate was so loose on its hinge it kept falling between the cog teeth when I let go. I held the plate open with one hand and tried to retract the cable with the other.

The crank handle slipped from my grasp and spun violently in reverse, releasing the pent-up cable tension. Its iron grip smashed into my forehead, crushed the straw in my cowboy hat, and slammed me to the ground.

I stumbled to my feet, dizzy, and pulled off my hat. A long stream of warm blood shot from my head in a wide arc over my eyes. Covering the wound with one hand, I grabbed my hat and butchering knife with the other and ran to the house to show Mom.

She looked at my knife then the gash in my head and screamed, "My God, Mark, what happened? I heard a shot!"

Rod and Tom rushed to the house, leaving the dead wether in the ditch. Tom stared in terror. "Betty Rose, I'm so sorry. He needs to go to town."

"A bit lower and you would have lost an eye," Doc Halsey told me later in his office. "You're lucky you weren't knocked unconscious, or you would have bled out."

Halsey's diagnosis proved to me that I needed to slow down and think before I acted, not only while working with sheep, dead or alive, but while living life itself.

When we shipped the last of our sheep in 1973, an elk calf mixed in with one of our bands. A hunter had shot her mom, so the calf imprinted on a small group of sheep, becoming tame in its own way.

She followed them all the way through our corrals, right up to the loading chute, until we spooked her away from the herd as we loaded the sheep into "pots" (stock trucks). The elk reluctantly ran toward the hills to fend for herself.

Three years later, I saw a lone ewe in the Haystacks we had missed when we shipped the last of our herd. Long, scraggly wool hung on her back and raging fire burned in her eyes. I tried to herd her toward the ranch, but she had lived alone so long she developed an uncompromising belligerence all her own.

That ewe, and even the calf elk, grew wild again out of necessity, finding internal power to face the world on their own. I thought about my own life without the herd of people I loved around me. How would I behave when the rest of my family was gone? What path would I choose?

Many years after we sold our last sheep, I asked Dad about his memories of them. "Did you like running sheep better than cattle?"

"Well, I did. More honest animal, I think."

"Easier to handle?"

"Uh-huh. They didn't mess up the water holes like cattle, didn't graze out the feed. They would go in and get a drink and go back out. Easier to gather too." Dad laughed. "Christ, you could go out there on the south end and holler, and they would all run to the north end."

I flashed back to the last time Bill and I had helped Kirk herd the ewes, when the bells on a couple of lead animals got them all to move. Sheep acted so much alike in a group that a single stimulus could send the whole bunch in the direction they needed to go. On careful reflection, we five grandkids behaved a lot like those sheep back then.

10.

Following Frank's Fences

I tied Cracker in the first stall at the barn and curried down his back after our short ride. I was about ten that summer. Across from me, Grandpa Kirk leaned on the hayloft ladder and reminded me again to use a slip knot on the halter rope when I fastened my horse. Kirk's signature wide suspenders draped over his broad shoulders and clipped to a pair of worn work pants.

"Cracker is a good horse around cattle," I said, feeding him some oats.

"When I was your age, I rode horseback everywhere. One time, I found lots of dead cattle."

I shot a glance over at Kirk. "Wow! You did?"

"Yep, I rode by a deep arroyo south of the ranch and saw hundreds of dry bones piled up in the bottom of the draw. The way I figure it, the animals had wandered during the bad winter of 1886 and '87, looking for grass and better weather. Ike had no fences back then to hold them at home where we could keep an eye on them. No one had fences in those days—they were against the law on public land."

Apart from being blown away by what that must have looked like, I couldn't believe there was a time we had no fences. That's mostly what Dad did: he was either building new ones or repairing old ones.

When I told him later about Kirk's story, he said, "Your grandfather knew we needed to put in fences so that kind of thing wouldn't happen again. As soon as we were allowed, I started helping him build them. That was before I was even in high school."

He and I were sitting at the dining room table eating hot tamales he'd brought back from town. Dad loved Safeway tamales.

"Then in 1934, we got really serious about it when the government passed the Taylor Grazing Act and set up grazing districts. We had to keep our livestock separate from other operators."

Eventually, Dad said, the law allowed ranchers to lease federal lands for grazing in combination with their own private holdings. The Bureau of Land Management (BLM) worked with stockmen to designate the boundaries of each operation. As the foreman at the time, Dad met with the BLM employee who came to the ranch shortly after World War II to assign our perimeter.

"I told him we needed to go on horseback," Dad said. "He didn't seem too thrilled about that, but we didn't have a choice."

The two men rode from the south end of the Haystacks across the east rim of the Great Divide Basin, north toward Bradley Peak, partitioning our allotment along the North Platte River watershed. They chose the simplest route that followed the most likely terrain.

When they finished, the I Lazy D, officially listed as the Seminoe Allotment, comprised approximately half federal land and half private and state. Dad could have requested more federal lease since the I Lazy D had plenty of privately owned base property, but instead, he helped outline a perimeter that gave adjacent ranchers more land to run stock. It was the neighborly thing to do.

After a long day of surveying, the two men rode past Annie Saltiel's old homestead toward the headwaters of Indian Creek and then turned their mounts east and trotted down the valley in the direction of our ranch house seven miles away. Dad spotted his father's horses grazing beside some willows too far from home and told the BLM rider they needed to herd them to the barn on their way back. Dad kicked his horse's flanks and loped toward the animals.

"Hell, I got in behind those horses and they galloped clear to the barn," Dad told me.

"What happened to the BLM man?" I asked.

Dad ate the last bite of tamale. "He didn't get back for three hours. I was worried we might have to send out a search party, but he just was riding so slow."

In his childhood photos, Dad is a carefree boy with an impish grin. He later enrolled at the University of Wyoming as an agriculture major, but near the end of the term before he expected to graduate, the Japanese bombed Pearl Harbor.

Dad enlisted on December 30, 1941, at twenty-two years old, and spent the next thirty-two months as an Army Air Corps photographer in Australia and New Guinea. He seldom spoke about his military career in later years, though he preserved much of it in pictures he had developed overseas: hundreds of detailed images of jungle scenes, beautiful native women, bombing raids, and the aftermath of brutal battles.

When he returned from the war, Dad spent countless hours on fence preparations, still a stoic Wyoming cowboy, long and sinewy, in tune with every quiet task he undertook. His demeanor, though, had been molded by experiences in two vastly different worlds—one peaceful and agrarian; the other, ruthless and chaotic. A small corner of his memory had been transformed by a loathing for Japan he hid behind an invisible barrier, creeping out on occasion during rare reminiscences.

His postwar fences carved several pastures from the open range his father had known when he was a boy. That allowed them to rotate grazing every spring, which protected the land and water holes from overuse, helping both the livestock and wildlife. And they could then control the drift of animals, so they didn't need as many riders, as well as regulating breeding by separating bulls from cows part of the year.

When my brother and I were kids, Dad worked silently at a steel-dipping vat behind the barn, filled halfway with creosote, old motor oil, and flushed antifreeze, a black concoction that preserved the cedar wood of thirty thousand fence posts he set after the war. The vat measured the length and width of a water trough but was built much deeper so he could submerge the bottom half of posts in the viscous lubricant for a week, given that they would remain buried eighteen inches deep in our pastures for decades.

Dad loaded dozens of barked cedar posts at a time. Thousands more were stacked in huge piles behind him, waiting their turn. Cottontails scampered through the nooks and crannies, and we kids watched them play while Dad worked at the vat.

One day, I spotted a brave rabbit scampering around the cedar posts. It had built a straw bed in the cracks of the woodpile. Dad eventually moved the posts that protected its home, grabbing one at a time until the straw bed was exposed and the rabbit had to leave. I stood mesmerized, watching how fast Dad could load and soak the cut lengths of cedar.

The now homeless animal hopped in my direction and then stopped and sat down, its long ears bent, damp nose twitching. I didn't move while it hopped closer and sat again. It stopped directly in front of me and stared, as if to get acquainted. I held out my hand, but the quick movement scared it away.

"Step off six paces between posts whenever you build fence," Dad said, interrupting my visit with the rabbit. He wiped a bead of sweat from his brow. "We need lots of cedar."

He eased another post into the tub of dirty oil, where it bobbed up and down before settling at an angle against the group already soaking there. The afternoon sun heated the metal vat nearly as hot as a burner on Mom's stove, so Dad avoided touching the sides when he slid each post into the pool. Sweat soaked the hair on his chest that billowed from the open V formed by two unsnapped buttons on his cotton work shirt.

Dad liked working alone, maybe because he had been on his own so much when his father managed the place. Solitude had taught him self-reliance, forging a confidence that required no input from peers, a mettle that sustained him all his life. Such qualities tempered in him while he built more than a hundred miles of fence. They helped him keep his mind off his father's hard drinking and mitigated the unrest caused by a world war.

When my brother and I were about eleven and ten—old enough to help fence—Dad had become the most deliberate man I knew. He built fence for eighteen pastures, one post at a time, six paces apart, each fence a straight line of tight wire and oiled wood that vanished into the distance behind him.

"The best help I ever had was a one-armed man who worked with me before the war," Dad told us. "He left Russia after the Soviet take-over and came out West."

"How did he fence with only one arm?" I asked.

"He was faster with one arm than anybody I knew with two." Dad shook his head. "He was driving the team one day while I sat beside him, and the front axle hit a rock. The wagon bed slammed to the ground after the axle broke away and the horses spooked, their harness tearing free from the tongue. They kept on running and yanked that old Russian out of his seat, but he wouldn't let go of the reins. They dragged him a hundred yards before finally settling down. Then he calmly stood up and led them back to the wagon. Most men with two arms wouldn't have cared—they just would have let go."

The two of them had built most of the fences up to that time. "I'd stretch woven wire," Dad said, "and he'd hold it between his chest and stump while hammering each staple with his only hand. I couldn't keep up."

He paused. "There were many good men before Pearl Harbor. After-ward, too many veterans acted like the country owed them something."

Dad never wasted a single motion, having performed the same tasks for so long he knew what to do better than anyone.

"Mistakes can be deadly," he told us often. "Our range gets hit hard in the winter. Don't stretch the wire too tight before you staple, or it will break under the weight of the snow."

There were many reasons not to stretch the wire too tight, and we kids didn't always heed his advice, unfortunately. One time I started to staple old barbed wire while my buddy stretched it ten posts away with a Goldenrod wire stretcher. The ratchet of iron teeth bit each cog as he cranked the handle to tighten the wire, drawing the length of barbs closer to him, stretching it like he was tuning the string of a guitar. The line had no sag for thirty yards across the undulating terrain between us. If we stapled the overtightened wire, its tension would pull the posts right out of the ground.

I was about to warn my friend about the danger when the wire snapped next to his stretcher and twisted into a bouncing coil that tumbled downhill toward me, kicking up dust on the way. I jumped free as the mass of barbed wire struck my fence post and wrapped around the wood, still humming from the speed of its flight.

During another fencing lesson, Dad grabbed three staples instead of the usual one. "Here's what you do for a fence in the high country," he said.

He pounded two staples partway into a post, horizontal to the ground, one underneath the other about the length of a knuckle apart, leaving them to project half an inch out of the wood. Next, he placed the loosely stretched barbed wire between them. Finally, he dropped one prong of a third staple into the gaps formed by the projected ends of the first two, like a padlock. The wire pressed the loose staple against the others, holding the barbs close to the post.

"Wire stapled like this will turn livestock fine," Dad said. "You and Rod come up here after we move the cattle and pull each loose staple from all the posts. Then release the wire and lay it down on the ground where it will be better protected from snow drifts that might freeze. No point having a four-foot fence up here in the winter when snow drifts are five feet deep and the cattle are gone."

One of the last fence lines Dad designed would span about two miles across a sand dune to replace an older segment he decided to abandon. He pointed to the old line. "That's a bad area. Two deeper fences are buried there, one under the other. The dune's covered all three. First one's under ten feet of sand."

Stabilized dunes were easy digging, and the soft ground allowed my friend and me to use shovels the entire distance. Dad already had set a post in the ground every hundred yards to give us a line to follow, so we sighted in each new post before we set it, confident our measures were straight and true.

Then we looked back on our line after we finished and saw a crooked, weaving path like the trail of a snake. We had missed Dad's route by fifteen yards despite the guideposts he set, leaving a bow in the fence that put too much meadow on the wrong side of the wire. We offered to redo the segment, but Dad only smiled.

Hard ground was a different story for posthole digging. Dad told me once to build a small stackyard during Christmas break while I was home from college. I'd hoped to relax and watch football, but he had me follow him to a place past the river canyon next to the county road where he needed to pile hay. The ground already had been flagged where each of four railroad ties would be set vertically as a fence corner.

"You might need these split tires to prepare the postholes," he said.

"What good are they?"

"The ground is frozen. Burn them over each spot to thaw the dirt so you can dig."

I moaned. "Got any matches?"

"Here you go. I'll keep the beer cold at home."

I piled dry grass and wads of old newspaper in each tire to burn them one at a time over the corners. Every twenty minutes, I slid the smoldering tire aside and, with a crowbar and spade shovel, chipped three inches of dirt from the slow-thawing hole. It felt like I only sharpened the crowbar rather than moved any dirt. The project took two and a half days.

True to Dad's word, ice-cold Schlitz awaited my return.

I seldom saw my father's fences after my family left the ranch in December 1983. But when I drove out there with a good friend seventeen years later, gnarled posts and rusted wire came back to mind.

We traveled down Firecracker Hill where long grassy meadows and sage-covered ridges stretched in parallel lines toward the old ranch house in the valley below. Coarse-grained sand dunes, white in the sun, crawled like snails in front of the wind.

Beside the meadow, a soft breeze blew through the bulrushes, just as it did when I was a boy. We passed the spot where Kirk parked his truck that day long ago to honk his horn and attract cattle to cubes of protein cake we supplied. It seemed all familiar to me, except for new fences.

I was remembering Dad's fences that followed ridgetops where snow didn't lie, that divided meadows with water holes on either side of the wire and directed the drift of livestock toward the next pasture or down to the barn. His fences had been the boundaries of my home. New employees, who arrived after we left, shifted the pastures around. Barbed wire was replaced with electrical fence, and metal posts stood where knotty cedars once were. Old gates and cattle guards were gone.

Then we saw the stone ranch house where it has always been and passed the barn corner where Dad's dipping vat once stood. Even without his pile of logs, I still recognized the place a rabbit wouldn't let me get too close when I got in a hurry to try. Dad had worked there to build the many fences in his life, some to keep things in, and others to keep things out. No two were ever alike.

"Your grandpa Kirk didn't like building fences," he told me during one of our many conversations about the ranch in his later years. "He always left it up to me."

"You spent a lot of time at it."

"There's much more to fencing than most people realize. You gotta learn where to build them—but you also have to know when to take them down."

11.

Posthole Digger

You can't ship cattle until you load them onto stock trucks for the trip to the sale barn in Torrington. But you can't load them until you have a shipping corral with pens to sort the animals, scales to weigh them, and a chute to guide them onto trucks. But you can't have a shipping corral until you dig postholes, connect posts with horizontal poles, and make everything strong enough to maneuver confined animals so you can perform the necessary tasks.

When Rod and I were teenage fence builders, Dad decided to build a new corral in the shipping pasture along Hurt Creek where our cattle rested in the fall. For years, we had shipped from the shearing pens corral several miles south of the creek, but the annual cattle drive from the shipping pasture to that corral always shrank the animals just prior to being weighed onto trucks. We needed a more appropriate site.

Dad picked a location adjacent to a good access road atop Windy Ridge, easily reached by cattle trailing down from the mountains in the fall. He turned water into the pasture from the Kirk Ditch to grow more grass for livestock waiting near the pens.

While we were building the enclosure that summer, Dad taught me proper handling techniques for animals confined in a man-made feature like our shipping corral. The more thought that went into the design, he argued, the more successfully it held the animals.

Our goal was to build the perfect corral.

Rod and I worked with other hired hands to gather hundreds of railroad ties from the ranch and set them in holes dug deep enough—about three feet—to withstand the pressure if a throng of animals leaned against them. We nailed horizontal pine poles on the inside of the ties facing into the pens, so the resistance of poles to herd crowding was supported by the vertical ties holding them up. Poles nailed on the outside of ties were more likely to break or loosen if hit by milling cattle.

We labored to build sturdy corral walls, alleys, and pens and carefully maintained them through the years. They kept animals right where we needed them and allowed us to perform any required tasks on them without threat of danger. The last time I worked on the corral, I was a second-year undeclared major at the University of Wyoming, still proud of what we had accomplished during its construction.

Despite my experience building corral fences, Dad told me one morning that winter, "Don't major in agriculture, Mark. No future in it."

He was keenly aware that the Miller family didn't have controlling interest in the I Lazy D. There was no guarantee I would always have a job on the place.

"Come with me," he said. "I want you to meet somebody."

We hopped into Dad's pickup and drove to Coal Creek Canyon in our yearling pasture south of Cheyenne Ridge. Towering cliff walls, laced with outcrops of Mesa Verde Sandstone, rose three hundred feet above the rock-strewn road. Marine organisms, prostrate and lifeless, lay fossilized inside the stones.

When we reached the canyon mouth, we turned north about two hundred yards and stopped on top of a low-lying hogback rim, a steep cuesta above a dry tributary creek. Four vehicles were parked there.

Dad and I walked to the foot of the cuesta and stared into a large, square hole recently dug a couple of feet deep into the terrace sediments. A few kneeling men brushed and troweled loose dirt into white buckets. Another worker carried the buckets over to a handheld screen where two people were shaking the loosened sediments through the screen mesh.

A tall man standing by the hole saw us and walked over. He looked to be in his late forties, about my mother's age, and his hands were the largest I had ever seen.

He and Dad smiled at each other, and the man said, "Hello again, Frank. How are the cattle doing?"

Dad turned to me. "Mark, this is Dr. George Frison, Wyoming State Archaeologist from the university. He came by the house last week to ask for permission to cross our land to this site. It so happens that he grew up on a ranch too."

Dr. Frison extended his enormous hand, and mine disappeared in it. I knew his name. I had taken an introductory course in anthropology the semester before, and he was department head, but I had never been introduced to him.

"Would you like to work with us today, Mark?" Frison asked.

I glanced over at Dad and he nodded. "Sure!" I said.

Dad looked relieved. "I'll pick you up on my way back to town."

One of the students handed me a trowel and bucket and showed me what to do. I tentatively moved a little dirt and hoped I wouldn't destroy any important evidence. There was a lot of detail to grasp, but Frison showed confidence in me by letting me learn on the job.

When we took a break, he gave me a tour of the place, what they called the Scoggin site bison kill, explaining what had happened there about five thousand years before. Prehistoric hunters had intercepted a small herd of bison passing by on top of the cuesta and coaxed them over the cliff, where many fell to their death at the spot Frison's crew was now digging. The hunters butchered the animals before sharing the meat and other byproducts among people who had participated in the kill.

Frison continued on, saying something that would forever change the course of my life.

He pointed to twenty small circular spots in the floor of their dig at the base of the cliff, each about eight inches in diameter, and containing lighter sediments than the surrounding soil. They aligned with each other in the shape of an "L," the long axis running parallel to the hogback cliff. The crew had cleaned out a couple of these small features, and one of them contained a bison leg bone embedded vertically in the hole.

"Those are postholes from a corral built to confine the surviving bison after they went over the cliff," Frison said.

Hunters had jammed the bison leg bone into one of the holes to tighten the post setting there. I understood the tactic. Rod and I employed the same technique using rocks on our own fence lines to reinforce them.

"Once the bison fell over the cliff, they were trapped inside the corral and finished off by the hunters."

My jaw dropped. I was standing in another corral on our ranch that had also confined animals where people needed them to be so they could perform required tasks with minimal danger. But unlike our shipping facility, this corral was five thousand years old!

I thought I knew everything about animal control structures after helping build our shipping corral. Instead, scientific evidence proved that human families had built them on our landscape millennia before we arrived. What could they have taught me?

I had taken so much for granted—and I had so much more to learn.

Returning to the University of Wyoming eager for spring semester, I declared my major in anthropology with a specialization in archaeology. Dr. Frison offered challenging summertime employment on his other sites, so I began to work less on the ranch. But then after I finished graduate school in December 1979, Dad hired me part-time. On my first day, he grinned, saying that I should be good help now because my PhD actually stood for "Posthole Digger."

Dad had been right in a way. It *was* a line of ancient postholes dug into our pasture that had pointed me along the career path I needed to follow. Twelve years after that fateful day at the Scoggin site, I succeeded Dr. Frison as Wyoming State Archaeologist and kept the job for thirty years until my own retirement.

12.

Cowboys, Cooks, and Cattle

One spring morning as young boys, Rod and I drove with Fred Wise, one of our cowboy heroes, to his place so he could clean it up for summer living. Cowboys are ranch hands hired to work with cattle, and Fred was the most genuine one I ever knew. A grizzled old man, he moved from ranch to ranch doing odd jobs in the slow winter months for little more than room and board. When the seasons changed and the trail drives began, the "grub-line rider" returned to his rustic dugout carved into the southeast slope of the Haystacks, only the front door and a corral visible to anyone outside.

Fred told us to stay in the truck until he had a chance to check things out. Striding over to the weather-beaten door, he pushed his arthritic shoulder against it to force the rusted hinges open, and then he disappeared into the dark hole of his cavernous living room.

Seconds later, he yelled, "Damn it! Get outta here!"

A live rattlesnake over three feet long flew in a twisted roll through the doorway and landed writhing on the ground by the corral, followed by a second and then a third. They had found the perfect den for the winter.

All kinds of noises came next—rickety chairs scraping the wooden floor inside, a bucket banging against a wall, pots and pans clanging. Fred's worn-out broom appeared in the doorway and disappeared again and again, clouds of dust billowing past the porch into the front yard.

And then silence. Rod and I stared wide-eyed. What would happen next?

"Come on in, water's hot!" Fred hollered. "Want some cocoa?"

The year we visited his home, Fred lived a lonely bachelor life, but he'd been married to three different women in his time. None of them ever tamed his restless spirit. His ex-wives were Tempest Charters, Badlands Mary, and Butcher Knife Lil, the last one named for the kitchen utensil she allegedly once used when negotiating marital issues with Fred.

All of us kids loved him, the way he took us under his wing and patiently answered all our questions about cowboying. He would wear a black Scotch cap, with fold-out earmuffs and a fluffy tassel on top, and a long black silk scarf around his neck, curled like the snakes he threw from his home. He always twirled it into a roll and then looped the bandanna twice around his neck before tying it off to protect his leathery skin from the stinging bite of Wyoming wind. He'd pull it up to protect his face if he was horseback riding in a windstorm or blizzard.

Crow's feet cut deep and long beside his eyes, just like the desiccated cracks that crisscrossed his wooden dugout door. The longest crease down each of his cheeks reminded me of scoured-out stream channels, but while our creeks ran water every spring, the wrinkles under Fred's eyes remained dry—the man never wept.

Fred taught Rod and me how to herd cattle without a single lecture. On separate occasions, he would take one of us with him to gather a pasture, line us out behind the first group of cattle he found, and then disappear over a hill. The young kid, left alone with fifty cows and calves, would ride back and forth behind them so the calves wouldn't turn, loping to the lead to keep them headed on course. There was no time to whimper or whine—or we would lose the entire bunch. A boy grew up fast herding cattle.

Every so often, another six or so head would come running out from little valleys that disappeared back into the hills. These newcomers mingled with the rest and soon moved in the proper direction. A few hours later, Fred would ride over another hill and pull in alongside to help the boy finish the day, having watched the young cowboy's progress from a distance while pushing small numbers toward him. Fred always struck an imposing figure, mounted on a favorite rust-colored horse that was so tall he needed to stand on a bucket to step into the stirrup.

One crisp morning in May, we pulled into the Tapers' ranch yard, as we usually did when we gathered cattle near their place. By then Rod and I were often going along with Dad and a few other cowboys to help herd.

Jack Tapers, an old-school cowboy, lived with his wife, Becky, and a few sheep and horses on a 160-acre homestead south of Cheyenne Ridge in the middle of one of our calving pastures. You couldn't miss the turnoff to their place. The weathered end of an old wooden crate hung nailed to a pine post beside the only two-track road around. Jack had painted bright red letters on the crate, cracked and peeling with age, that read, "Tapers 3 miles." Every half mile or so, a similar sign listed decreasing distances so rural travelers could track their progress through our pasture. Jack and Becky had a monopoly on visitors—no other neighbors were on the road.

Our six-member riding crew climbed out of the pickups. Dad backed the stock truck up to Jack's loading chute and prepared to unload the horses.

"Hold on there, Frank," Becky called over. "Come in and have a cup of coffee first."

She stood at the door of their ancient, paint-chipped trailer in her best town outfit, always prepared for guests because she knew the schedule of our rides. Wearing a bright flowered dress, she had her gray hair done up and her ruby red lipstick caked on as thick as mud on our tires after a rain. She never changed the shade. It was the same color she used to mark their sheep every year to distinguish them from our own. The patriotic Becky once painted the back of one ewe red, white, and blue to celebrate the Fourth of July.

"How are things at the I Lazy D?" she asked.

"Good, good," Dad said. We all nodded our heads.

Whenever we stopped by their place, Becky made our crew sit in their cramped trailer to discuss current events while she pulled a handful of cups from the plywood cupboard and set out some sweet rolls she had made. She poured scalding coffee, thick and black, but barely strong enough to soften the layers of dark red lipstick caked along the rim of each cup. I rotated my mug looking for a clean edge and found none, but I drank as a courtesy anyway.

She spoke of rare trips to town, eyeing the new cowboys we'd hired on the crew. Jack talked about the weather and livestock prices, his gnarled hands waving in the air. He and my family went back decades. After Charley Wagers moved on in the early twentieth century, Jack had gathered the last wild horses on our ranch.

"Need any help riding today?" he asked.

"We're fine, but thanks anyway," Dad said, rising to his feet.

We couldn't leave until I asked the question I always asked when we stopped by. "Found any arrowheads lately?" I blurted out. Dad frowned, in a hurry to get started.

"As a matter of fact, we did, just last week." Jack rummaged through a coffee can on the floor by his feet. "Becky found this arrowhead and a piece of pottery. They came from O'Brien Spring near your shearing pens."

The sand dunes on their homestead attracted all kinds of local arrowhead hunters, most of whom I would meet in later years. Like many ranching families, including our own, the Tapers also hunted artifacts to pass the time. They had pretty good luck finding sites with artifacts, except in one windblown depression behind the dune east of their ranch. Even though it seemed a perfect place for an Indian camp, they never found anything there.

"I finally figured it out," Jack told us with a smile. "The Indians were too busy with other things at that spot to waste time making arrowheads. I call it Honeymoon Dune."

We all laughed, even Dad, though by now, he was standing by the door. We had work to do.

Saying our thanks, we piled out of the trailer. Jack followed us to the loading chute, the only structure in reasonably good condition amid a jumble of age-inflicted neglect. A strong wind could have toppled their ramshackle barn and flimsy outbuildings. Even the wobbly corrals needed repair. The posts and poles had been fastened together with rusty bailing wire instead of nails.

The Tapers divided their small pasture with woven wire hung from bent staples embedded in old, untreated cedar posts. Two of the posts, rotted off at ground level, were suspended above the meadow by tight wire stretched between two railroad ties. An afternoon breeze would rock the hanging fence posts back and forth until they swayed in tempo with the wind. Passing through their homestead one day on horseback, I stopped close to the bouncing wire and listened to it sing.

Though quite elderly at the time, Jack faithfully repaired the chute on a regular basis. That was especially good for us. In the years before we pulled horse trailers, we needed his chute to unload our mounts from the high-clearance stock truck. Without it, we would have had to ride on horseback a number of extra miles or unload at a less suitable spot. Then the Tapers would have had fewer visitors at their secluded ranch, and they didn't want that.

Standing not much over five feet, Jack might have been taller in his youth, but he was stove-up when I knew him. His spine had been hammered low by the pounding bucks of a hundred different horses.

I once saw a picture in Rawlins of Jack at a rodeo riding a saddle bronc named Sunday Morning. He was sitting on top of the horse during a high buck, raking his spurs from front to back—pommel to cantle—and stretching his free arm skyward, eyes glued to the horse's neck and withers. Sunday Morning had bucked so hard Jack probably shrank an inch when his butt slammed back in the saddle.

One day when Dad and I were repairing a windmill near the Ta-pers' place, he told me that Jack could ride two horses Roman style. "He would use bridles but no saddles and stand with one foot on the back of each, holding the reins to move 'em in tandem as part of a team, just like in the movies." Dad shook his head. "I've never met anyone else who could do that."

And no one knew more about horses and horse equipment. At the ranch, Dad took one of my old belts, folded it into a figure eight, cut a slice in the side at one end, and twisted the other end through the slice, making a slip knot. Then he tied a piece of twine on the long, twisted end and held it up to show me.

"This is what Jack made with a leather strap to hobble a horse so he could release it after he was mounted." He yanked the lengthy twine that pulled the twisted leather out of the slice, and the belt fell loose.

The last time I saw Jack, Rod and I were building fence a couple of miles below Tapers' corrals, near where old Sefarino Gonzales once had his sheep camp. A horse whinnied on the other side of the north-ern horizon, and then a large bay stud loped toward us. A beaten felt hat and the head of a man bounced above the horse's dark silhouette with each lunge of the animal's forelimbs. Jack was riding over to say hello.

The stallion's strong neck dwarfed most of Jack's frail body. Rod and I walked over when he reined in and visited as he sat in his sad-dle, one leg hooked over the fork.

"How's the fence coming?" he asked.

"We're almost done," Rod said.

None of us had much to say, but such meetings were a sign of mutual respect among neighbors in the country. Before he left, Jack reached down and shook our hands. He never dismounted, didn't have to—he was more at home on horseback than anywhere else on earth.

Trailing cattle remains one of my most vivid ranch memories. Soon after a heavy late March snowstorm when I was a teen, I helped herd a bunch of fifty tired animals plodding north out of the winter pasture on the way to their calving grounds. Their backs hunched from the stress of the storm and their necks drooped, barely holding tired heads off the ground. They were so weak their tails wouldn't even swat flies.

The lead animal shied away from the week-old carcass of a bloated cow when she passed it, as if fearing proximity to those who hadn't survived the recent cold. Half an hour later, forgetting all she had seen, she gathered an old cow bone in her mouth and chewed on it for the calcium it held.

Her near-term fetus had received most of her nutrients over the winter, and now it rolled from side to side in her belly as the cow just waddled along. We always let the animals creep slowly toward the calving pasture each spring, hoping not to lose any weak stock on the way.

Our back trail faded in an irregular line of broken ground, scalloped by hundreds of hooves zigzagging around sagebrush and rocks that we passed. Early-season flies circled drying cow pies behind us, while others hovered over the back ends of walking cattle, patiently waiting for a fresher reason to land.

We crossed high ridges of dry ground, where our trail dust settled on old patches of snow still hiding in the shade. Thump . . . plop, thump . . . plop, as heavy hooves struck thawed ground and sank to deep frost before sucking air from the soil as each foot retracted. Cows too tired to moo meandered along as we neared the calving pasture.

The last cow through the gate was a ten-year-old Hereford with no unborn calf of her own, a "dry," as we called them. A ball of cancer the size of a grapefruit covered her left eye. Dad and Shorty team roped her after closing the gate and gave her a shot to quiet her down.

As their horses stretched the two ropes tight, pulling the cow's head in one direction and her hind legs in another, Dad cut the blackened red mass from her socket before pouring coagulant into the hole, the purple disinfectant we used when dehorning. I held Dad's horse and loosened the ropes while the cow was still groggy.

Ten minutes later, she stood shaking her head. The doctored hole in her face dripped like a melting grape snow cone. She ambled off to the meadow, where she turned her nose to the ground sniffing for grass, ignoring the worried cowboys around her.

"She'll probably make it till fall," Shorty said.

"Yep. Let's get a cup of coffee," Dad said.

The toe tips of Dad's boots gripped stirrup leather when he remounted his mare, barely inserting his boot through the stirrup, always prepared to pull his feet out if an emergency occurred. He never wore spurs, bumping his horse into a trot using only his worn boot heels. In contrast, Rod and I liked wearing spurs because they made us look more like the cowboys in the Western movies.

"If you need them," Dad said, "you probably have the wrong horse for the job."

He paced his mare whenever he rode, never working her more than she could handle, and still returned to the ranch without her being "wind broke"—wheezing from an overworked airway. Dad didn't even own chaps.

"They're made for the brushy thickets in Texas, not Wyoming," he said, though our big sage grew as tall as some trees. The cowboy in Dad reached much deeper than any clothes he wore.

Dad watched Westerns on television with Rod and me, unimpressed with most portrayals. "Oaters," he called them, because so many horses showed up on every set.

One oater we all watched together was *Red River*, starring John Wayne. He leads a cattle drive from Texas up to the rail head on the Plains. When gathering the herd, all the Hollywood cowboys yell "Yeehaw" at the top of their lungs. The animals raise their heads from the grass, bunch into a herd, and run full blast toward the river.

"Those actors are too noisy around livestock," Dad said. "The animals will figure out what to do if you give 'em a chance."

Young, hired hands at our ranch were even noisier than those Hollywood cowboys, so Dad cautioned us to calm down, not to yeehaw around livestock. He was a cattle whisperer. His motions were slow and deliberate, maneuvering animals with an internal karma and guiding them wherever he wanted them to go.

Unlike us boys, Dad never made animals nervous. His patience earned their acceptance, so they did whatever he needed.

We always tended to our horses before setting out to work cattle, even waiting to eat a hearty breakfast until after we fed our mounts. Breakfast ended by six each morning, and we thanked Red, the cook Dad hired from the Square Shooters restaurant in Rawlins after I graduated from high school. His name came from the bright hue of his nose.

For his first breakfast at the ranch house, Red followed the menu he had used in town, including fried eggs, ham, bacon, sourdough pancakes, hash browns, coffee, and juice. Good cooks were hard to keep on a ranch, and we figured Dad had found the perfect man this time. Eight of us sat around the dining room table and ordered from the menu, but after Red's first trip to town, our choices shrank.

Funny thing about him, whenever he went to Rawlins, he took two suitcases light enough for a child to carry. On his trip back, the suitcases weighed almost too much to budge. He had taken several trips to town before we solved the mystery.

The stash of whiskey hidden behind the cleansers under the kitchen sink tipped us off. After Red fed us breakfast and we left for work, he would start drinking. Once he had his fill, he'd sleep on the couch for a few hours before preparing supper around midafternoon.

One day, my buddies and I finished ahead of schedule and came back to the ranch early. I sneaked past our sleeping cook to move the dining room clock ahead to suppertime. Then all of us pushed the door open from the front yard and rushed in. "We're back! Supper ready?" we hollered. "We're starved!"

Red rolled over on the couch, squinting at the clock. "Christ!" he said, falling to the floor.

He scuttled on hands and knees to the kitchen to start cooking, cussing all the way for having slept in. His red nose turned even brighter when we explained the trick we had played.

I learned soon enough that you never cross a ranch cook. They have too many ways to get even with the surprises they can put on your plate, like undercooked pancakes laden with Ex-Lax that made a day in the saddle particularly painful.

Our federal grazing lease let us run one cow-calf pair for every five sheep we used to own. By 1974 we had finished replacing six thousand ewes with twelve hundred cows, a slow conversion we had started a decade earlier. Dad bought black Angus bulls and bred them to Hereford cows starting each Fourth of July. They produced a good genetic mix.

We always picked a relatively level pasture with good cover and water to use in breeding season. The bulls could move more easily through the cows and do their duty in earnest.

Black Baldy calves were born in late April or early May, each weighing about four hundred pounds when we shipped in the fall. Crossbreeding produced larger calves, and their darker hides eliminated most of the cancer eyes so common in pure Herefords.

"Hybrid vigor, that's what we want," Dad said.

Calves fattened all summer on our range, and then we shipped them out before the first snow, often in late October or early November. Dad kept good mothers over the winter and fed them hay when snow drifts got so deep no animal could graze. In the spring, we trailed pregnant cows to calving pastures where the next generation was born, and the life cycle began again.

I learned to ride horseback much quicker than I learned how to recognize subtle behavior in cattle. Like the time I left the ranch with a friend to look for cows bedded down near Seminoe Reservoir. We were young teens when we rode on our own for two hours while the older men searched for cattle in several nooks and crannies at the far reaches of the pasture.

My buddy and I gazed down from the top of a hill onto a green meadow dotted with twenty black calves asleep at the feet of a single brown cow. I didn't find out until later that the adult had been babysitting this nursery herd, assigned the task by the other cows through their own social hierarchy. She watched over unbranded calves while their moms lounged down by the water a quarter mile away after going for a drink.

My friend and I charged down the sand dune, loped in back of the calves, and whooped it up just like in the movies. We didn't even see the mother cows behind us.

"Yeehaw!" we screamed.

The babies ran away from the noise, but got hungry and scared before going very far, so they sniffed the air for Momma's milk. Black Baldy calves ran every direction for half a mile, eventually turning back to the place they last sucked, bawling for mom.

The lounging cows hurried from the reservoir when they heard their calves and finally met up with them at the previous night's bed ground, the place we had begun. Twenty pairs were now mothered-up after a couple of boys' noisy impatience had cost two hours of valuable herding time. Had we first mothered them up, we could have moved the herd on time to where the other riders were waiting.

When we caught up with the older riders, Dad just looked at us and frowned. "Glad you could make it," he said.

A young man could hardly be considered Western unless he knew how to roll one of his own cigarettes. But where could I practice without getting caught?

My buddy and I found the perfect hiding spot: the old Lemaster place just above Rankin Creek.

Like most homesteaders, Lemaster had picked a well-watered spot to settle down, scavenged barbed wire and fence posts from earlier homesteader claims, and built his American Dream on his own soil. Kirk eventually bought him out, as well as several others who started the same way but failed when the economy slumped.

"Hell, I bet I paid for the same posts and wire eight times through the years," Kirk told me one day.

When each homesteader moved on after being bought out, the

next homesteader came in and scavenged the posts and wire from the earlier occupant before Kirk could recover the materials. They built their own fences and corral facilities even though Kirk had already paid the earlier homesteader for those same materials.

When I was a teen, the Lemaster house and root cellar lay crumbled in ruins. Tall meadow grass twisted around its boards, pulling them deeper into the sod, reclaiming the land Lemaster once owned.

One of our best corrals was strategically located about a quarter of a mile away, where the spring and summer pastures were adjacent to each other. While the older boys did some repair work in preparation for branding, my friend and I hid behind the leaning north wall at the Lemaster place instead of helping them. Bull Durham tobacco and thin papers rested in our pockets, lifted from back at the ranch.

Dozens of Prince Albert tobacco tins lined our pantry shelves for use in the bunk house and sheep wagons where men typically relaxed and lit up after a long day of work. We also kept Bull Durham tobacco for cowboys to smoke while riding horseback. They could stuff the more portable cloth pouches in their breast pocket, letting the yellow draw strings dangle down the front of their shirt. The paper tag at the end of the strings swung like a pendulum from their pocket when the horse trotted away, as common a trait on our working cowboys as the weathered Stetsons they wore.

On that summer day at the Lemaster place, rusty nails poked through sun-rotted boards, and shards of broken bottle glass shone purple and green in the sage. We looked toward the corral to be certain we were alone and then laid cigarette makings in front of us and tore papers from the book, bending them concave around the index finger on one hand.

"Make sure to stay behind the wall where they can't see us," I said.

My shoulders scrunched to block wind gusts from hitting my hands as I loosened the pouch strings and poured an uneven line of cut tobacco leaves onto my paper. Fred Wise would hold the pouch to his face after a pour and grip the draw strings between his teeth, pulling them tight before stuffing the bag back into his pocket, so I did the same.

I moistened the exposed flap on the side of the cigarette with my tongue. Rolling the wet flap over the other side of the paper, I twist sealed each end to hold the tobacco inside. Fred could ignite a stick match with the flick of his fingernail, but I needed to scrape one against the teeth of my zipper to get a good spark.

My friend and I lasted half an hour before we started feeling sick.

Just as we were about to take off, we overheard two older boys walking by during a break. One of them had just returned from a military tour in Vietnam and came out to help Dad for the summer. When the two stopped near the old ruins, we scrambled to bury ourselves in the damp meadow grass.

"Viet Cong everywhere," said a muffled voice. "Ambushes at night. Mines and booby traps during the day. I was scared out of my mind."

The other guy said something I couldn't hear.

"We'd march for days, sometimes weeks. It was so damned hot and wet. All the time. I was never dry. Slogged through rice paddies up to our waists and hacked our way through the jungle. We were covered in leeches. And the mosquitoes? Jesus Christ, they never quit."

I shivered. A few more years and that could be me. I nearly threw up from the smoke and fear.

Now I understood why Dad hardly spoke about his time in New Guinea during World War II. My sympathy grew for the veteran, and I didn't consider him just an older kid anymore.

He had been lucky to survive, unlike the brother of my childhood friend who had died in country a year or so earlier. I never did understand the rationale for that overseas war, or why so many citizens in an ungrateful nation treated the veterans poorly when they returned home. After all, they landed back in America leaving the innocence of their youth behind them.

When the two guys walked away, my friend and I waited a few minutes and then ran to the corral to help finish the work, never smoking again.

13.

How to Lose a Cow Herd

We branded in early June, always the busiest time of year on the ranch. I was ten in the early summer of 1962 when we branded calves at the shearing pens. At seventy-four, Kirk still worked the cattle from horseback, roping each calf from his horse and dragging it over to the fire. He rode Pick, an aging black gelding as quiet as a ghost floating among the cows. Pick knew not to disturb stock or scare calves away from their moms, like Dad.

My job that day was to gather sagebrush and greasewood into a pile next to the fresno, an iron slip that looked like a giant spoon with no handle. Dad pulled it into the corral with a rope attached to an O-ring on a towing bar at one end. The slip would hold the burning wood and hot coals that kept the irons hot.

We added sagebrush fuel to the fire, the dry branches popping and cracking when the flames spit embers into the sky. The business ends of three different brands turned red hot where they were buried in the coals, and an eager cowboy stood near the slip waiting to carry a hot iron to the next calf.

Kirk nudged Pick through the milling herd, gliding toward a mother cow from her left side so he could check her brand. Old ranches like ours registered their brands long before many new outfits began, so they enjoyed the early choices of brand designs and where to place them. In my childhood years, our cows wore several different brands, and the only way to determine which one belonged on a "slick" was when it was mothered-up with a branded cow.

Ike had chosen the left side since most cowboys were right-handed and needed to see a cow's markings before throwing a loop. Left-side brands didn't require right-handed cowboys to cross the rope over the horse's head if they ever needed to capture the cow from behind.

The nearest cow in the corral that day glared at Pick, raised her head, and called her baby out of the crowd. A lonely bawl resonated behind her, and a slick calf hopped stiff-legged through the herd over to Mom. His tongue dangled from a wide-open mouth as he rammed into her udder, knocking her so hard she had to reposition herself, and his lips closed in a viselike grip around one of her nipples. He slurped milk until foamy drool covered his nose, dripping to the ground whenever he moved.

The calf now mothered-up, Kirk checked the cow for her brand. "I Lazy D!" he hollered toward the cowboys gathered at the fire.

Someone stoked the sizzling coals, stabbing the appropriate branding iron into the base of the flames. While Pick nosed between the mother and calf, Kirk stretched a heeling loop and tossed it in a soft arc under the calf's belly so it landed in front of the hind feet just as the calf stepped into it. Kirk yanked the rope tight, securing both ankles, and then dallied the rope around his saddle horn and dragged the slick to the fire. Two cowboys flanked the animal down before slipping the loop free so Kirk could ride back to the herd and capture another calf.

Even though I was still a pup, those early years of branding allowed me to contribute a little effort to the cause. When I entered high school, Dad started hiring several of my buddies as a crew each summer. He would keep the hardest workers through haying in August until we needed to return to town for two-a-day football practice. Rod and I never had to look far to find friends eager to wrestle calves at the ranch.

By that time, we were using only one brand. Dad would wean the calves the night before, and the next morning, our buddies herded a group of them into a small corral where we legged each one by hand and dragged them over to a propane branding stove before flanking them down.

One boy would rest his knee on the calf's neck and grip the left foreleg into a tight flex while another boy would sit behind the calf, grab the left pastern above the hoof to straighten the leg, and press one boot against the calf's rear end to plug any unwanted emissions. His other boot locked between the calf's hock and thigh, pushing the right leg up toward its belly.

By the 1970s, Dad had moved the branding to the shipping corral in the Hurt Creek pasture. Rod and I continued to help, and Shorty was still our foreman, branding the last time for us in 1977.

"Steady her, boys," he would tell us.

Rod and I held the calves for him so he could administer the hot brand to the hide across the left ribs. Shorty wore gloves for branding, one of the few jobs when he wore any. He would grip the looped handle on the end of the iron to steady the hot letters when they burned the calf's hair, sending a funnel of rank smoke into the air. I Lazy D seared into the hide, a symbol of the ranch the cow would carry the rest of its life.

Heifer (female) calves moved quickly through the ritual after Dad slit their left ears halfway down and burned an age brand on their hips to let us know the year the animal was born. A bull calf required more attention. Just like Kirk, Dad kept a razor-sharp blade on his Old Timer to castrate the bulls, slicing the scrotum, pinching each testicle through the hole, and then laying them on the propane stove to cook.

"Take five," Dad would say after we finished the first bunch. "Smoke 'em if you got 'em."

We'd stand and brush the corral dust off our jeans. Some cowboys lit cigarettes and leaned against the corral to smoke while others pinched chewing tobacco under their lips. Rod and I always kept a watch on the bloated nuts sizzling on the stove. When their spongy contents erupted through scorched membrane, they were ready to eat.

Hot testicles, "bull fries," are hard to handle with bare fingers, but their gray contents are a protein rush that swallows easy with a cold swig of beer.

During our final years on the ranch, Rod and I switched back to roping calves when we branded. We had our own families by then, but our kids were too young to help, and high school boys no longer seemed interested in ranch work. But the main reason we returned to roping was the tradition it honored, a tribute to our grandfather's way.

After Kirk retired in 1963, Dad became manager and vice president of Miller Estate Company and continued running some cows in addition to the existing herd of sheep. That's when Dad hired thirty-three-year-old Ed to fill the foreman job he had just vacated.

One of Ed's first big jobs was to trail boss the gathering of four hundred cows and calves from a holding pasture adjacent to the shearing pens and herd them north over Cheyenne Ridge to Indian Creek and the summer pastures where they would fatten up for the fall. Dad wouldn't be riding with us that day because a newspaper reporter was touring the ranch with him and needed an interview.

A young cowboy had already wrangled horses for the eight riders who would move the herd the required five miles. Rod, Bill, and I were excited to be part of the drive. I woke up at four thirty that morning without an alarm clock, which I never had to use on the ranch.

Climbing out from my wool bedroll, I lit the kerosene lantern bracketed to a bow slat on the wall of my sheep wagon. The flame warmed the wagon, filling the air with the scent of hot oil and drying canvas recently moistened from the chilly morning dew of summer outside.

I hopped around on my left foot while my right stabbed at the entrance to a sock. My knuckles loosened their frigid grip when I buttoned my shirt, and then I remembered to check the back pocket of my pants for a bag of stale chewing tobacco I wanted for the ride.

It was quiet and calm when I walked to the barn, passing the stagnant pond that bubbled beside a culvert under the old ranch road. Lazy frogs squatted in the wet foliage on its shore, jumping into the water as I walked by. No wind bent the tall grass. Stars twinkled in the sky clear to the distant horizon, unhindered by clouds. We needed this early start to move the cows before the day got too hot.

I grabbed my halter and walked toward the round corral where the unsaddled horses were milling around, waiting. "Will the cattle still be bedded down when we get there?" I asked Ed.

"Sure thing. It'll be a fun day." He tied his horse in the stall.

Cracker stared at me as I walked through the corral and approached him. He blinked, his black eyes shining like orbs of polished obsidian. I held out my hand to scratch his nose, and his snicker scared adjacent horses away. Normally, I hid the halter behind me when I approached a horse, an innocent deception to draw them under my spell, to make them think I was there only to offer oats from my hand. No need for trickery with Cracker—he didn't care what I did.

He nudged his nose into the rigging, bent his ears forward, and bowed his head to let me fasten the throat latch under his jaw. Blowing warm air in my face, he curled his upper lip, sniffing for oats.

Earlier cowboys had painted his name across a century-old timber nailed above one of our stalls. I tied him there with the slip knot Kirk taught me to use and then fed Ice Cream's offspring a half gallon of oats. He came from hardy stock and could handle the upcoming ride.

"You ready, Cracker?" I whispered.

I combed a cocklebur out of his mane and pulled spear grass from his coat. If I missed a single blade, it would drill beneath the saddle and dig into his flesh all day. After laying the horse blanket over his back, I adjusted the saddle Dad bought me from my godfather's Colorado Saddlery shop, but I drew the cinch only half tight before tying my bridle in the saddle leathers and looping the earpiece over the horn. Cracker's belly always expanded when he ate oats, so why cinch tight until it was time to climb into the saddle? The chore finished, I walked to the ranch with Ed for our five o'clock breakfast.

After a full plate of eggs, bacon, and pancakes and a last cup of coffee, we loaded our horses into the stock truck, and eight of us packed into two different cabs for a trip to the pasture, as tight as sardines in a can. The youngest of us rode between older boys who sat by the windows and challenged each other to produce the loudest fart. Middle riders grimaced at each fusillade.

Our headlights chased jackrabbits running across the road before the truck caught up with them. Why didn't they just wait until after we drove by to cross? The country, silent beyond our yellow beams, rested before sunrise. I didn't like disrupting the slumber of predawn, but we needed the early start.

Cattle were easier to gather in the cool morning before all the calves nursed and while their moms were still nearby. If we arrived too late, the calves would have eaten and the cows gone off to graze, leaving another nursery herd and a babysitter at each bed ground.

We reached the shearing pens half an hour after leaving the barn, unloaded the horses, and walked off their morning bloat before tightening our cinches. Ed pointed in three directions, telling each of us where he wanted us to ride, even though most of us had ridden this country several times before he was even on the payroll.

Splitting up, we covered a wide swath across the south end of the pasture and sneaked up on relaxed cattle still bedded down. Then we softly nudged cows and calves together, letting the young ones drink some milk before moving each pair ahead.

"Hyup," I whispered just loud enough for the nearest animal to hear.

We made a slow trot north toward the rising slope of Cheyenne Ridge. In under an hour, we had four hundred pairs walking slowly through the sage-covered dunes, the easy part done and the day still cool. By midmorning, we had bunched the herd at a gate that opened into our Seven Pines country.

"Hold 'em up on the other side," Ed remembered to say.

After the last pairs walked through the gate, we rested them in the corner before starting over the ridge. Several calves stole another drink from Mom.

"I'll take point," Ed said, loping to the front of the herd.

Dad had warned us at breakfast to keep a point rider in front of the herd before it reached the top of Cheyenne Ridge and the lead started down. "Ed, if you don't hold that position and slow the herd, faster cows will smell the water at Indian Creek and run ahead, forgetting their calves on the south side of the hill."

Bringing up the rear, the youngest boys rode drag behind the cattle, where the dust from hundreds of hooves exploded up from broken ground and hovered around us in a throat-choking cloud that assailed our nostrils. The congested mass of cattle pushed a small calf against the east fence where it slipped through the lowest barbed wires into the next pasture. There was no gate between us.

"Don't worry about him," Rod said. "He'll follow along on that side."

Other calves began to lag toward the back of the herd when the day lengthened, the slope steepened, and hunger returned. They searched in vain for lost mothers who had already moved to the front of the herd a hundred yards away, in a hurry to reach cool water ahead. The cattle bogged down from the stifling heat building around us.

"Keep the calves' heads turned north," I reminded the rider beside me, not wanting them to stare at where they had been or ponder where they had last sucked.

"It's getting thirsty out," I heard somebody say.

Older boys on sharp-witted horses rode swing on the left flank, keeping the cattle lined out along the east fence leading to Indian Creek still three miles ahead. The herd bulged away from the fence when the side hill steepened, and the lead cows found diagonal paths up the rocky slope.

The swell and dip of brown and black cattle moving over each hill resembled a ragtag army marching in defeat from some distant battle, their heads bowed low as they plodded ahead. Flank riders coaxed wandering cattle back toward the fence, straightening the western edge of the herd until it paralleled the wire. They brought half a dozen cows to the drag to mix with the weary calves and get them focusing on wet udders nearby.

Ed had kept the lead moving slowly, as Dad directed, bunched with the rest of the herd. But when they reached the ridge crest, Ed's head bobbed along the skyline and then dropped out of sight, several cows hot on his heels.

The herd stretched nearly the full length of the ridge. We loosened our bandannas, fastening them over our faces to keep dust clouds from clogging our lungs.

"Go doggies . . . up that hill," we hollered in frustration this time. More cows should have been grouped at the summit where the calves could see and hear them.

Blazing heat formed the mirage of a water pond dancing on the nearby slope that vaporized when cattle approached. The drag was now half the distance to the top of the ridge, but our effort slowed when fifty calves huddled together in the rear.

A flank rider pulled in alongside to help press the herd on ahead. "Spread out!" he shouted. "We can't be so close together—like we're riding the same horse."

Each time a calf looked over its shoulder, one of us loped to the spot and turned it around, wishing we had more fingers to plug this dike.

"Hyah!" we screamed.

Dad would be angry that so many hungry calves were bunched up too far away from their mothers.

"Where the hell's Ed?" a voice shouted from somewhere in the billowing dust. "The lead should be at the top of the ridge waiting for us to catch up."

"I'll go up and look around," Rod said, probably dying for fresh air.

The drag slogged behind a thick dust cloud fifty yards from the crest. More calves hung back, their heads bent toward the holding pasture and meadows they had sucked at that morning. Rod topped the sandstone crest, reined in near the weathered trunk of an old pine tree, and looked down into the valley of Indian Creek. Then he loped back.

"The cows are scattered for two miles ahead, spreading out all over the valley. The lead's clear down at the creek. It's a total wreck!"

One flank rider who had been nearest the point was standing on the ground, bent over, and pulling prickly pear spines from the cheeks of his ass. His horse had slipped on loose rocks and dumped him into a thick cactus patch. Foreman Ed, our trail boss that day, had disappeared.

Suddenly, half a dozen calves broke through the horsemen in the drag and ran headlong to the holding pasture behind us, hungry for milk. Every rider chased a calf, trying to turn it back to the herd, as twenty more escaped.

The dike broke, and a flood of calves poured down the hill toward their last bed ground. I helped one rider cut twenty cows out of the herd and run them toward the gate we passed earlier that morning, figuring the calves might see them and come back.

Our surrogate mothers didn't work. Calves crazy with hunger were frightened from being away from Mom for so long. Their flapping tongues jettisoned spit that splashed back in their faces when they ran.

Beating us to the fence, they crashed through the stretched wire as if the steel barbs weren't even there. By the time we opened the gate and herded our handful of cows through, Black Baldy calves were back at their morning bed ground bawling for their moms.

"We've lost 'em," Rod and I moaned.

We left the gate open, and my brother and I rode side-by-side in silence to the top of Cheyenne Ridge, sunk in our saddles under the weight of failure at a task Dad had counted on us to perform. Fred Wise would have been disappointed in us as well.

It was too hot to regather the cattle. We lost the herd and an entire day's work. What would Dad say?

"We better find Ed," Rod said.

We rode down the north side of the ridge through milling cattle, their heads buried in grass, oblivious to the calves they had abandoned. The lead cows had raced clear to a tributary of Indian Creek over an hour before. Ed stood behind a cut bank alongside the draw with a rope in his hands, staring at two cows stuck in the mud at the bottom of a narrow arroyo.

"What happened on point?" Rod asked him.

"The lead got away from me after crossing the ridge. Damn cows ran straight for water. These two got hung up in the mud. We gotta get 'em out before they sink any deeper."

We coaxed the shallower cow free after ten minutes of tugging and pulling, but the other animal only twisted, digging herself deeper into the muck. Every movement sucked her further into the rancid mire that lapped at her belly and buried her legs.

Two saddle horses and two ropes couldn't break her free. If her nose stuck in the mud, we knew she would smother. It was late afternoon, long after we should have been back at the ranch.

"We can't get a four-wheel drive in here to tow her out . . . the country's too rough," Ed said.

Unknown to us then, Dad had driven to the ridge above Indian Creek in his two-wheel drive pickup looking for us because we were late and saw in his binoculars the scattered herd and two cows stuck in the mud. We sent a rider to the ranch to get some help, and he intercepted Dad on the road back toward the headquarters. Dad harnessed Prince and Dan in the barn, the last team of workhorses we owned.

Meanwhile, the rest of the crew dug wet mud from the cow's mouth to keep her airway clean. Exhausted from her lengthy ordeal, she slipped slowly into the bottomless pit until somebody crammed a wooden plank under her chin, keeping her head up and buying more time.

Fourteen hours since breakfast and everyone was starving. Rod found a small sandstone outcrop where he could sit, a place already occupied by a rattlesnake who warned him of his unwelcome intrusion. Rod jumped back, gathered a handful of stones, and smashed the snake's skull.

He started skinning it. "Anyone got a match?" He built a pile of sage to cook the pink-gray flesh, and several of us tried a bite, grateful for food and something to do besides wait for help.

Near dusk, Dad arrived with Prince and Dan all harnessed and ready to tow. He said nothing to Ed as we dug sticky muck away from the cow's forelegs and then looped a couple of ropes under her belly before tying them to the harness rigging that hung behind the team.

Dad snapped the reins over Prince and Dan's rear ends. They tugged in unison against their collars, stretching the traces tight and pulling the cow from her sticky prison onto dry ground.

It took twenty minutes for her to get circulation back in her limbs. She hobbled off toward a nearby group of cattle as the last light of a setting sun shimmered on drying mud stuck to her sides and belly.

We were exhausted. Cows had scattered to every corner of the pasture, belatedly calling for their missing calves, their udders tight and swollen from a day's worth of undrunk milk. Some walked back toward the ridge looking for their calves and losing weight as they wandered.

Bill and I climbed into our saddles, prodding our weary mounts for the long ride back to the ranch together. The last of us arrived at the barn about eleven thirty that night, eighteen hours after we had begun. Not a single cow finished the drive, many calves were alone, hungry, and scared, and our horses were totally spent. It was the longest workday I'd ever had on the ranch, and it ended without getting a damn thing done. I hated it.

It would have made a good story for the newspaper man who had come to see Dad. That reporter should have ridden along.

I collapsed on my wool bedroll in the sheep wagon and lay there wondering what the hell Ed had meant that morning when he said it would be a fun day. His disregard of Dad's specific instructions to manage the lead cattle convinced me to always be prepared for contingencies whenever I directed a crew.

14.

Pets and Friends

Way before my time, our family treated sheep for scabies at a dipping works built on a terrace above the Kirk Ditch near the Seminoe Mountains. One summer day in my late teens, I was cleaning the ditch with Dad and we took a short break to visit the ruins. The interior chutes and pine panels had long since collapsed into rubble. Old posts were rotted off at ground level, and long, wiry grass protruded up through deep cracks in the wood, the thick stems pinning the crumpled walls against the ground.

"When did the outfit stop using this place?" I asked.

"Let's see, 1937 or a bit earlier, when sheep stopped getting scabies. The last year we used them, I had a pet goat that died in one of the pens. Sweet little guy." Dad shook his head and smiled. "That put me out of the goat business."

On our way back to work, we reminisced about my own childhood pets. Dad said, "Remember the time your grandfather dyed the lambs?"

I laughed. "How could I forget?"

When you live on a ranch with so many animals, a few are bound to become treasured members of the family. Most of ours weren't goats but other young livestock: bum lambs, orphaned calves, or an occasional steer.

Dad built a small cage by the ranch porch one year where we kids kept little bum lambs until their strength returned so they could be released into the herd. The pen became Mom's domain, and she cared for all the animals there. Each of Kirk's grandkids helped her feed them every day with warm milk from Coke bottles Mom had capped with rubber nipples.

She taught us to turn the bottle upside down, shake a drop onto the inside flat of our wrist, and let our bodies measure the temperature before giving any to the lambs.

"They need it warm, not hot," she said. "Pay attention to what you're doing when you feed them."

When I was about seven, I picked a black lamb among four white lambs to feed. I stood her between my legs and pressed my knees into her belly to hold her in place, cupping her chin with one hand to keep her head still while inverting the milk bottle toward her mouth.

A drop of milk leaked from the nipple and landed on her nose. She exploded in a burst of energy, pinched the nipple into her mouth, and pulled hard, pushing back into my grip to force more milk down her throat. The impact rammed the bottle against my nose and forced the nipple to slip from her mouth and squirt milk all over her face until she could recapture it. I could tell the milk was flowing again by watching the high-speed circle she wagged with the undocked length of her tail.

It was later that summer when Grandpa Kirk dyed the wool on each of the white bums—red, blue, green, yellow—just for fun, creating a colorful herd resembling a pen full of fluffy Easter eggs. He told us that by turning each of the white lambs a different color, the black one wouldn't feel so alone. Kirk knew how to make diversity cool.

One year, my cousin Susan raised a yearling steer she named Jimmy who got so fat we shipped him. She groomed him, but he was tougher to handle than bum lambs. Susan loved all the livestock and became one of the hardest workers on horseback.

She and her father, Uncle Chad, often rode together during our cattle drives. Once they were late leaving the ranch with the rest of the crew and parked their own horse trailer in the wrong pasture, the one we were filling with cattle.

We put cows through one gate while just as quickly Susan and her father were over a small hill pushing them back through another to where they had started. We all laughed when we discovered the problem and finally got the livestock where they belonged. The cattle probably wondered what the heck we were doing.

Whenever possible, Susan slept with Grammy Peg in her sheep wagon to be ready for every morning adventure. The old woman and young girl were a lot alike, both waking up with the sun. Peg was too old to help gather the livestock, though she had often ridden on her own in the lower meadow in her younger years. She and Susan were kindred spirits born in different generations, and they were the best of friends.

By the time Rod, Bill, and I were teens, we had turned our emotional attachments to the horses we rode. They became our pets, like Ice Cream was to Kirk. And to Mom's infinite relief, as I grew older, my social circle expanded to include many of the two-legged variety.

My Rawlins friends loved coming to the ranch. We didn't work cattle and sheep all the time, and once our daily chores were done, we explored the vast landscape of mountains, streams, and valleys on horseback. When I was a young boy, I felt sorry for my town friends who had to play in small sandboxes framed with two-by-fours in their backyards, while Rod and I traipsed over a thousand acres of active dunes, searching for arrowheads and lost treasure.

My best friend was Gary. Our families had known each other for years in town long before he and I were born. Barely a teenager when his mom got sick with cancer, Gary came with me to the ranch while she fought for her life. One day, my aunt drove to the ranch to deliver the heartbreaking news and tell Mom and me to take Gary to town. After a long, silent drive, we arrived at his house, and Gary's dad, Swede, walked out to the car and hugged his youngest boy, soothing the sadness both of them felt.

Gary found happiness again working summers on the I Lazy D. Herding livestock with our hired hands gave him a purpose and helped alleviate the pain of losing a parent at such a young age. He worked hard, quietly undertaking any task assigned to him, building a self-confidence and resilience that served him well in life—like my father after he came home from the war.

The year before we graduated from high school, Gary and I drove with Dad to Joe Martinez's sheep camp on Deweese Creek to deliver supplies. Joe had parked his wagon in a picturesque aspen grove above a deep beaver pond where we often went to fish and swim. His corpulent wife visited Joe on weekends, and when the two of them were in the wagon together, they filled it completely.

"Would you and Gary like a sandwich?" she asked, squeezing through the narrow door.

"Sure, thanks."

We expected a real Mexican treat when she pulled tortillas out of the cupboard, raised her skirt, and slapped them flat on the naked skin of her inner thigh. But then she reached back into the cupboard and grabbed bologna and cheese.

"There's watermelon for dessert," Joe said after we finished.

Gary was slicing the melon with a butcher knife when the blade cut through the rind, carving a deep gash in his hand. My first instinct was to clean his bleeding wound, so I poured cold water over it.

His knees buckled when the frigid water hit his bloodstream, and he leaned heavily against my side. I thought he was just kidding around, so I pushed him away. Off-balance, he blacked out and fell to the ground. I felt terrible and apologized.

Many decades later, Gary and I still talk about that incident. He carries the scar, and I still think about using water more wisely.

In early May of our senior year, Gary drove his girlfriend to Dutchman's Grove for a picnic. He loved the area, having ridden by it several times while moving cattle to their summer range. But he didn't arrive home when expected, so Swede called me early that evening to ask where his son might be. I had no idea but offered to drive him out toward the ranch to see if Gary had gotten into any trouble. We drove past the aspens at Dutchman's Grove in the dark, and neither of us saw a vehicle or any signs of life.

"Let's look in the RS Meadow in case they picnicked down there," I said.

The road into Deweese Creek valley leading to the RS was rocky and steep.

"Are you sure their car could make it down here?" Swede asked.

"Gary could if he wanted to. We better check to be sure."

Had I been thinking clearly like Swede, I would have known that a low-clearance vehicle like Gary's couldn't possibly travel that mountain road. Swede had been too kind to insist we turn around. Since neither of us saw any vehicle lights up ahead, I made another ill-informed decision. "There's an old building across the meadow. If they aren't there, we can go back to the county road and check at the ranch house."

The damp meadow sank when our truck began to cross, and our front tires slipped into muddy ruts so deep the transmission case rested flat on the ground.

"Don't spin the wheels," Swede said, getting out of the cab to check the soft ground.

We labored for over an hour jacking the axle up, piling sagebrush beneath the tires, and rocking the pickup between first gear and reverse.

"It's too dark to work anymore, Mark. Let's wait until daylight to finish digging out."

All conversation ended in the cramped cab as both of us tried dozing off. Well over six feet tall, Swede had to bend like a pretzel trying to find a comfortable position. My stomach churned with guilt for putting him though such distress.

When the night turned chilly, I restarted the engine to heat the cab and looked over at the folded mass of Gary's father, the man whose comfort I had robbed in an ill-fated search for his son on a soggy meadow no city car could cross.

We woke at first light to the sound of a truck motor's balanced cadence behind us. My folks had driven out from town to search for their own wayward son. Mom looked worried as she sat beside her husband in their cab. She relaxed when Swede and I stepped stiff-legged from our truck.

"Are you two, okay?" she asked. "I brought you coffee and something to eat."

Mom always cared for her children, nieces, and nephews on the ranch. I never felt safer than when she was around.

Dad grinned at our predicament in a way that conveyed no outward emotion. As I walked over to help with the tow rope, I saw how he held his mouth, a habit he got from his father, a wry, tilted smile and lightly pursed lips.

"Have you seen Gary?" I asked.

"He got in last night after you two left. Couldn't get his car started at Dutchman's Grove, so he and his girlfriend walked to the ranch. Shorty brought them to town. He said they passed you two in the river canyon."

"We were looking for his car. It was too dark to see anything by the time we got to the grove."

"Mark, you know the RS Meadow is wet this time of year. Weren't you paying attention?"

My mind had needed to see things that my eyes failed to note. I learned another life lesson from the ubiquitous grin of a man so familiar with every acre on the place, he could find his impulsive son in the pitch-black darkness of a remote mountain valley.

Despite my carelessness that night, Dad agreed to let Gary and me have a weeklong camping party with a few friends right before graduation. We would stay in a grassy bend of Hurt Creek across the channel from the old dipping works, the same place Dad once taught Rod and me how to catch fish with our bare hands.

"Put the beer in the creek to stay cool," I said, while Gary helped arrange tents in the grove and park vehicles on the side hill above our camp.

A car full of girls came by, but we made them leave when the party died down. Bachelors like us were not going to break our own rule of no couples allowed. Everyone went to bed about two in the morning after losing only one six-pack in the creek. The sounds of splintering wood and tearing canvas woke us an hour later.

"What's that?" Gary asked.

A friend's truck had slipped into neutral and rolled into the side of a nearby tent. Our classmates were just beginning to crawl out of the mess when Gary and I walked over.

"That truck missed me by six inches," one of them said.

A quick inventory showed everyone safe, so we went back to bed laughing. We all felt immortal then.

After drinking the rest of the beer, we drove to Seminoe Boat Club to resupply. A tall guy in loose-fitting cutoffs was kicking his car's front tire and cussing, his face beet red. He had gotten stuck in the beach sand on the way toward the shoreline, near where he planned to swim. We watched him get behind the wheel, start it up, and spin his tires trying to pull free, the one thing Dad taught me never to do in sand. My buddies and I grabbed a tow rope and pulled him with our jeep onto solid ground. He thanked us and asked what he owed us for the favor.

"A case of beer," we said.

Our jeep driver hit a bump on the way back to camp that bounced one of our friends out of the back seat and onto the dirt road behind us. We had been traveling less than twenty miles an hour when the kid completed his reverse, 360-degree flip that landed him on his butt without spilling a drop from the beer in his hand. A few years later, he was killed in a car accident after drinking most of the night and trying to drive. He proved none of us were immortal after all.

On our final evening in camp, another friend started having convulsions. He had suffered from a history of physical problems, but we thought he had paced his drinking so well that none of us were worried about him the entire week.

Panicking, we laid him down in the back of a truck bed and put a pillow under his head. The driver sped to the hospital in Rawlins while I sat in back giving our sick pal mouth-to-mouth resuscitation the entire way. As he rested in the emergency room, I asked the attending physician what had gone wrong.

"He's drunk."

That was it? All I could think of was my mouth pressed over his in the back of the truck, and the kids parked on main street staring at us driving by, me bent over another guy with his head on a pillow.

Everyone had hangovers the next morning, but we still needed to clean up the mess we created. Dad had made us agree to gather our trash before we broke camp, his only condition for letting us use the shaded stream bank for our party.

We piled into one of the trucks and drove three miles back to the county road, where we jumped out and picked up cans as the truck crept back to camp in first gear. Dad told me later he never saw the road so clean.

"You picked up beer cans over twenty years old," he said.

A couple of months later, Randy, another friend, and I hauled a small load of hay on the same rocky road I had taken with Swede, over the divide between Bradley Peak and the Seminoe Mountains. The entire route was dry this time and we had a higher profile vehicle. We crossed the meadow and drove toward an abandoned round corral near the ruins of a dilapidated ranch outbuilding.

The RS had been a British-owned outfit that ran cattle in the valley during the mid-1880s. Aunt Kit told me their manager once bought a herd from a dishonest seller who drove the animals past the front porch for a head count and then pushed the lead around a small hill to bunch them again in the rear. The maneuver formed a continuous circle of cattle, tricking the manager into counting the same animals twice and causing him to pay more than he owed. A couple of years after the sale, someone shot the manager dead during a brawl in the nearby community of Sand Creek.

Randy and I rolled down our windows to let the fresh air cool the cab on the way to the RS Meadow. Hot sun cracked our lips, but we had loaded some cold beer to drink at the end of the job. The Casper radio station was broadcasting the Selective Service draft lottery for the Vietnam War. Someone picked a number for each birthday out of a revolving basket and read it aloud over the radio to let young men know if they would have to serve.

They selected my birthday as a high number 310 in the draw. The year before, my brother's number had been drawn high as well. Dad would be relieved that neither of his boys would likely have to serve in some jungle conflict as he did in World War II.

Then they drew Randy's birthday. Number six. He would be called up right away.

Silence filled the cab as the weight of it all sank in. Randy let out a deep breath and leaned against the seat, resigned to the news. I handed him a beer as my mind wandered back to the horror stories about combat I had heard from the young cowboy at the Lemaster place a couple of years before.

I didn't know what to say, so I unloaded most of the hay while Randy drank most of the beer. Later that afternoon, we drove back to the stone ranch house so he could prepare for military service.

15.

Keepers and Shippers

On a clear fall afternoon, four hundred cows crowded into the holding pens at the shipping corral. Their erratic movements would make even the most seasoned hands nervous as they tried to maneuver inside the pens. Heavy, bovine bodies pressed against one another, cows sticking their noses above the melee just to breathe fresh air.

I coaxed them forward through one of the lanes toward the gates up ahead. My boots slid on slick cow manure, and I fell to my knees, ducking under jets of wet snot that shot through the air when the cows threw their heads back swatting at flies.

The congested herd rocked back and forth in unison, each cow waiting her turn to break free toward the pastures beyond the gates up ahead. A short, hairy black leg shot from a calf in the crowd striking my shin just under my knee, causing my body to buckle in agony once more. My eyes watered, trying to drown out the pain.

After we cut the calves away from the cows, Rimrock, one of our hands, guided a nine-year-old Hereford into the squeeze chute so Nick, the vet, could perform a pregnancy check. Rod and Dad trapped the cow in the chute and closed it against her head and sides. I splashed a dose of Warbex on her back to prevent her from getting ticks or lice.

She leaned into the bars as Nick pulled a long plastic glove over his arm to do his medical duty behind her. When he raised her tail and explored shoulder deep for an unborn calf, the cow curled her back and threw her head against the squeeze chute. The entire contraption clanged as she twisted against Nick's penetrating curiosity.

"She's open," he said, finding nothing inside.

The chute door released, the sides fell away, and the unbred cow trotted down the lane toward an open gate that led to the rest of the dries.

Next came a six-year-old. "This one has a calf," Nick said.

I had tilted a cup of Warbex over her haunches to let it drip onto her hide, but when Nick goosed her, she kicked high and the medicine splashed back onto my face and into my eye.

"Clean that out right away!" Dad hollered.

Our water jug was empty, so Buddy, our brand inspector, poured half a cup of lukewarm coffee from his thermos and handed it to me. "This is all we have left," he said.

Tilting my head back, I dripped the coffee onto my forehead so it would cool on its way into my eye, and flushed out the medicine before Rimrock nudged another cow toward the chute.

Buddy wandered among the cows bunched in the small holding pen next to the scales, checking brands, a ritual we had followed for a century. Ranchers needed him to verify the ownership of the stock before they shipped. He checked hundreds of thousands of animals during his career and worked so hard we treated him like one of the regular crew. His sense of humor kept us on our toes.

He pointed to the left ribs of a cow and the shallow, healed-over scar of bent hide and knotted hair that needed to be the capital "I" part of our brand. "You must have branded that one, Mark," he joked. "A little thin, don't you think?"

"It looks like you read a brand better than you rope," I said, referring to the time he threw a loop at a calf and caught a cow around her midriff instead. We both laughed.

❧

Afterward, we herded thirty calves onto our scales. If a cattle buyer attended, he stood alongside while we weighed each bunch and the scale printed out tonnage on a slip of paper we handed him. If calves were to be trucked to the sale barn in Torrington, we gave the weight of each lot to the driver who then turned it over to the auction boss.

Once the calves were loaded onto trucks and sent down the road, the crew began handling the mothers. We turned pregnant cows into our pasture to keep for another year and gathered the dries so Dad could inspect them and decide if each one might produce another calf before becoming too old to breed.

Dad stood at a spot in the center of the fenced lane, facing the oncoming cows thirty feet away. Of all his ranching skills, Dad performed this task perfectly, culling shippers from keepers. His decades of time around livestock gave him the credentials to make such critical decisions.

Two kids positioned themselves at separate gates, one to Dad's left and the other behind him. He communicated to each boy at a gate using subtle hand gestures, pointing with a finger from waist level to the left gate that led to Indian Creek, where keeper cattle would go. Or he pivoted, nodding toward the chute behind him, where shipper cows would load onto a truck bound for the sale barn.

Each movement was deliberate, lenient, gentle, but rapidly calculated. He stirred no more than the grass stems in the softness of a morning breeze.

As I think back those many years ago, I realize how subtle all of Dad's lessons were on the ranch, how his quiet manner kept us centered, making us concentrate on the details of every task before we performed them. I like to think I inherited some of his subtle, methodical focus.

Dad kept cows about ten years, although other outfits held breeding stock longer. The I Lazy D had too much coarse sand in its pastures. Loose grains would blow over the range until the grit stuck to the grasses our cows ate. Dirty grass would wear down a cow's teeth faster than grass grown on firmer soil, and cattle would starve when their teeth were gone.

The lead cow glared at Dad when she moved away from the crowd, searching for freedom beyond one of the corral exits around her. They stared each other down, Dad's body still, his voice silent, doing nothing to frighten the stock. As she moved, he focused on her from head to tail.

His mind sorted through a dozen observations in moments: healthy eyes with no evidence of infection; strong conformation, no hunch or sway in her back; and four well-formed hooves, not long like two pairs of skis. He read a single numerical brand that indicated she was seven years old and found no sores on her udder. She was fat and healthy, even though she hadn't been bred. The bulls had simply missed her.

Dad's decision could not be impeached. A quick gesture and the gate to Indian Creek opened. In the blink of an eye, he rendered a verdict to keep or ship every cow. We needed confident, educated decisions for our ranch to survive, and Dad showed us the precision required.

I tried sorting keepers from shippers that day, but my untrained mind fumbled with each verdict. The first cow trotted past and then stood behind me waiting for one of the gates to open so she could move on.

"Bring her back around," I said. "I didn't get a good look."

Dad smiled. I never attained his split-second mastery of quality or potential. A successful cattleman like him analyzed cows—he didn't just see them. He understood the range where they lived and didn't simply ride over its surface.

Unambiguous reasoning was no task for a tenderfoot unwilling to learn, so I taught myself better ways to observe the world around me. In later years when I instructed undergraduate students in archaeology at the university, I found myself in situations somewhat similar to Dad's. I closely observed the behavioral traits of each person in class and assessed their likelihood to remain successful in academics for another year.

Truck trailers contained distinct levels of pens divided into several compartments for confining shipper cattle during each trip to the sale barn. The driver backed his pot up to the loading chute with precise steering, jumped from the cab with a battery-powered prod in his hand, and called for the number of cows he wanted in the first compartment.

The cattle disliked trucks, so they stalled in a crowd at the bottom of the chute and tried turning around. Young cowboys got anxious, yelling at them, "Yeehaw! Yeehaw!"

"Shh. Quiet down," Dad said. "Let the herd find its leader."

One brave cow took a long look at the gangplank leading up to the trailer, stepped onto the chute floor, and trotted into the compartment. The rest of the cattle followed close behind. When the last truck left the corral, a calm settled over the ranch.

Haying finished, fencing done, and the weather still favored the grasses so no need to distribute supplemental hay. We had some breathing room at last. Perfect timing, because autumn in Wyoming was ideal for a leisurely horseback ride through the Seminoe Mountains to enjoy the vastness of the ranch.

Late-season rain painted new green into the pastures, creating a welcome Indian summer. Bred cows fattened for the winter ahead, untethered by the demands of recent motherhood, their unborn infants still small and quiescent, asleep in their wombs.

Paperwork, piled up in drawers and closets, still needed our attention. But first, we spent time with family and enjoyed the big paycheck the company took to the bank.

This was when Kirk went to the bars.

PART 3

People and Culture

Dad at the barn dance. September 21, 1979.

Robert "Bob" Meldrum mug shot, 1916. One of the
outlaws who worked at the I Lazy D.

16.

Battle over Grass

Soon after finishing graduate school, I sat with Mom in our Rawlins home as she rummaged through a box of keepsakes. With a smile, she pulled out my baby book and started flipping through it.

"Look at this, Mark."

She pointed to a page where years ago she had written down my first official ranch chore: hauling buckets of coal from the shed to heat our living quarters in the ranch house.

"That was 1954. You had just turned three. It was a big bucket, and you did it all by yourself." She touched my arm, her eyes glistening.

With Mom's support, I had been able to contribute to the family workload at an early age. And later, she enthusiastically supported my college education. She had profited so much from earning her own degree—her business skills were always in demand in Rawlins. Focus on achievable goals, she would tell me, stimulating not only my intellectual growth, but also my work ethic as a young cowboy.

As I grew older and my ranch duties evolved, I came to understand that my family and the animals under my care experienced the full consequences of my actions. I needed to carry my own weight so other cowboys didn't have to repair my shortcomings. Whether fencing with barbed wire or riding horseback behind a herd, I used the techniques

I'd learned from Dad while watching him manage the outfit. Ranching was never a game to him or a fabricated movie scene.

When I earned my PhD in 1979, so did hundreds of others in anthropology, but only a few tenure-track teaching positions were open for application nationwide. I was married to Leona then and had two stepchildren, so I chose not to chase gypsy scholar positions across the country. They were typically available only for a year with no chance at academic tenure.

Instead, I started working part-time for Dad on the ranch and planned to do Wyoming archaeology in the summer. Rod was now foreman of the I Lazy D, and Dad still managed the place.

Within months, the outcome of a Nevada lawsuit weighed heavily on all of us. Environmental groups had argued that too many livestock were grazing public lands. In response to the court decision, the Bureau of Land Management (BLM) began conducting an inventory of all the vegetation in the American West to determine whether there was enough to support the herds.

As a boy, I had known that good ranching involved much more than moving cattle from pasture to pasture or riding horseback in the lower meadow. Now, I was about to put my research skills to work while learning the political ropes of the business.

Luckily we had a mild winter that year, allowing my family to focus on administrative duties, most importantly, doing everything we could to understand the BLM effort. Mom loved having her men work in town every day for a change, and she furnished a vacant bedroom with an office desk, filing cabinet, and other business essentials.

"What else do you guys need?" she asked.

We looked at one another and shrugged. No clue. We had never undertaken such an extensive project before.

"Don't worry, I have some ideas."

She bought relevant research books on Wyoming grasses, took notes in shorthand when we found an important fact, cooked three meals a day, managed every phone call, and offered useful insights from the perspective of a business school graduate. Our whole family worked together organizing the data of our ranching operation, making that time the most enjoyable of my early adult life.

We also helped build the newly reorganized Carbon County Stock Growers Association (CCSGA). The group had been active in the 1880s but declined in influence before the end of the nineteenth century. Rod was elected president, and for his first official act, he formed a committee to monitor developments in the BLM inventory.

"Segundo, I want you to chair the committee," Rod told me, using the nickname Dad had given me as the second child. "We need to make sure ranchers get a fair deal."

"I'll do what I can, Primo."

The BLM planned to compare the existing vegetation on individual ranches with a theoretical computer model of the plants that would have been present in pristine, natural conditions before European colonization. The result of that comparison would address how many head of domestic livestock the vegetation could support.

For decades, the agency had issued permits to ranches specifying the number of animals allowed to graze on public lands for set periods—without the aid of a computer model. But now, if that model rated those ranches in poor or fair vegetative condition, the federal agency could reduce the number of animals permitted to graze there.

County ranchers would face a significant loss of income if their stocking rates were reduced.

As committee chairman, I learned all I could about the BLM inventory method and the computer model, but we needed more help. Given the potential dire consequences, Rod and I talked about bringing in professional support. "Let's hire a range specialist," he told the gathering at our annual Carbon County Stock Growers banquet.

He took off his Stetson, put a few hundred dollars in it, and gave it to me to walk around the tables for donations. I put in a like amount, and the rest of the county ranchers pooled their resources. We raised more than $8,000 that night.

The independent consultant traveled all over the state, monitoring the BLM range technicians hired to conduct the on-the-ground plant survey and checking the accuracy of their work. Several crews were needed to cover such a large geographical area. Federal helicopters landed in ranch pastures and unloaded teams of students who wandered through the country counting grasses and forbs. The consultant told us that many of the young hires were from back east and knew little of the semiarid intermountain west or the plants it sustained.

Up to my elbows in lists, charts, and graphs, I soon discovered that the proportional representation of plant species observed on the ground was significantly different from the computer model's forecast for healthy range sites. Such a disparity would adversely affect the ecological ratings for most ranches and prompt the government to scale back the number of livestock allowed.

At an external review meeting in Denver, our representatives came to an alarming conclusion: the model was inaccurate and couldn't support the objective assessment of current range conditions. It appeared that BLM hadn't allowed for natural fluctuations in vegetation. Stockmen knew that the percentage of plant species changed over time for lots of reasons—they had seen it happen during their years in the saddle. Some plants increased, some decreased, some invaded, and some disappeared.

We had to present this fact in our argument that the computer model was faulty—and we needed a good example. The plant threadleaf sedge (*Carex filifolia*) came to our rescue.

Dad had shown me the species the year before during a trip to our middle winter pasture. As we crested a ridge in his pickup, he pointed to the forage in front of us. "See those plants?"

I looked across a hill slope blanketed with low clumps of grasses. "Yes, they're everywhere."

"That's threadleaf sedge. I call it blackroot." He got out of the truck, knelt down, and fondled the thick green blades of one plant as though they were made of byssus silk.

He went on to tell me that threadleaf thrives at high elevation in semiarid, shallow sandy soils typical of the western Hanna Basin. Its network of black roots spreads out like a mat just beneath the ground surface, enabling it to gather most of the moisture when it falls, even if only eight inches drop each year.

"Let me show you," he said.

Dad dug up one of the threadleaf clumps. He laid down his spade shovel and brushed away the dirt, tenderly massaging the root system.

"See that?" He pointed to the shallow roots bound beneath the blades of grass. "That's why blackroot survives even the harshest droughts. It outcompetes deeper rooted plants in country like ours that gets so little rain."

I learned that other species, like needle-and-thread grass (*Stipa comata*), need moisture to percolate further down into the sediments just to reach their root system. Threadleaf actually increases in moisture-stressed range areas because of its competitive advantage—not because of domestic livestock overgrazing, as some had speculated. Throughout history, many wildlife species have also enjoyed threadleaf. Bison ate it for thousands of years before cattle even arrived.

After numerous discussions and debates, BLM range specialists finally admitted to University of Wyoming scientists that threadleaf occurred on nearly three million acres of rangeland in south-central Wyoming, affecting range condition for many ranching families, including our own. They conceded that forage adjustments penalizing high percentages of the species would hurt a tremendous part of the local ranching economy.

Their direct admission scared ranchers, especially when BLM acknowledged that even though high percentages of threadleaf could occur in natural plant communities, those high percentages hadn't been allowed in their model. The species comprised nearly ninety percent of some range sites, yet BLM's inventory method allowed only five to ten percent occurrence in many pastures. Its natural dominance in Carbon County could singlehandedly give a ranch a poor rating.

If the model was implemented, stockmen would face dramatic reductions in livestock numbers for reasons unrelated to overgrazing.

At one of the CCSGA committee meetings, I pulled Rod aside. "We need to halt this program. There's no way ranchers will get a fair measure from it."

"Check with the university," he said. "They're working on the problem too."

Dan Rogers, University of Wyoming Extension Specialist, had labored tirelessly on these issues, and his efforts nailed the coffin shut on the computer model as a forage allocation tool. BLM ultimately withdrew it from use.

Ranchers who leased federal grazing lands in Carbon County could finally breathe a huge sigh of relief. The BLM also deleted the "elimination of livestock" as an alternative action in their Environmental Impact Statement, disappointing those who wanted livestock permanently removed from public lands.

My family and many other rural ranchers helped expose these concerns, as did range scientists at the University of Wyoming. Carbon County awarded Dad, Rod, and me Rancher of the Year honors for our research efforts, and later the three of us were recognized by the Wyoming Section of the Society for Range Management for Excellence in Grazing Management. The agricultural community appreciated what we did, and even some BLM friends joined us for a drink.

Older stockmen nicknamed Rod and me the Carbon County Mafia for our tenacious defense of ranching. Grandpa Kirk would have been proud of the whole family.

Considering Wyoming had been the first place worldwide to incorporate women's suffrage in 1869, gender equality would have been much better served had Mom also been recognized in those grazing awards. She stood with us toe-to-toe through every tribulation, and I regret her omission. But like she was while taking our photographs through the years, Mom was a silent force too seldom acknowledged by those who benefited from her contributions.

17.

A Network of Roots

Rich wetland grasses thrived in our lower meadows. Parallel fields of tall, green plants meandered between linear dunes for two miles east of the barn. Every year, we harvested 240 acres for baled hay and fed it to the cows during the winter, when the snow drifted to six feet or more.

Our native plants anchored deep in the sandy soil, along with introduced European species, all of them reaching for the sky. Many of them looked different from one another out in the field, but their hidden taproots were interlaced in a tangled network beneath the surface. They had integrated so well during their lifespan that Miller meadows supported a single, diverse community of grass.

It was similar to the way America had become a melting pot of diverse human populations who called it home.

Migrating geese ate the tops from Garrison creeping foxtail in the meadow, so it never grew in patches as thick as it should. Black Baldy calves bedded down in the smooth brome and timothy grass under shaded willows at the edge of the dunes. Some mornings, deer mice scampered among the redtop stems as if lost in a miniature forest, their tails knocking dew drops from the canopy of leaves arching overhead. And sweet clover grew every other year adjacent to the irrigation ditch, luring pronghorn to wander the banks for the special treat.

We cut hay every fall, watching mice run for cover under raked windrows, followed closely at times by rattlesnakes lurking in the grass. The baler would gather loose hay from the windrows—and sometimes the snakes—and compress rectangular blocks tied with twine and spit them back out onto the meadow.

In their free time, high school kids would buck the bales onto a wooden slip dragged behind a tractor to the stackyard. They always reached for each bale in the meadow with steel hooks before grabbing the twine, wary of any live snakes that might have survived the plunger.

All the plant species depended on my family to irrigate and help them grow. Dad learned the fickle nature of our streams, anticipating the crucial timing of the runoff from the Seminoe Mountains. For an optimal hay crop every fall, he had to divert the maximum flow to the meadows.

We irrigated in early spring and continued until just before the harvest, if the water in Hurt Creek lasted that long. Our goal was to raise three tons of hay to the acre, but we never managed to do more than a ton and a half—water was simply too scarce and our soil nutrients too poor.

On a bright, blustery morning in March, Dad and I drove to the ranch and stared at the bifurcated peaks on Bradley far to the northwest, white with snow. A bumpy layer of frost coated the road beneath our wheels. Crusted ice sheets hid the meadow grass from the healing power of the sun.

"Let's work the Supply Ditch today," Dad said.

"So soon? The ground's still hard, and the ditch is buried under ice."

"Let's get a head start this year. I want to fix the ditch so it's plenty ready when the water gets here. Use your shovel to break through the ice."

We dug for a couple of hours, clearing the channel of debris, though the water wouldn't flow for two or three weeks, maybe longer. But that was how Dad captured every drop. "You can't irrigate after it's gone," he'd say.

As we moved along the ditch, he plugged frozen mole holes in the walls to keep them from diverting water to the wrong place on the meadow. We returned every day and dug, waiting until the snow melted in the high country, listening for the oncoming rush of cold mountain water before we could see it.

One afternoon in April, Dad suddenly stopped digging and cocked his head. "Do you hear that?"

He had barely gotten the words out when a foamy white wave roared through the head gate and rumbled around a tight bend in the ditch, spitting out twigs and leaves it had carried. Thick, airy froth slopped over the banks, spilled onto the edge of the meadow, and disappeared in the torrent of water that rushed in behind it. Cold runoff raced through the channel while Dad leaned into his shovel and threw dirt down another burrow before the water flooded the spot.

I hurried to shovel along the lower portion of the channel adjacent to the meadow.

"Up here, Mark. Always dig from the high side of the ditch."

The older I got, the more details he shared about proper ranching techniques. There were a million of them it seemed.

The water flow turned shallow when it seeped into the dune, carrying nutrients to grass roots out in the meadow. Our sandy soil sucked up water like a sponge, so we never had to dig turnouts anywhere along the way.

During our many irrigating trips over the years, Dad would instruct my brother and me on water management. We'd stare at him, mesmerized, as he moved water to where it needed to go, his manner calm and deliberate, just as he was when sorting livestock. His teaching style rivaled any graduate class I ever took.

When the sun dipped low behind Bradley Peak on that day in April, Dad stood with his chin resting on the handle end of his shovel. He watched the water flow gently toward the next dry spot in the meadow and smiled.

18.

Barn Dance

When Rod and I were in our late twenties, the Marlboro Man came out for a photo shoot. The company wanted to photograph scenes at our barn to use on cowboy billboards for smokers back east. For several hours, the Marlboro Man lit cigarettes in various places.

The shoot was almost over when someone from the camera crew noticed the barely visible sign nailed to the main ceiling beam. It read, "No Smoking. This Means You."

They threw away an entire roll of film. Years later, we found a much earlier message painted on the back of the sign: "Private Land. Please Keep Off."

A notice to trespassers as old as the building itself.

The main barn entrance is a timeless portal into my West. An old wooden door still hangs there, heavy on rusty hinges, covered with peeling paint, barely sliding open when we enter. Over the decades, hired hands carved brands and initials into the wood, inscribed at a time far beyond the distance my memory travels.

Soon after finishing the barn in 1890, workers poured the concrete patio in front of the door. Before the damp matrix hardened, they stuck metal objects into it to protect the foundation from tromping hooves.

A rusted auger bit, heavy horseshoes laid on edge, and gear wheels sheltered the concrete from the slice of shod horses and gave traction when muddy animals entered the barn.

Every cowboy who worked on the ranch has walked through that door. Five generations of Millers stood there. Dad taught Rod and me how to ride horseback in front of it. Fred Wise sat there when he showed us kids how to wrap black silk scarves around our necks so we could look just like him. Even though time passes and people change, that barn door remains the most immutable nexus of my past country life.

Mom and Dad chose September 21, 1979, to hold a barn dance at the I Lazy D, sixty-one years after my grandparents had celebrated with a similar shindig at O'Brien Spring.

We had a lot to celebrate. Miller livestock investments were over a century old, my folks had been married for thirty years, and Dad would turn sixty that fall. Rod had returned to work full-time at the ranch after spending a few years in Europe, and I had just finished my doctoral program at the University of Colorado. We all migrated back to the ranch from different directions, as if wanting to nurture our own roots once again. We were ready for a real party.

A barn dance, a quaint country tradition, is a time-honored means of social interaction for rural families who live miles apart, but still consider themselves neighbors. New immigrants and old natives come together and mingle. They may look a little different from one another in the circulating crowd, like those unique stems of assorted meadow grasses, but they are all there for a common purpose.

Everyone at the shindig swaps lies, shares recipes, and kicks off the trail dust of summer. Some even meet eligible members of the opposite sex, and new relationships begin.

Mom and Dad wrote up a guest list that numbered over a hundred, inviting kin and acquaintances from both sides of our family. We asked golfing buddies my folks met after they took up the sport, hired hands who worked for us before moving on to other careers, cattle buyers, brand inspectors we had known for decades, and neighboring ranchers from both sides of the river.

We even invited Aunt Lil, the last surviving guest of the 1918 O'Brien Spring party, a widow by then for many years.

"I would love to go," she said, "but I'm afraid the barn dance would bring back too many memories of my husband and me at the shearing pens." She decided to stay home, passing the torch to a new generation.

We spent two days preparing the barn and corral for festivities. Mom's brother-in-law, Uncle George, was an expert carpenter and probably my closest friend in our extended family. He built a sixteen-step staircase leading from the ground up to a wooden door in the hayloft and fastened extra boards to windowsills to stabilize the handrails on both sides of the steps. The only better way up would have been an elevator.

As I helped him, he taught me a valuable lesson about carpentry—and life in general.

"Always measure twice, and cut once," he said.

Uncle George's cautionary tale proved appropriate for an impetuous young man who never thought enough before he acted.

We rearranged hay bales to the side of the floor in the loft, keeping a large area open for dancing. Rod nailed four-by-eight pieces of plywood to the wooden floor planks, and his oldest son scattered sawdust across them.

The day before the big event, we dug a six-foot-deep trench in front of the round corral, piling the back dirt off to the side. Younger hands gathered old cedar fence posts, sagebrush, and cottonwood to build a bonfire in the bottom of the pit. The flames quickly oxidized the sandy walls a bright orange. We added fuel until red hot coals were two feet deep.

Next came the side of beef. After Mom basted it with barbecue sauce, we tied its fore limb and hind limb to a long steel pole with baling wire. Holding opposite ends, two men lowered the meat until it hung over the coals inside the pit. Then we added a tin roof and shoveled dirt over it, allowing the beef to cook for twenty-four hours before the crowd arrived.

Our cowboys swept out the horse stalls and piled "road apples" behind the barn. The double-wide stall to the right of the barn door held card tables piled with whiskey, tall glasses, and ice. A chilled beer keg sat in one corner.

When the first of the crowd arrived in midafternoon, we opened the earth oven and removed the cooked beef. Meat easily peeled away from the bone.

Ice cubes crackled in glasses under the warm flow of bourbon, single malt scotch, and rye. The smell of good whiskey mingled with the century-thick horse sweat that saturated our barn wood. Visitors ascended Uncle George's staircase to take their places on the dance floor, while the four-piece band from Hanna warmed up: a drummer, a saxophonist, an accordion player, and the best fiddler I ever heard.

We ate, drank, and danced for hours, long into the night. Old friends renewed acquaintances, and old disputes were forgotten. Former employees swapped half truths about the tough years they had endured while working on the I Lazy D.

Dan, the bunkhouse singer, attended. So did Rob and Gib, two other top hands. They had all worked together on the ranch many years earlier.

A tough, square-jawed cowboy, Gib had changed from a hard drinker to a gentle family man during his years on the I Lazy D. The country did that to some people, taming them almost like Dad tamed the livestock. The country brought out the kindness in their character.

At an earlier time, Gib had worked as a roughneck on an oil crew until a fellow worker let the sucker chain slip from his grip when the drill rod was spinning. The chain uncoiled and hit Gib in the face, breaking his jaw, but the impact never knocked him down. He shook off the injury, walked over to his coworker, and decked him with a bare-knuckled fist.

His reputation for strength and frontier justice preceded him, so we never messed with him on the ranch. After he survived all of life's challenges, Gib's final words shortly before he died years later were "Where's Peanuts?"—the horse he had ridden so many times on the ranch.

Mom took dozens of photographs at the party and kept them in a three-ring binder. Without her dogged attention, too many memories would have been lost in the silent, unlit shadows of the past.

My favorite image from the party shows Dad, slightly out of focus, walking across the corral yard in front of the barn. Hunched under his Resistol cowboy hat, smiling his ubiquitous grin, he unsuccessfully tried to avoid Mom's camera. One hand was stuffed in his front pants pocket—the only time I had ever seen him do that.

Dad always admonished Rod and me, "You can't get any work done with your hands in your pockets."

Mom captured that watershed moment in Dad's ranching career, preserving the biggest day in his life when he shared his home, his ranch, his accomplishments, and his heritage with all his family and friends.

Crouched under his hat on a mission, he was halfway between the barn and the snubbing post he set as a teen, just uphill from our hay meadows where those flowing, diverse grasses were all connected by interlocked roots. Dad had paused while he headed toward an equally diverse crowd of ranchers, golfers, and townsfolk mingling with one another.

I suddenly knew why his hand was in his pocket.

He had put it there for a reason—because his work was finally done for the day. He was standing right where he belonged.

19.

Footprints

Every time I rode horseback through our pastures, I thought about the countless riders who had ridden the same range long before me. What was on their minds when they looked for cattle? Did they ponder their own family, or maybe dream of girlfriends? Which horse was their favorite? What had actually happened out there during the last century?

After I started studying archaeology, I had even more questions and pestered Dad whenever we worked together. One day, while we were down in the garage—Dad called it our cathouse—repairing a Caterpillar tractor, I asked him about our hired hands.

"You must have known many of the cowboys who worked for the outfit. Most are gone now, but I swear I can feel their ghosts out on the range."

"Some shifty characters were with us over the years," he said, greasing a zerk on the axle. "A couple of them were pretty hard to talk to."

"Tell me."

"Well, at least one of our hired hands had been an outlaw. A guy by the name of Bob Meldrum. He worked out here during your granddad's time. Kirk remembered him well."

Dad told me that Bob was a loner who kept to himself. "When

he walked into the ranch house, he headed straight for the corner of the living room next to the gun closet. That's where he always sat."

Actually, I liked sitting there too. A single wooden chair rested in front of the closet, bare walls on either side. Someone seated there could prevent anyone from sneaking up to grab a stored firearm from inside.

"Bob faced the outside door and the windows, his back to the gun cabinet, watching every cowboy come and go, as if measuring their intentions," Dad said. "He never turned his back to a window."

Meldrum's gun-fighting days had earned him too many enemies, and the other hired hands knew not to approach him from behind. If they wanted to get his attention out in some pasture, they would yell his name from a safe distance and wave their hands well beyond revolver range.

I later found a 1916 portrait of Meldrum shortly after his sentencing to the Wyoming State Penitentiary for fatally shooting unarmed cowboy Chick Bowen in Baggs. He got five to seven years. Meldrum is unhappy in the photo. His wrinkled countenance maps the rugged topography of a lifetime spent in the saddle. Tousled hair matches a gray shade of moral indifference. His cold, brutal face frames the piercing stare of a man to whom life means nothing.

Steel-gray eyes shine from hollow sockets as if he is looking right through the photographer, condemning the man to death with his gaze. For an outlaw who supposedly carved several notches into the handle of his Colt revolver, Meldrum's stare is no idle threat.

But he was a Jekyll and Hyde outlaw. He transformed himself in a later photograph into a clean-shaven gentleman with neatly combed hair, dressed in a nice suit and tie. His eyes were subdued this time, his mouth bent in a slight, unpracticed smile. It looked to me like a portrait you might circulate if running for a political office.

Well known in western states at the end of the nineteenth century, Meldrum had ridden into Colorado mining towns to quiet labor unrest using his skill as a professional gunman. He also worked in

Idaho alongside Pinkerton detective Charlie Siringo during the trial of Harry Orchard for the assassination of former governor Steunenberg. Meldrum had hired out to protect "Big Bill" Haywood, the labor organizer Clarence Darrow defended as an accused accomplice to the crime.

I began reading books about Meldrum's various escapades. When I discovered that he might have ridden with the legendary stock detective Tom Horn, I flashed back to a day I was with Kirk in the barn.

He brought up the time he'd been riding horseback to the ranch from Rawlins when a lone rider reined in beside him. "I couldn't have been more than twelve or thirteen at the time," he said. "The man rode with me for a couple of miles and then broke off and headed toward the Ferris Mountains."

"Do you know who he was?" I asked.

"Said his name was Tom Horn."

According to family lore, two men from the John Coble ranch near Bosler spent a night in Ike's town barn then, and one of them was Horn. His ride with young Kirk the following day no doubt prompted my grandfather to hire Horn's friend, Bob Meldrum, when he was released from prison several years later.

Meldrum never did spend his full sentence behind bars. Some friends secured an early release through an honor system that placed him as a laborer for area ranchers.

The Daley Ranch and our Miller Land and Livestock Company were two of his employers during the period following World War I. About the time Meldrum worked for the I Lazy D, oil and gas development in the Lost Soldier area north of Rawlins attracted many local investors. Numerous families bought interest in the production company. Even Kirk pulled together some savings and went to town with Meldrum so he could buy some shares, but both men ended up in a bar instead. Apparently, they drank up Kirk's savings. He never did purchase interest in Lost Soldier.

Meldrum developed a real skill at leather work, creating fashionable gloves, belts, holsters, and horse tack. He made some items while working on our ranch, and his pieces command a premium today with collectors of Western memorabilia.

As a kid forty years later, I rode a beautifully tooled saddle Grandpa Kirk kept in the tack room. It had a narrow seat between fork and cantle, built for a small boy. Its fenders and stirrups hung close to the skirt, dangling from clean, folded straps. Stamped into the stretched leather on the back of the cantle were Meldrum's initials, "RDM."

Meldrum had made the saddle as a gift for Dad's older brother, Isaac, after he was born. He was a toddler when Meldrum worked at the ranch. Uncle Bus, as we called him, hated ranch work and left it when he was a young man, seldom visiting the place after World War II. His childhood saddle still hung in the barn until I was about ten or so and then it disappeared.

By the late 1920s, Bob Meldrum had finished with ranching and was operating his own leather craft store in the railroad town of Walcott, twenty miles east of Rawlins. He enjoyed a good business for a few years but dropped out of sight shortly after his shop burned down.

Nobody heard from him after that. Some say an old enemy dry-gulched him out in the country. Others say he went back to New York City where he had family. His whereabouts remain a mystery to this day.

Wherever Meldrum went after Walcott, he stayed gone. So did the saddle he made for Uncle Bus. Tom Horn was gone too. Only their stories remain.

One day, I received a call from George, a university colleague. "We have a human skeleton in Carbon County," he said. "Might be on your ranch. Want to help with the recovery?"

"Sure!"

I enjoyed the forensic archaeology we did together, especially when we had an unsolved mystery where I'd grown up.

A few days earlier, a coyote hunter had found the bleached bones of a man murdered in our pastures over a hundred years before. Some people speculated he had been a missing person, but to be a missing person, people needed to know he existed in the first place. Otherwise, how could they tell he was gone? We just didn't know who he was.

Preliminary descriptions suggested that his life had ended during a time the range was unfenced and horses were the primary mode of transportation. The rest of his story was an unsolved mystery I hoped our recovery team could address. George and I organized a field expedition to the site.

We met in Rawlins with the county sheriff, a younger man I remembered from high school, and a forensic group from the Wyoming Crime Lab out of Cheyenne. Together we drove north toward Muddy Gap and turned east on a two-track road crossing Separation Flats, heading toward the murder scene.

The sheriff's Bronco bounced over rutted tracks across sand dunes baked hard in places, blown soft in others. He stopped at a gate. "You're riding shotgun, Mark. Hop out and open it."

I had repaired this fence several times in my youth, the boundary between the Stone Ranch and the I Lazy D. The remote post and wire line stretched through the middle of an arid basin where people and livestock seldom crossed. Nobody had driven through this gate for some time, so the stretched wire had pulled tight in the gate between fence posts on both sides of the road. I grabbed the barbed wire in the gate's center and yanked until it sagged, prompting two loops around the gate post to loosen their grip.

"This is one of our spring pastures," I said when we drove through.

Ten minutes later, the sheriff parked beside a high, active dune. "We walk from here," he said.

Southwesterly wind yanked small sand grains from the back of the dune and propelled them eastward until they landed on the lee slope, stinging our faces. Tenacious wind had scoured out the ground behind the dune for decades, leaving an oblong blowout in its wake, like the one that once held the waters of Loch Leven.

Over the centuries, erosion exposed things once buried beneath the dune and ignored by most people living today. The dune trough opened toward the afternoon sun, its abraded surface smooth and flesh colored.

"Over there." The sheriff pointed at a white lump lying on a low pedestal near the center of the trough.

"That's the guy," said a member of the crime lab team who had already visited the site.

After waiting agonizing weeks for final permission from the appropriate agencies to remove the evidence, we didn't want to lose more of its context to wind, predators, or artifact collectors. George, our physical anthropologist, walked over to where the skull had been found, downhill from the pedestal that held the rest of the corpse. John Doe's skeletonized knees were bent, one arm folded, the other straight. His head had faced downslope in the dune trough, exposing a .45-caliber bullet hole in the back of the skull.

"They found the bullet under the cranium," someone said.

I took a few steps closer. "I wonder if my family knew the man."

The leader of the crime team muffled a laugh. "I hope your family had nothing to do with this."

We pounded a rebar in the ground to help us record each bone in place. Measuring tapes opened, compasses were set, and the pages of notebooks flapped in the wind. We would map and document each discovery before removing anything to the lab.

"What do you make of that?" I pointed to a trail of dispersed human bones heading away from the pedestal toward a nearby arroyo.

My colleague Rick called out, "There's another line of bones over here."

He and I inspected the bones. Those in his line were small and light, aligned with the long axis of the dune trough. Strong winds had blown them northeastward away from the man's body, bouncing them along the blowout toward the top of the dune where they eventually settled.

My trail was oriented perpendicular to the wind, leading to an arroyo north of the blowout. Human bones here were heavier than Rick's and chewed on their ends. Canine scat littered the ground. Coyotes.

Rick and I recorded the lines while George observed the arrangement of pedestaled bones. "Looks like he was kneeling when someone shot him," he said. "The murderer held a gun to the back of his head, like an execution."

"Was he stripped?" someone asked. The question went unanswered, but there was no evidence of clothing.

The only other artifact besides the spent bullet was a small, corroded piece of metal found beneath the deepest bones. We couldn't identify it or how it got there.

According to the ballistics expert at the crime lab, John Doe was probably shot between 1880 and 1920. That was well before anyone owned Social Security cards or similar forms of identification. Clues to his name and background remained hidden in the sun-bleached bones, the victim of an unsolved homicide more than a century ago.

Was this man an innocent traveler or an unlucky road agent or what? A human life had been taken in secret, and we needed to figure it out. The discovery drove home to me how many events on the I Lazy D had never found their way into a history book. So little information had been recorded.

The physical anthropologist's report identified the body as "Caucasian, male, forty-two to sixty-five years old. Gunshot entry wound on the posterior left parietal. Exit wound above the right ear." It was a brief, impersonal epitaph for a man nobody remembered.

Scientists who study the rate of dune migration in the Seminoe field argue that these dunes move downwind as much as five meters a year. We measured the distance from the front end of our dune's nose back to the skeleton in the blowout. If the dead man had been shot at the front of the dune, as we suspected, the distance between that spot and the skeleton suggested the man was murdered around 1890, based on the dune movement rate.

That made sense. No one would intentionally bury a homicide victim in a dune blowout. The surface there constantly erodes, and a body wouldn't stay hidden. The shooter probably buried the victim in the accumulating sand of the dune nose, and it took a hundred years for the dune to migrate over the victim to its present exposed position downwind.

The outlaw Bob Meldrum disappeared when he was about the same age as the dead man in the dune. Those who thought he had been dry-gulched speculated that this skeleton belonged to him. But a facial superposition of Meldrum's photograph over the victim's skull didn't match, and Meldrum lived past 1920, the minimum limit of the estimated date of death of the dune murder victim. Still, Meldrum did work on our ranch about the time John Doe was buried in the sand and may have known something about his death.

More research led us to B. F. (Frank) Buchanan, the missing eyewitness to the 1889 lynching of Ella Watson and James Averell in the nearby hills to the north. Buchanan disappeared about the time of the dune murder, after not appearing to testify at the grand jury hearing in Rawlins for the suspects.

According to his account, Buchanan had been sitting in Averell's roadside store that fateful July day in 1889 when two boys rushed in and told him some ranchers had just grabbed Ella Watson and James Averell. They were driving the two away in a wagon. Buchanan ran to his horse, tightened the cinch, and stealthily rode to where he could watch the wagon's maneuvers. The wagon pulled into a narrow canyon in the Sweetwater rocks and came to a stop.

Buchanan had paralleled their path, staying behind boulders and trees. As he peeked over the rock crest, he saw Averell and Watson with ropes around their necks being taunted by some of the men who had abducted them. Buchanan took aim and emptied the cylinder of his revolver twice, wounding one of the captors in the leg. When return fire cracked against the rocks near his head, he scurried back to his horse and galloped toward Casper to alert authorities.

He was the only nonparticipant eyewitness to the double lynching, so his sworn testimony at the hearing would have been crucial. His absence clouded the outcome, an injustice that still echoes throughout Wyoming today.

My great-grandfather Ike had been named foreman of the grand jury that heard the case against local ranchers arrested for the lynching. True to their charge from the judge, neither Ike nor any juror ever divulged testimony from the hearing. But the most useful evidence would have come from Buchanan himself. Without it, Ike couldn't sign a true bill of indictment.

Our initial analysis suggested John Doe might have been a bit older when he died than Buchanan was when he vanished. Whoever he was, his body had been dumped in a dune less than a mile off the old wagon road between Rawlins and the Seminoe gold mines, a road also leading to the I Lazy D Ranch headquarters.

Did Frank Buchanan meet his fate in the dunes on the I Lazy D at the hands of someone not wanting him to testify? An anonymous person must have thought so. When I visited the scene a few years after we removed the victim's skeleton, a metal cross stood there with the iron initials "FB" soldered onto its frame.

It would be ironic, indeed, if Ike had driven his horse-drawn buggy to Rawlins for grand jury duty in 1889, unknowingly passing within a quarter mile of the dead body of his primary witness along the way. Carbon County continues to yield its historical secrets grudgingly.

Other nefarious individuals lived on the ranch during my own time. When I was a teenager, a hired hand named Donald wandered out from town one summer to work at the ranch. He kept to himself, never speaking about his past.

Dad gave him the corner room upstairs in the stone house, and I walked by once when his suitcase lay open on the bed, crammed full of watches, jewelry, and pocketknives, more than any one person could use. I figured he had been a traveling salesman before he came to work for us.

Donald owned a well-balanced throwing knife and showed it to my brother and me, much to Mom's dismay. It felt good in my grip when he let me handle it. After he had been at the ranch a couple of weeks, he took Rod and me to the coal shed next to the house, closed its wooden door, and paced off several steps. Turning around, he said, "Watch this, boys."

When he extended his arm, the knife flew from his grip and stuck deep into the coal shed door. He retrieved the knife and walked back to us. "Here, I'll show you how. Hold it like this." He gripped the blade and bent his elbow. "Focus on the center of the door."

Donald handed me the knife, and it stuck when I threw. Mom came out after Rod took his turn and told us to wash up for supper, ignoring Donald when he walked past her to his room. She followed him out of the corner of her eye.

A few days later, Donald, Rod, and I had just finished grooming some horses at the barn and were walking back to the house when Donald stopped to use the privy next to the corral. A plume of dust rose from the road leading into the yard, and we watched the county sheriff drive up and park next to Dad, but I couldn't hear what they were saying to each other.

Donald exited the outhouse, saw the parked patrol car, and walked in slow motion toward the sheriff. Muffled words were exchanged between them, and then the sheriff turned Donald around, handcuffed him, and put him in the back seat of the patrol car.

I heard later Donald was sentenced to serve time in the state penitentiary. Apparently, those watches and jewelry weren't his after all.

20.

No Home for Kittens

"When did your father come to America?" I asked Aunt Kit during one of our Park Manor conversations.

"In 1865. Papa told me he was twenty-one when he landed in New York."

"Do you know why he left Denmark?"

"Prussia had invaded the year before, so he decided to start over somewhere else. I think he might have been avoiding the draft."

By 1911, Ike was sixty-seven and had earned time to reflect on his Wyoming accomplishments. One day that summer, he drove Kit in his buggy over to his Buzzard holdings in the Sand Creek country on the northwest edge of the I Lazy D. The team of horses pulled hard through a dry patch of loose sand on the way.

"Those were lovely animals," Aunt Kit said. "Santa Claus and Christmas. Two perfectly matched white horses."

During the drive, she looked over at her dad and told him she was worried about how hard he was working. "Will you ever sell off some of the ranch?" she asked him.

"No, honey. I built exactly what I wanted. I won't divide it up, but I might sell the whole place to a buyer in Salt Lake."

Obviously, that sale didn't happen.

At the peak of Ike's ranching enterprise in the early 1900s, the vast country of the ranch must have seemed incredible to him, considering the small farm his parents once worked in Denmark. His combined properties were about twice the size of the I Lazy D alone.

"Papa died in Long Beach the year after our ride." Aunt Kit frowned. "The board of trustees sold the Buzzard part to two ranch speculators."

Apparently, the trustees had the authority to sell the Buzzard property and keep the proceeds in the trust. That money would be available to those who inherited the estate in later years.

"What about Ada?"

"Mama died three years earlier, in 1909. She and I were riding home on the train from a visit to family back east when she got very sick. I didn't know what to do. The conductor gave me a little pouch of money Mama had kept with her, and I brought her body back to Wyoming."

Ada had filed on a 160-acre homestead under her name sometime after she married Ike Miller. They built a house there on the terrace overlooking the North Platte River. The HO, as the Millers called it, sat at a convenient location, especially in winter. When heavy snows came, the livestock would gather for protection on the adjacent bottomland.

Ike, Ada, and their children spent many days in that house at the end of the nineteenth century. Ike never filed on a homestead in his own name, even though he had lived in Wyoming since 1868. Elected Rawlins' first mayor in 1886, he waited until the following year to establish his official US citizenship. Formalities seemed unimportant to him.

Aunt Kit remembered living at the HO homestead as the youngest child in the family. Her memory had locked onto a single event that happened when she was only six years old.

Her cat had just given birth to several kittens, far too many to keep as pets in the small home. Ike and Ada planned to destroy them before they grew up and took over the limited living space. Ike put them in a gunnysack, tied off the end, and carried them to the edge of the terrace above the swift current in the river fifty feet below.

He held the bag with the same hands he had used many years

earlier to hang a man convicted of murder. Lifting the gunnysack, he dangled it over the river cliff, but stopped when the kittens wiggled inside, unable to throw them to their death over the terrace.

Ada scowled, marched over to her husband with the same resolve she had exercised when firing Charley Wagers, grabbed the bag from his hands, and heaved it into the river. The kittens landed with a splash and were swept downstream.

Our family abandoned the HO river home after Ada and Ike passed away. By then, Kirk managed the ranch and used the old building to store hay for the winter. Local fishermen often took shelter there to get out of the cold, building a fire on top of the wooden floor to keep warm. One blaze flared up in the 1930s and burned the place down, leaving walls lower than the seed heads on Indian rice grass growing nearby on the terrace.

Kit's childhood home is now a disheveled line of sparse foundation stones next to a scatter of broken glass, stove parts, and charred wood. These artifacts mark the spot where my ancestor's home once stood, and it is slowly disintegrating, just like Annie Saltiel's place.

An occasional stump remains from the stock corral on the other side of the two-track road we traveled on when heading to the river. Most town folks pass the area without knowing the homestead or abandoned corral are even there.

My elderly artist friend, Bill Scoggin, often fished below the ruins and hunted arrowheads on the riverbank. He remembered walking down the slope to a single fence post still firm in the ground but leaning downwind. Barbed wire clung to it by a diagonal staple pounded into the weather-beaten pine a foot from the top. The stretched wire's weakening tension suspended the post, keeping it from falling into the river.

One morning, Scoggin watched a meadowlark fly down from the homestead and land on the post, extending her claws to grip the soft wood. She pushed her bright yellow breast with black crescent collar into the wind and folded speckled wings to her sides. Her eyes were wide open and wary when she sang a sonorous chirp.

"I painted that scene," Scoggin told me while we were having coffee at the Square Shooters in Rawlins.

Bill gave me one of his prints, Wyoming's state bird perched on a post where Ada had thrown a bag full of kittens into the river, the place Kit and Kirk had lived as children. Where little lives had been swept away while others had just begun.

That day at Park Manor, Aunt Kit fell silent after finishing the kitten story. She looked out the window and back at me, her eyes tearing. "I was sorry to hear about your baby daughter," she said softly.

Her abrupt shift startled me. It had happened over a year and a half before, but the pain still gripped my heart—and always would.

I had woken on October 30, 1978, Mom's fifty-fourth birthday, and reminded myself to call her that evening after I got home from campus. My daughter, Tanya Rose, was only three months old then. I'd been researching my doctoral dissertation, consumed with academic work, leaving for campus each morning while Tanya was still asleep, and seldom getting home until after Leona had put her to bed. I had cataloged so many artifacts that I hardly spent any time with my daughter at all.

I rode the bus to my office that morning and no sooner settled into the workday than my phone rang. The secretary where Leona worked told me to hurry home right away. I arrived just ahead of my wife and stepdaughter who brought me the tragic news.

"I wish I'd gotten to know Tanya better," I told Aunt Kit. "We took her middle name from my mother's, Betty Rose."

Tanya died of Sudden Infant Death Syndrome (SIDS) a week before my scheduled defense of a dissertation prospectus. I'd been poring over physical evidence of archaeological sites, contemplating theories about prehistoric settlements, and calculating the influence of vegetative diversity on human subsistence when I heard about my daughter.

My mind went into shock.

The graduate committee offered to let me postpone my defense so I could recover from the grief, but I turned them down. If I had walked away from my academic program, even temporarily, I knew I'd never return.

I presented to the committee shortly after Tanya's funeral. How I managed to get through it without breaking down, I will never know. The coroner had requested an autopsy to learn more about SIDS by studying Tanya's little organs. I agreed but suspected we wouldn't learn anything new since SIDS was such a great scientific unknown.

After the autopsy, the coroner returned Tanya's personal effects. Nothing could have prepared me for that.

He handed me my daughter's baby blanket, stained with massive pools of dried blood from the autopsy he had performed. I took the ruined blanket home, folded it into the top drawer of my great-grandfather's rolltop desk. A friend and I had hauled it to town from the ranch years before. I wrote my dissertation there.

Work was the only thing that helped.

I dedicated myself to defending my finished dissertation before the first anniversary of Tanya's death, beating the self-imposed deadline by a couple of weeks. After earning my degree, I took the blood-stained blanket from my drawer and threw it away so no one else in the family would ever know about it.

Aunt Kit stirred in her chair, shaking me out of those tortured thoughts.

"I had a brother named Isaac who I never knew," she said. "He was born in 1879 and died when he was only a few months old. A sickly boy according to Mama."

I thought of Isaac as a baby in 1879 and Tanya as a baby in 1978, each young life extinguished nearly a century apart before they ever had a chance to really live.

It was getting late, and I needed to head home. I hugged Aunt Kit and then paused at the door, seeing in her tear-stained eyes the profound impact those two heartbreaking events had visited on different generations of my family.

I waved goodbye to Aunt Kit and never saw her again.

21.

El Viento

Carbon County sits in a powerful wind corridor squeezed between towering peaks of the Central and Southern Rocky Mountains, where fifty-mile-an-hour gusts sweep over the Continental Divide, crisscrossing the region and propelling almost everything in their path. Centuries of people have forsaken their eastern homes to wander this windy basin on a journey in search of their own West, taking trails, railroads, and highways, leaving behind loved ones in places they passed.

The wind travels too, mostly in the opposite direction, uprooting pieces of the western landscape, dropping them farther east, burying the tracks of immigrants who faced into the storm. Zephyrs muffle their migrating voices, confounding every story they try to tell. In this way, the wind has long protected the rural history of the American West, concealing closely held secrets by burying them beneath windborne sediments and frightening timid interlopers away.

When I talked with Aunt Marggy, Dad's sister, about the Wyoming wind, she told me a story about a man named Clyde. A new immigrant hired in the Rawlins school system, he went to Kirk and Peg's house to discuss teaching music in town.

The faculty knew my grandmother as an accomplished pianist, so they sent Clyde to interview her for curriculum suggestions. When he entered their mudroom, he closed the heavy door against the howling wind outside, barely winning the battle against gusts that hammered the house and blew his tie over his shoulder.

Peg had been playing her Steinway piano beneath a brass pendulum that clicked back and forth, keeping time without hands for a task where hours and minutes didn't matter. She and Kirk looked up at the visitor.

"Boy, it's windy today," Clyde said. He stared out the front window and down the street, as if wondering whether it had been a good idea to take a job in Carbon County. "Does the wind always blow this way?"

Kirk had spent his life in the wind. Stiff currents sculpted character into his face and tousled thin hair on the back of his head, but no tempest ever dulled his keen sense of humor. Smiling, he joined the newcomer at the window and pointed in the opposite direction up the street. "No, Clyde, sometimes it blows the other way."

Kirk built the windmill beside the ranch house that pumped water for our family to drink. The rhythmic push and pull of the sucker rod coaxed cool liquid to flow. Years later, he taught his son, Frank, how to build windmills too. Kirk's boy learned to harness even more of the wind when he grew into a man and raised two sons of his own.

As I reflect on my years working with Dad on windmills, I believe he saw ranch life in layers. Water flowed in deep aquifers underfoot, locked in the earth out of reach. Wind blew over the landscape, sucking surface moisture away from the plants. Livestock weakened when summer Chinooks turned our reservoirs into dust, until the animals lacked strength enough to graze four miles from the last place they drank.

Cattle would shrivel in that limbo layer between too much wind above and inaccessible water below, trapped in a sort of vertical asymmetry in the West. Dad worked to join these rangeland layers together through the propellers and pipes of steel windmills, persuading each breeze to pump water to places where earlier winds had stolen it away.

He hired Vince and Galusha to dig wells and build mills at the mouths of narrow canyons where the wind funneled through and consolidated its force. The two men drilled for eleven dollars a foot, but their dysfunctional friendship was priceless.

They moved around each other like two magnets facing identical poles, each effort producing a whole outcome less than the sum of its two contributing parts. Neither knew which man was in charge. They resembled Laurel and Hardy out West as Dad and I watched their shenanigans from the comfort of his truck.

"Here's the crescent wrench, Vince. Climb up there and tighten the nuts on the vanes," Galusha grumbled from the base of the windmill's legs.

"Okay, but it's your turn next," Vince said. He stared at the blades overhead, scampered up to the top of the ladder, and stabbed the long wrench at the windmill as if he were Don Quixote.

Minutes later, he hollered, "Watch out!" The crescent was falling toward Galusha's head.

The wrench struck galvanized steel in its descent, whistled past Galusha's ear, and slammed to the ground by his feet. Galusha glared at Vince through the crossbars of the windmill frame.

"Damn it, be careful. One of us could get hurt around here."

"Got that right," Dad whispered to me. "I hope we finish this job without having to bury someone."

Our windmills transformed violent gusts into pools of calm water where wildlife and livestock could drink. New water holes only two miles apart spread animals more evenly over the range, keeping them healthy longer so they fattened for harsh winters ahead. The same natural power that once had dried out the land now nourished it once more, as though the wind always gives back whatever it has taken away.

After the curtain closed on the last Vince and Galusha act, Dad modified his GMC pickup as a workover rig to maintain finished windmills they had built. He welded on a sturdy frame to store sucker rods, bolted on a pipe cutter, and packed away tools, chains, nuts, bolts, and washers. Dad planned every detail on his own with little explanation, still teaching me by his example. Watch and learn.

We drove in his converted truck from town to the ranch every morning, checking to see if any windmills along the way needed repair after strong windstorms. When livestock moved out of each pasture,

I would close the brake handles and tie them off to shut down the pumps. We would reopen the flow a few days before cattle or sheep returned, so the troughs could fill before the animals grazed adjacent side hills and broad meadows. Our windmills pumped like mechanical hearts, and range life responded to each pulse.

Dad designed shut-off valves to conserve water when each trough became full. At the end of the outlet pipe, he attached a toilet float with a swivel gasket that fell open when each trough was empty. Then he disengaged the windmill brake so the vanes squeaked into motion. Galvanized blades captured the sun's glow, angled its glare, and dazzled bright rays in our eyes.

When the windmill blades turned, water rushed through the pipe to the trough, the increasing depth raising the float. As soon as each trough was full, the float closed and shut off the flow. It stayed that way until the next animal drank. Dad's design worked well if hunters didn't shoot the floats full of holes or leave gut piles in the troughs when they butchered game.

One summer, Dad and I checked the windmill in one of our pastures south of Cheyenne Ridge, where we found a closed float, a full trough, and a dead mouse floating in the water. The rodent had crawled to the edge for a drink and slipped on the metal surface, falling into the trough. There was no traction to help him climb out.

Dad built small wooden bridges that winter and laid them across the troughs so they hung over the water where swimming rodents could grip them and move to dry ground. His design worked well if hunters didn't burn the little bridges in their campfires.

In 1981, the BLM sponsored a hearing to discuss livestock grazing on public lands in the West. We listened when federal employees, many of whom were our friends, claimed water was very important. We listened when they suggested ways for ranchers to improve the use of their windmills.

Windmill troughs, they said, needed built-in escape routes in case small animals fell into the water. Rod and I smiled at the ingenuity they had borrowed from Dad.

Even though windmill troughs are unbiased oases where every animal drinks, some of our BLM friends thought ranchers should just drill flowing wells, rather than letting nature water the land by powering windmills. They worried that windmills distorted the public's view of the true Western landscape, as if stock-raising facilities didn't belong out there.

Ranchers and bureaucrats sat in that hearing room until smiles turned to frowns on all our faces, faces that had been sculpted that day by air conditioners instead of the wind. Ranchers should paint windmills the color of the land, we read in some report, so the steel blends in with the terrain.

"What about this policy?" I asked. "Who'll pay for all the paint and labor? It's a waste of time."

"It's a good idea," a bureaucrat said. "Then the recreating public won't see the impacts of ranching when they drive by."

"My family would need to paint thirty-six windmills white for winter, green for spring, yellow for summer, and brown for fall. Which hue did you have in mind?"

It must be hard for men to manage a land when they don't even know its color. Silence answered my question that day, and the meeting came to an end. There was too much confusion over wind, windmills, and water. So many friendships were strained.

I felt sorry for those well-dressed officials who sat in that room as if the blood flowing to their brains had been strangled by their tight ties. But then I realized all of us see the West from different perspectives. We must all walk for a time in one another's boots. Instead of meeting in town that day, we should have invited everyone to the country, where Kirk taught Dad how to build windmills.

22.

Danger in the Haystacks

At the University of Wyoming, stone buildings towered above me, hiding the sky and the stars, their rigid proportions and architectural conformity dwarfing any structures I saw on the ranch. Well-watered lawns replaced sagebrush and migrating dunes. Instead of rolling hills, I found parking lots and a place academics called Prexy's Pasture used for students rather than livestock. Landscape became a verb on campus, some service you hired a contractor to perform.

Students learned about ranching from the perspective of a white-collar science, the instructors standing behind podiums instead of leaning on fence posts. Stock raising was a theoretical subject. Despite this alien world, I had met many new friends who understood some aspects of agriculture much better than I did.

On a fall day in 1983, a bearded professor sat behind a long oak table in a dingy seminar room in the corner of the student union. He resembled a stuffy intellectual but proved to be friendly and open with an audience. Three walls around him were plastered with torn posters of coming campus events, and the fourth housed a water-stained window with cracked and dirty panes of glass.

Twenty chairs scattered around the table for the too few students who wandered in to attend his lecture. At ten past the hour, only four of us sat in front of the instructor, and I wondered why others had so little interest in the topic he brought to our group.

"We announced this all over campus. I can't imagine where everyone is," a troubled student said, frowning at such poor attendance.

Perhaps nobody cared.

"That's okay. Let's get started anyway," the professor said.

He had volunteered his time to discuss his thoughts on the ecology of the American West with the students and public. We listened for an hour, posing many pertinent questions.

His lecture exposed a serious omission from the research of the 1960s when many ecology theories were first formed. Studies back then had focused on systems of energy exchange in nature absent any human influence. Humans had been treated as an outside force that threatened the existence and diversity of life. People were an unnatural element attacking a natural order.

He argued that this myopic approach to ecology was a mistake, and I agreed, baffled at such intellectual oversight. Humans are a biological species, so how can scientists ignore them in any study of the ecosystem in which they try to survive? We're all part of the same energy flow. No parallel universe exists.

The professor completed his seminar amid comments on mineral extraction, population growth, and endangered wildlife species. He saw humans as integral to the world, with both positive and negative contributions, a critical link in the chain of life.

We must think creatively about what people do before we pass judgment on the value of their deeds. After all, humans have lived in Wyoming for over thirteen thousand years, and researchers are nowhere near understanding all their possible adaptations to the region's ecology.

Some human behavior is relatively obvious, like plant introductions during nineteenth-century migrations from Europe. Immigrants brought crop seed to America for food and fiber production. Other plants came as ship ballast or packing material during ocean voyages. Foreign plant species arrived and interacted with native communities already growing here. Some escaped their primary habitat and evolved into troublesome weeds.

Livestock and domesticated pets were introduced as well, adapting in many ways. Most found a safe place to live, so why should human immigrants be any different? We just need to understand how they all relate to one another.

A new book by a man named Wolf came out in 1980, a hiking guide to the Continental Divide Trail. The author had trekked the entire route across Wyoming, keeping a journal about his daily experiences in nature. He described details of the rural landscape, locations of potable water, and patterns of land ownership.

But he had not contacted any of the landowners for permission to travel on their private ground. His route crossed several miles of the I Lazy D, but we never knew of his trip until I saw his published book for sale in town.

I bought a copy of the paperback. It had a yellow binding and resilient cover so it could survive the outdoor weather perils of back-packing trips. It told of hiking conditions, fences, and the hazards of cow manure. Points of interest were listed in measured increments between places of departure and each destination.

How this author could know so much about private land and so little about landowners was beyond my comprehension. His traveling advice wasn't thorough enough for the average backpacker, either. We would have told him so had he contacted us ahead of time about his proposed route.

Our ranch is a harsh land. To the seasoned cowhand on a good horse, it isn't too difficult to travel. But to a pedestrian tenderfoot with forty pounds of hiking gear on his back, wearing camouflaged shorts and low-cut boots, trusting only in a yellow book, the landscape could be a gateway to exhaustion—or even death. The Haystack Mountains, in particular, are a very hard place for the uninitiated to survive.

One hot August day, Rod, Dad, and I encountered three hikers sitting on jagged rocks along the east face of the Haystacks. They stood up slowly as we approached, their lips dry and cracked. Trendy sixteen-ounce water bottles hung empty at their sides. One trekker was flipping through his yellow guidebook.

"There's no water out here," he said. "We ran out hours ago, and the book doesn't help worth a damn."

"That's why we have windmills and reservoirs. Streams up here are dry this time of year," Dad said. "You better get in back, and we'll drive you to the county road. You'll die of thirst out here on foot."

The backpackers jumped into the truck. Dad turned around and drove seven miles back to the paved road. "This is as far as I can take you. We've got work to do. Too bad that author didn't call me or I could've warned him about the limited water."

The young backpackers thanked Dad for his kindness, promising to write the author about how they'd nearly died and ask him to communicate more openly with landowners along the trail. The Haystacks loomed in the distance behind them, parched and dry, a rugged terrain where all sorts of dangers waited to forcefully educate those too stubborn to learn on their own.

A few days after we dropped off those hikers, I was checking the fence across Coal Creek below the Haystacks. I walked through the sagebrush back to my truck just as a rattlesnake struck from its lair under a bush, injecting venom into a cottontail rabbit chewing on a leaf.

The young rabbit shivered beneath the canopy of sage, stumbled forward on paralyzed legs, and stared at the snake through overcast eyes that no longer blinked. Toxin penetrated each nerve, causing all motion to cease, except for the wounded beat of his heart.

Coiled in the summer shade, the viper rattled its interlocked joints of shed skin dangling at the end of its tail, his only acknowledgment that I stood behind his bush. Then he unhinged wide jaws, engulfed the head of his prey, and swallowed the poisoned animal whole. Burdened by the weight of an undigested hare, this snake was easy to kill.

The following week, Leona and I were gathering yearling heifers in Little Shoe Canyon and herding them north to Coal Creek along the foot of the Haystack Mountains. A hundred head ran in unison toward the gate until a dozen in the middle jumped and fanned out as though they had stepped on hot coals.

When our horses passed the spot, a rattlesnake twisted in the grass striking at every shadow that moved. Sixteen times those heifers tormented wandering snakes and not a single yearling was bit. The horses, though, were wound extra tight, their muscles flexed, nerves tuned to a high pitch—even the hair on their fetlocks stood erect.

"I hated to ride horseback through the Haystacks," Aunt Kit had told me. "My friends wouldn't go with me to the country for fear of rattlesnakes there."

"They gave me nightmares," I said.

These serpents symbolized hell, and I wished every one of them gone. Older cowboys had shown me how to kill them with no remorse for their deaths. But after I grew older, indecision began to replace my childhood terror, and I eventually started to see snakes for what they really were.

One morning over black coffee, a professor friend named Dave told our family, "The Miller ranch contains the densest concentration of pit vipers anywhere on the globe."

No one who visited the Haystacks argued against his assertion or questioned the snakes' uncanny ability to survive and reproduce.

"I watched two snakes wrestle at the mouth of a canyon," I said.

That day, the dust billowed up from a large rabbitbrush I was passing. When I jumped aside, the head of a rattlesnake poked from inside the cloud and then beside it, the head of another. Two tangled bodies twisting like strands of a double helix, locked together in fury.

The rattlesnakes writhed past my feet, oblivious to my presence and the rest of the world. Never had I seen snakes so aggressive and vulnerable at the same time—like humans when they fuse with similar passion.

Free-ranging snakes crawled everywhere on our ranch. They would wander onto the porch in front of the house from their hiding places in the cracks of the coal shed's rock walls before we tore those walls down. Killing snakes when I was young became an inherited duty no different from gathering eggs, a necessary chore we sometimes enjoyed.

We would cook snake meat for an occasional meal, wear their stretched hides as hat bands, and nail amputated rattles beside the cracked mirror on the south bunkhouse wall. No matter how many we killed, they would return time and again in numbers greater than before. They lived close enough to be our neighbors, but we never wanted to visit their homes.

The rocky slopes of the Haystack Mountains were deeply dissected by several stream channels, the place Aunt Kit would never ride. Coal Creek Canyon flanked Wild Horse Mountain there, fed by streams gathering high-country rain and guiding it downslope to converge in one channel at the head of the narrow valley.

The creek had carved deeply through the rugged canyon walls of Cretaceous-age Mesa Verde sandstone. Those exposed cliffs became an appropriate place for countless snakes to hide, under ancient rocks that formed when their ancestors ruled the earth.

A hundred yards below the canyon mouth was a stone circle site where Indian hunters had lived in bison hide tepees a thousand years before. Loose rocks and cobbles from the abandoned camp had been arranged into rings seven feet across, now overgrown by grass.

One spring, I directed an archaeology crew to map these features and record architectural evidence of the ancient village. We flagged each circle, pounded an iron rebar into the ground, and measured from it the angles and distances to the center of each ring.

"Snake!" a colleague yelled as it slithered over the threshold of one rocky circle.

The variegated rattler inched over the site. Its layered-on scales rolled like armor when its belly bent over the stones.

"Kill it!" I yelled back.

We would be working there most of the day, so the animal had to die for the safety of the crew. My colleague shot it with a revolver he kept holstered at his waist for such an occasion, and we moved on to mapping the next circle of stone.

"Another snake!" the nervous archaeologist hollered moments later. It was headed in the same direction as the first. We killed it too and then went back to work.

"Snake!" he yelled again.

The day turned tense and bloody. Revolver shots echoed through the canyon until the air soured with gunpowder that had propelled bullets into the bodies of eight different snakes.

Our maps were wrinkled from fighting the wind and dampened by the stress of the day. Everyone was eager to leave once our measurements were done, though we cautiously looked through our backpacks before reaching in to put away tools.

It was easy back then to tell my crew to kill snakes. When Rod and I were kids, we had a black Labrador named Dinah. A rattlesnake bit her in the throat, and she died a year later from the pain of a venom-tainted liver. I killed many snakes after that.

The last time I killed one with no twinge of regret, I had been riding Tabasco on a grown-over trail at the foot of Bradley Peak. Tabasco's hooves kicked through bent grass with each step until a loud hiss drowned out the rustle of foliage.

I jumped from my saddle, gathered a handful of rocks, and stirred the grass with my boot to prod a hidden snake toward bare ground. My first stone struck the top of its head, thwarting any escape. I threw rocks until my shoulder hurt, flattening the snake into mush, and then ran to my horse and untied his reins from the branch of a nearby aspen.

When I led Tabasco clear of the tree, he shied from the dead snake. I stabbed my left foot at the stirrup and swung my right leg over the cantle, but Tabasco's muscles tightened from his flanks to his withers. He bucked two feet off the ground before my butt hit the saddle, tossing me off his back and onto the dead snake, where I missed poison-drenched fangs by an inch.

The following year, Mike, a University of Wyoming graduate student, drove to the ranch and asked Dad where he might find a den of rattlesnakes. He wanted to study their secretive nature for his thesis. Dad had killed snakes all his life, though never hunted for dens.

A UW alumnus, Dad encouraged research whenever he could. He directed Mike to a fence near the river where Rod and I had earlier stumbled onto a den, unaware we had burned it out. Mike found nothing when he arrived but the empty hole we had torched and new repairs on a woven wire fence.

He returned to the ranch to ask Dad for further suggestions. Rod and I were back from chores by then, so I told Mike about the eight snakes we killed in one afternoon at the mouth of Coal Creek Canyon. He drove there the next day and in thirty minutes followed the path of migrating rattlesnakes up a stony slope and over to a crack in the cliff that opened to a den in the side of the mountain, just under the crest of the ridge.

Geometric rocks lay jumbled in loose heaps along the ridge slope, resembling a collapsed stairway to the heavens. They contained fossils of odd marine life, plants and animals that had lived when water prevailed before livestock were there to drink.

Those dead organisms transformed into stone were mute testimony to ecological changes our rangeland had known. Piled rocks, cracked and broken by the ravage of a million frozen winters became the tumbledown house where the crawling serpents reside.

Spring warmth touches these stones and slumbering rattlers awake, pour out of each breach, and spill onto the rocky slope. Dozens of them, then scores, then hundreds, rolling over each other, and spreading out in the sun. From a distance, the canyon wall seems to move.

Mike studied these migrating snakes traveling back and forth from their den. He captured a barrel of vipers in less than two days, sedated them on a makeshift table, implanted subcutaneous transmitters, and put them in a container to recover from the drug. After freeing the recuperated snakes, he tracked their movements with a handheld, thirty-channel receiver that homed in on the distant beep.

He pinpointed each snake, flagged its location, and recorded the distance and direction of movement. Two weeks of tracking produced three distinct paths marked by orange pin flags leading from the den to each destination.

Migrating pit vipers would leave Coal Creek, crawl toward the river over the stone circles we had mapped, and then stop at small mounds of windblown sand drifted under canopies of sage. These sandy bumps were homes for families of deer mice, the summer diet of hungry snakes on the prowl.

One day, Mike convinced me to help him search for a particularly transient snake, a male in search of food as well as a mate. We located the orange-flagged pin from the previous day and turned power on to the receiver. He handed me the instrument. I rotated the antenna through a wide arc, scoping the landscape as I faced toward the river, seeking the predator's vernal movements. A faint beep registered on the instrument panel, and we walked toward the sound.

Moments later, a louder, more frequent beep. Twenty more feet and "beep . . . beep . . . beep." Another ten feet and "BEEP! BEEP! BEEP!" The snake was right there, but I couldn't see it, hidden despite its noise. My hands sweat, the receiver shook, and I stared at every sagebrush and pebble, looking for the "voice" at the end of my line.

"Here he is," Mike said, pointing to the tip of my boot.

A three-foot rattlesnake lay tightly coiled in the shade beneath a low branch of rabbitbrush, his black-forked tongue flicking out at me and his rattles buzzing a million notes in my ears. I concentrated on the beat without moving a muscle.

"Fun, huh?" Mike asked from a safe distance.

"You take this damn radio!" I yelled, as the rattler crawled away on his own.

I might not have been great help, but I did better than a member of the campus research office who visited Mike the following summer. That scholar stopped to kill a foraging snake in the road and brought the limp carcass back to camp.

"Here you go, Mike. Study this one," he said.

The dead snake had a radio implant.

The first year of Mike's research ended when we followed snakes back to the den in the fall. They crept along a trajectory as straight as the one they had taken in the spring. I stared at the horde of rattlesnakes slithering past my feet toward the shadowy crack in the cliff.

"There goes a garter snake," I said. "Don't rattlers eat them?"

"Normally, yes, though not when they enter the den."

If rattlesnakes ate this late in the year, I learned, the food wouldn't digest. Decomposing flesh in their belly would rot and kill them during hibernation. Mike watched the garter snake crawl into the crevice and laughed. "But I bet he's the first one out next spring."

I thought of Mike's research every subsequent opportunity I had for a kill. Was this wriggling tube of cold-blooded scales saddled with a radio transmitter? Perhaps I was standing on his trajectory right now, the land of my tracks destined to be marked by an orange pin flag by some future scholar.

In the name of science, instead of deciding on death, I let each serpent slink away toward the dark recess of its den.

The last time Dad and I cleaned the springs in the Haystack canyons, we drove through the big sagebrush forest that defined Blind Canyon, traveling under thick shrubs taller than the Stetson on a man riding horseback. The only paths through this gnarly maze were the two-track road we were on and a narrow stock trail leading to the water below.

Dad parked on the road, and I swung a shovel over my shoulder and walked down the trail to clear a clogged spring in the draw. The cattle route to the meadow floor had cut a worn trench into the terrace deeper than the height of my chin. I reached the plugged water source, dug ten minutes to open its flow, and started back to the truck, muddy, slouched, and breathing too hard.

When I reached the deepest part of the trail halfway back to the truck, I heard the familiar sound of interlocked rattles. Raising my head, I looked too late at the path I had taken. At eye level, only a foot from my nose, was the cocked head of a rattlesnake startled by my noisy intrusion.

I froze. A venomous strike in the face or neck could be fatal, even for a young adult like me. Dad sat in the truck thirty yards away, hidden behind the forest of big sage. He honked the horn, oblivious to my predicament.

"Hurry up, Mark," he called out. "We haven't got all day."

The snake and I ignored his request for a suspended moment. Then the patient reptile lowered his head to a resting place on top of his uppermost coil and lay there slow rattling a hollow, agitated tune.

I inched sideways toward the top of the terrace without taking my eyes off his. He finally rested his tongue and his tail and let me pass by safely.

Snakes had brought out the worst in me as a child. I had killed without question until Mike showed me how knowledge could overcome fright. Snakes are likely to strike only when they're surprised—a spontaneous reaction without malice.

But there is something more principled in rattlesnakes than self-defense. I had clearly surprised that Blind Canyon pit viper, yet he consciously chose not to strike when he could have killed me. His passive acceptance of my presence during his clear tactical advantage taught me to weigh my own options before making hasty decisions whenever I had the upper hand. Climbing back into the truck, I smiled, relieved that I had vowed never again to kill snakes on the ranch.

A long ridge of red sandstone outcrops in the Indian Creek pasture below Saltiel Corral, a few miles north of the Haystacks. Rocks there are big and flat. Many had been used in the past to build homesteads, their abandoned ruins now dotting our pastures. That craggy ground was the only place on our entire ranch where Wyoming winters never stayed frozen.

Buried deep in the spine of that ridge, beneath the weathered cap rock, burns an ancient coal seam. Nobody knows how or when it ignited, but it burned when Kirk was a boy, burned when Dad managed the ranch, and burned throughout my career. We never even tried to put it out. It still burns today and will probably burn on until all its fuel is gone.

Snow melts when it falls on that ridge. Heat from the underground coal fire warms the rocks from within, turning ice-cold Wyoming blizzards into pools of fresh water. An unusual place where the landscape is always thawed, a thermal ridge that explains the odd character of rattlesnakes who live in its cracks.

One day, I got a call from the manager who had replaced Dad after we left the ranch. "The snakes on that ridge are bigger than any others out here," he said. "Very tough snakes. Hard to kill."

"Natural selection, I suppose," trying to remember if I had noticed the fact when I lived out there.

"Maybe they're bigger because they can live longer in a warm environment," he said.

A place where intractable nature comforts a poorly known species that threatens all others around it. Ancient reptiles at home in a hostile land, their life history too often distorted by nescient visitors who pass. I had been just a visitor too. An interesting spot, we both agreed.

Mike would have enjoyed studying that ridge as well. I thought about his research when I walked across campus after that ecology lecture in the student union. I stared at the engineering building and its familiar credo carved in stone above the main door, "Strive on, the Control of Nature is Won, Not Given."

That limestone facade tells a story quite different from the piled rocks on the I Lazy D. Ours was an untamed country where rattlesnakes had lived forever while watching everyone else who tried. Indians, homesteaders, and stockmen eventually abandoned their homes built with those stones. The misunderstood rattlesnakes were the most enduring residents of them all.

Their legacy in our rocks is clear. Snakes will thrive on our ranch long after the last cowboy is gone.

PART 4

Family Archaeology

My mom and dad in Rawlins. 1981.

The snubbing post in the round corral at the I Lazy D originally placed by my dad in 1935.

23.

Trial and Error

Fifty white-faced heifers loafed in the thick, wild rye beside the shallow reservoir at the mouth of Coal Creek Canyon. Half of them stood in ankle deep alkali along the shore, their ears twitching at dragonflies trying to land. They buried their noses in the stagnant pool and sucked water in rapid bursts. After quenching their thirst, they bedded down beneath the sage canopy suspended over both sides of the arroyo. Flies were less bothersome there.

A dozen wet tongues rose from the water when I rode past on Bally, the gelding's iron shoes clicking against flat rocks resting on top of the earthen dam. I reined in beside the spillway to ponder the scene, the other riders already four miles ahead of me at the shearing pens. Coal Creek Canyon stretched in the distance behind the heifers, the same canyon where several years earlier Dr. Frison had introduced me to the Scoggin site bison kill and a career in Wyoming archaeology.

My boot heels touched Bally's flanks, nudging him over the edge of the bank until he stepped stiff-legged down the water side of the slope, his hooves slipping in loose dirt and gravel. He lowered his butt toward the ground to gain more balance in his descent while I stood in the saddle to take weight off his kidneys. The cattle stiffened and then jerked when Bally's front hooves splashed the dark water, sending concentric ripples to where they were drinking.

It was 1982, three years since my last day of graduate school, and I still loved helping Dad on the ranch. My evolution from cowboy to archaeologist was nearly complete. Professors had lectured in my classes about prehistoric strategies for hunting large game, and Dr. Frison had taken me to several excavations at bison kills all over the state, including the site just up the canyon from where these heifers now stood.

At many kill sites, hunters bunched animals into tight arroyos like the one along Coal Creek, where they finished them off with arrows or spears shot from above. That was a more sensible means of procurement than cliff jumps, because the hunters could more easily control the number of bison killed.

Bally stopped to drink, rolled his curb bit on top of his tongue each time he swallowed. He stretched his neck to reach deeper water and shook from head to tail, nearly knocking me over his withers and into the reservoir.

The movement woke me from my daydream about arroyo kill sites. The heifers started drinking again and watched Bally and me through the corners of their upturned eyes. I tugged the reins. Bally raised his neck, jerking his front legs out of the muck.

"Come on, boy. You've had enough," I whispered, heading him toward the cattle.

Scattered heifers moved away from me as my mind wandered back to the classroom. Dr. Frison was internationally known for his skill with experimental archaeology. He once used stone-tipped spears to test how deeply they embedded in the flesh and bones of a dead African elephant. And he butchered several bison with sharp quartzite stone flakes, just as prehistoric hunters had done for thousands of years.

"Hyup, cattle."

I prodded the heifers up the draw toward others bedded down in the shade. We had plenty of time for my own experiment. Dad would never know.

Bally and I nudged the herd up the Coal Creek arroyo in the direction of the old bison kill. Wild rye and slough grass broke under their trampling hooves.

The lowest branches cracked on the sagebrush canopy that hid part of the meadow and underground spring from the sky. High earthen walls alongside the drainage narrowed into a steep funnel the farther we moved up the draw. The cattle packed tighter. Several twisted their heads over their backs to steal nervous glimpses behind them.

"Go, cattle."

I didn't need flank riders since I had cut banks twice the height of the herd. No need for a point rider either, given that the lead had only one direction to go. It was all moot anyway, because no rational cowboy would have helped me if he knew what I was doing.

Spring water erupted from the meadow in front of a vertical earthen slope where the sides of the arroyo met to form the head of the draw in the shape of a box canyon. This is a knickpoint, the place where stream down-cutting has carved the sediments away. Lead heifers reached the spot and bunched as tight as any stock in our shipping corral.

No space existed between them. I could have walked from one side of the arroyo to the other just by stepping on their shoulders.

It worked! If I chose to drop piles of sagebrush behind them, they would have no place to go. The perfect arroyo trap.

Dust swirled from the ground beneath them, all the grass beaten away by sharp hooves. Muffled grunts echoed in the canyon from skittish cattle as they waited impatiently for the next thing to happen.

Bison arroyo traps must have looked something like this. Unfortunately, Dr. Frison's lectures had focused on hunting strategies, not on removing live animals from a trap. I tugged Bally's reins until he backed out of the arroyo toward the open meadow behind us. Then we followed a stock trail up the slope and rode to the knickpoint where I peered down on the herd from the top of the cut.

"Back, cattle," I called out.

Agitated white faces bobbed up and down below me. Their stares conveyed confusion until the tail end of the bunch finally backed out, making room for others to turn around. Bally and I stayed with them while they settled down once again in the shade near the reservoir.

That half hour of unnecessary herding convinced me I was better off as an archaeologist than a cowboy. Turning Bally toward the shearing pens, I looked over my shoulder at the cows quietly feeding in the pasture once more.

By late July the next summer, my stepson, Shawn, had turned sixteen and wanted to help herd cattle. When Dad sent me out to scatter ride for heifers in the lower Coal Creek pasture, I brought him along. New to ranching, Shawn hadn't ridden much, so I put him on a tame horse, still learning how to be a stepfather.

I was the adult in charge this time, and it felt different than when I was on the same riding crew as Dad. The new responsibility weighed on me more than I had expected. I needed to make all the decisions—and do so quickly.

Had Dad felt the same way when Rod and I were young and learning the ropes? I doubt it. Authority and decisiveness came naturally to him after so many years around livestock. They were innate qualities in his personality.

Forefront in my mind was the erratic behavior that the cattle sometimes exhibited. Dad's hybrid stock had became well adapted to our range, but we had to keep on our toes whenever we herded them. They could turn our country paradise into a chaotic hell in the blink of an eye.

We found the young heifers grazing on the south face of Cheyenne Ridge, strung out along the fence line a mile away. Our orders were to push them through the gate right in front of where we now sat on horseback and turn them loose in the south pasture near the shearing pens, where Dad and Shorty had fixed that cow's cancerous eye when I was younger than Shawn.

"Wait right here on your horse," I told my stepson. I positioned him about thirty yards east of the gate. "I'll open the gate, get in behind the heifers, and herd 'em down the fence line. When they get opposite you, turn them into the pasture to the west. We'll close the gate afterward and then we're done."

"Sure thing," Shawn said.

He sat on his horse facing the open gate while I rode north for the cattle. Half an hour later, the skittish heifers started down the fence and lined out well ahead of me, running directly toward Shawn.

I loped behind them, watching for him to turn the lead, but the cattle ran right past the gate and followed the fence on south. I galloped toward Shawn.

"What the hell's going on?" I hollered. "Why didn't you bend the lead into the open gate?"

Shawn jerked in his saddle and looked up with a start. "I—I fell asleep. I didn't see them coming."

We rode to the other end of the pasture, turned the confused heifers back to the gate, and pushed them through together. Afterward we trotted our horses toward the spot where Shawn had fallen asleep.

An old cow with crooked horns and a tight bag stood on the spot, lured away from the hidden arroyo by the noise of heifers when they passed. She stomped the ground once and stared wide-eyed at the pasture around her.

"She must have lost her calf," I said, looking at her bloated udder. "She hasn't been sucked for a day or more. Let's put her in the pasture with the rest of the stock and tell Dad she's there."

The belligerent cow didn't budge when we rode alongside her. Getting desperate, we both shouted at her to move, but she didn't react, not even when I snapped my rope on her ass.

Shawn started getting pissed. "Move, you son of a bitch!" he yelled.

She just stared at him, immobile, as if in a trance. Shawn sprang from his horse and grabbed a rock to throw at her. He was so quick in his anger—I couldn't stop him.

Every lesson I ever learned from Dad about working cattle exploded in my brain. "Shawn, get back on your horse right now!"

Too late. When Shawn's rock hit the Hereford in the shoulder, she came to life and bellowed a loud guttural groan, spooking Shawn's horse while he stood there. When he walked back to the mare and reached his left foot up to remount, the horse shied away. Sensing the cow's growing irritation, she yanked the reins away from Shawn with a jerk of her neck and galloped toward the safety of a nearby hill, his empty stirrups slapping at her sides.

Now Shawn stood alone in the open pasture thirty yards from me, trembling, facing the belligerent cow just a few feet away from him. She snorted at him through flared nostrils, dug a front hoof in the ground, and scraped loose dirt into a cloud that rose under her belly.

Shawn looked at her and back at me, the color draining from his face. My stepson was wide awake now. His pleading eyes melted my heart.

"Don't move!" I yelled.

Riding quickly between him and the cow, I used my horse to shield him from the danger he had invited when he dismounted. The tight-bagged cow charged us, bumping her crooked horns headlong into my horse's left shoulder, and then backed away to paw at the ground once more. My horse screeched, bleeding from a shallow scrape, and slumped forward, but quickly regained his balance.

Shawn grabbed my arm, and I lifted him up behind my saddle before the cow could strike a second time. We rode to his horse still standing a safe distance away. The old cow wandered back to the draw, bawling for her calf once more.

"Sorry," Shawn said. "It won't happen again."

I thought of every mistake I had made growing up around livestock and how Dad had patiently taught me by his example. After Shawn climbed back into his own saddle once his horse had settled down, I forced a nervous smile. "Don't worry, son, we'll get her tomorrow. It's time to go home."

24.

Our Last Day

On a September morning just a few weeks later, the board of directors of Miller Estate Company completely shattered my world.

President since 1967, Dad chaired the meeting that day. In a swift, unexpected decision, three of the five members voted to sell off our livestock and advertise the entire ranch for lease to a new cattleman with his own cowboys and herd, thinking lower operating costs might increase company profits.

Dad's ranching career would end on the last day of the year when he was sixty-four.

How could that happen? Why would the board divest the company of significant assets without calling for a full vote of the shareholders? Why had they not scheduled a special meeting? Shareholders should have been able to seek relief from unilateral board decisions like that.

Dad, Rod, and I had worked hard our entire lives to make the ranch a viable enterprise, and we had succeeded in the eyes of our peers, winning recognition for our achievements. Nonetheless, a couple of the board members had shown concern about cattle losses and lower income in recent years. But Dad had used any profits to pay off the land debt the outfit incurred after purchase of the DO range in the middle of our winter pastures.

The resulting lack of dividends might have angered some shareholders. Rod and I were angry as well, but for a different reason, suspecting some backroom deal had prompted the board's move. We knew little of any discussions, so we wanted to pursue a legal complaint against them.

Dad said no. He would not challenge Miller Estate Company in court, a ranch named after his grandfather that had been managed by the family for generations. Instead, Dad explained to the rest of the board that they needed to schedule a full shareholder meeting before voting on such a consequential motion. The board finally agreed.

Rod, Dad, and I joined the other shareholders as they gathered in a large room at the Rawlins National Bank on November 9, 1983. The three of us sat together, took off our cowboy hats, and set them crown down on the conference table. I glanced at the dozen faces around us, my heart in my throat, trying to convince myself we still had a chance.

The meeting was called to order. Wasting no time, a distant cousin read the resolution to be placed on the floor for action. With a show of hands, her family and the nonfamily members in the corporation cast the majority of votes to lease the ranch.

A groan from the corner of the room broke the silence. Our corporate attorney, involved with the company since the 1930s when he was a young lawyer helping settle Ike Miller's estate, looked hopelessly over at Dad.

How could something that took a century to build be destroyed in a matter of minutes?

It was poor consolation that the vote ending Dad's career had no effect on our inherited shares in the company.

To this day, that meeting cuts deep into my conscience. I hated to see Dad treated in that manner. He deserved much better from all the shareholders and their families who had benefited from his decades of dependable service.

The first potential lessee of the ranch was Elmer, a friend of Dad's from his high school years and my brother's godfather. He met Dad, Rod, and me at the ranch to discuss the outfit and its economic potential, something Dad had dedicated a lifetime to sustain.

"You know the operation," Dad told him. "The grass is good. There's water in every pasture."

Elmer wore an expressionless face. "It's a nice place, Frank."

Dad looked over to Rod and me and then back to Elmer. His boot swept the ground. "Rod and Mark know this place inside and out. They're good hands, and if you keep them on, I know you won't be disappointed."

Dad never asked favors of any man. Entreaty was not a gesture he admired, but he was thinking now as a father, not as a ranch manager. Only the security of his family could draw him out of his stoic, independent shell. Necessity compelled his request.

The man answered too quickly, as if he had anticipated the plea. "They're fine boys. I just can't hire them if I lease the place. I already have a full crew."

It didn't matter to Rod or me whatever the man said. We probably wouldn't have worked for him anyhow, considering the ill-informed vote against us.

Plus, I had a potential archaeology career to consider, and Rod and I both had growing families to raise. Rod and his wife, Linda, were bringing up four sons, Tom, Isaac, Kirk, and Victor. Leona and I had Josh. What did matter was that Dad showed Rod and me his love in a way he had never verbalized before.

Sunset, Saturday, December 31, 1983. It had been like any typical workday in the middle of winter. But that day, my family would leave the I Lazy D for the last time, one hundred and ten years after Ike Miller had first entered the livestock business.

We had picked up Rod in Sinclair where he rented a place for his family after moving from the stone house at the ranch. Beyond the river canyon, a soft sun had melted snow on the asphalt, even though crusty drifts still blanketed the countryside.

"Coffee?" I asked Dad as the three of us sat in the cab of his truck. I poured us each a cup from the thermos and handed one to him.

"Thanks."

The winter had been harsh on the livestock. Icy snow and frigid wind forced cattle onto feed grounds early in the season and threatened to exhaust stockpiles of native hay we had stored.

My brother and I were in our early thirties, the fourth generation of Millers to operate the I Lazy D. Both of us were reluctant to end our ranching careers on that wintry New Year's Eve, and we didn't approach the task ahead with our normal enthusiasm.

An aura of surreal tension filled the air. We were living through the end of a family tradition that had been started by an immigrant war refugee from Denmark in the late nineteenth century. The weight of family history hung like a millstone around my neck. I seethed inside with hostility toward the board, barely able to maintain my composure.

After gassing up the two-ton Dodge stock truck parked at the ranch, we checked its box rods and chains to ensure the side panels were secure. Then the three of us drove through the gate toward the nearest haystack in the lower meadow.

I rubbed my hands together under the fan attached to the temperamental heater in the cab, and it blew dusty warm air onto my palms. Dad rolled down his window, letting fresh air in the cab so the glass wouldn't fog. The sun tried to thaw things a bit.

Dad downshifted to buck through snow drifts in the trail as they blew across it diagonally, each one aligned by southwesterly winds tracking down the valley. I bounced against the cab ceiling when the front wheels hit a frozen rut and the tires dropped into its trough. But with Dad at the wheel, the ride was never uncomfortable. He downshifted again and drove through deep snow on the meadow.

Frank Miller fit here. If the rangeland had been an ocean, he would have been ruler of the sea. He would sit tall in any saddle when he rode over his domain, his back straight, knees slightly bent so he could absorb the shock of each horse's gait, protecting the animal from the impact of his weight on its back. He could drive a two-wheeler pickup over loose sand where the rest of us couldn't go in a four-wheeler.

Years earlier, when my friend and I had been building a fence near the Tapers' place, we got our four-wheel drive truck stuck deep in the dune slope. We were digging out when we heard the steady whir of a small pickup in the distance just as it topped the dune ridge above us. Dad sat in his two-wheel drive looking down at us with a smile. "Never spin your wheels in sand, boys," he always said. "There's no bottom to these dunes."

On that last day of 1983, Dad stopped the two-ton Dodge at the stackyard fifteen minutes after leaving the house. Rod, riding shotgun, opened the gate toward us so the truck wouldn't need to travel so far into the yard before he could close it. Dad backed up to the stack of seventy-pound bales to load for feeding.

This was the same haystack where earlier that month Dad and I had brought my two-and-a-half-year-old son, Josh, to help feed the cattle. Knowing by then that this would be our final year on the ranch, I took Josh along on each type of chore Dad and I did together. While too young to remember, my son could honestly tell his friends someday that he had ranched on the I Lazy D as a boy.

I set him behind me on horseback when we herded cattle at the shearing pens. He walked with me along the irrigation ditch and rode in the tractor when I stacked bales of hay. I showed him how we branded and how Dad taught me to mend fence, but I kept him away from the wire. Before the weather got too cold, Dad and I took him to the stackyard to help feed some heifers.

"Why are we here?" Josh asked.

"To feed hay to the cows," I said as Dad and I started loading bales into his pickup.

"Okay." He grabbed two hands full of hay and ran out the gate toward the heifers standing on the frozen meadow fifty yards away.

"Wait! Not like that!" I yelled.

I jumped from the truck and chased after him, worried he might spook the cattle and they'd trample him when they moved. Josh had almost reached the herd when my legs crashed through the snow and I sank up to my knees in the drift.

My little son had run over the same spot without breaking through, but it took me five minutes to catch up to him. By the time I reached him, he was holding hay stems for two heifers that stood there nibbling the feed out of his mittens.

"Just leave that hay, Josh. Let's go back to Grandpa Frank and get 'em some more."

Dad couldn't stop laughing. Walking back to the truck, happy Josh was with me, I thought about the time long before when I was with Grandpa Kirk and got out of the truck to run behind the herd with protein cake before he stopped me.

As the winter sun hid behind the clouds, Rod and I tossed bales to Dad, who stood on the bed of the two-ton Dodge so he could pile a maximum load. The stack in the hay yard was eleven bales high. Those on top were good, though drifted over with snow.

When I reached for the upper tier to pull down a bale, a wet skiff of snow fell onto my face, slipped inside my coveralls, and melted against the skin of my chest. I spit dirty snow from my mouth and brushed the rest away, stirring up hay chaff into a dusty cloud overhead. Rod sneezed from the stifling congestion of chronic hay fever.

Dad positioned each rectangular bale in a predetermined pattern, easily keeping pace with Rod and me, locking them together in tight tiers to minimize their movement when we drove. Center bales in the lowest tier lay parallel to the axles, and perimeter bales aligned with the side panels. Bales crisscrossed one another in subsequent levels so none of the gaps between them extended deeper than one tier. Every cowboy I ever knew took great pride in his skill at stacking hay.

Rod and I could quickly gather the middle bales in the haystack because they were free from snow and piled well above ground. The bottom layer was a different story. Tons of overlying hay had pressed bottom bales against the ground for three years since the haystack was built. They absorbed ground moisture that saturated the stackyard during each thaw until their bottoms had become rotten and mildewed.

That last day, they were frozen to the ground. We tugged and nothing happened. We yanked and kicked at their sides. Finally, I rammed my shoulder into one with a heave that broke the first bale free. I lifted it into the truck, weighing twice as much as the dry ones. Portions of some bottom bales were nearly inedible due to the rot, but in hard winters you fed all that you owned.

We hauled the load to the mature breeding stock on the winter range twenty miles from the house. Many of our cows had spent years on the ranch and were familiar with our pastures, water holes, and feed grounds. The savviest had already begun to congregate at the HO Bumps by the time we arrived. It was our best feed ground in the big winter pasture, characterized by small, stabilized sand dunes for cover and a broad field ideal for scattering out hay. Dad honked the horn, calling those not yet in attendance, while Rod and I climbed in back and prepared to feed.

The baler had wrapped each bale with plastic twine instead of the wire we used in the past. Twine was less expensive and easier to handle while feeding, but we still needed to salvage it after we broke up the bales. Cattle could swallow the loose pieces, and any plastic caught in their intestines might block their digestion and kill them. At least it didn't tangle in their feet as badly as carelessly discarded wire. Dad would never let us leave bailing twine of any kind behind.

He crept the truck ahead in first gear, overlapping the feed ground up the draw and back again. His fenders rubbed against the nearest animals, parting the herd until cows surrounded the Dodge like a hungry mob.

Rod and I stood at opposite sides in back to feed out our load, each of us armed with a pocketknife to cut twine. After more than twenty years, I had finally honed my knife well enough to keep the blades sharp. Kirk would have been proud.

We peeled generous slices of hay and scattered them to the stock, careful to wrap each plastic strand in our hand as it fell away from the bale. After the last hay dropped, we tied the twine into a bundle, left it in back of the truck, and hopped into the cab for a hot cup of coffee.

"We'll do one more load and give it to the heifers and weak cows in the hospital herd," Dad said.

We often kept young and suffering animals in the meadow next to the stackyard. By the time we loaded the last bale into the truck, white-faced heifers had wandered from the far reaches of the meadow to their position in the chow line near the haystack. They stared at our approach, panting warm breath that rose in clouds from their nostrils, gathering into a fine mist. We fed one bale for every three animals before stopping for a last cup of coffee.

I took over and drove toward the ranch house in the fading light, retracing our blown-over tracks barely visible on the trail. The old Dodge pulled heavy up the cold slope of the last dune beside the meadow, a hundred yards from the house. Softening snow blanketed the frozen sand.

Our dual wheels sank deep into the white drift when we crossed. The hard sand underneath would give way if I spun the tires, so I rocked the truck back and forth, shifting between first gear and reverse, exploiting the weight of the Dodge as it moved in the direction of each gear. But despite my effort, we sank even deeper, and the three of us got out to inspect the ruts.

It was New Year's Eve. Rod and I were young and eager to party with our families. Neither of us would have to wake at five the next morning to feed cattle, something we would never have to do again. Besides, we were only stuck in soft snow, not too deep in the bottomless sand. By dusk we were still an hour's drive from town where our families waited for our return. Some new manager would be in charge when the sun came up tomorrow.

"Hell," Rod said. "We're close enough. Leave it here. Why can't they free it in the morning before they feed?"

"Right. They can see the truck from the ranch," I said. "What can they do if we leave it, fire us?"

Dad stared at Rod and me, not grinning this time. He had lived the answer to our question long before we ever asked it, an answer he had understood as a child working for his dad.

The I Lazy D was his home, the home of his father, and his father's father before him. Dad's entire life had focused on making Miller Estate Company one of the best livestock operations in Wyoming.

Only the year before, he had earned recognition from his peers for his efforts. He was not the type of guy who would leave a company truck stuck in the snow.

"No, boys," he said. "We hired out for a job. We won't quit until it's done." Then he gave us our final order as manager of the I Lazy D. "Park this truck in the yard."

The three of us spent the next hour shoveling away snow to unbury the wheels. We packed the ruts with handfuls of mildewed hay for more traction and rocked the truck until it loosened from the icy grip of the drift. Dad sat behind the wheel and drove the rest of the way into the yard.

His final act on the ranch reflected a dedication to the only professional life he had ever known, an untarnished fulfillment of his family's legacy. For more than sixty years, there had been no acre on the ranch he hadn't worked, no horse he hadn't ridden, and no cow herd or band of sheep he hadn't helped brand. Leaving that truck in the snow would have dishonored the company that bore his grandfather's name, and he wouldn't have yielded such satisfaction to those who wanted us gone.

Dad had lived his life with strength of honor, a moral integrity visible in his military career, in his marriage and family life, and in the lasting friendships he made. He reminded his two shortsighted sons of that profound dedication on the last day, the last hour, when he silently dug out the dual wheels of the company Dodge.

Looking back on that time now that I am much older, I am eternally grateful Dad didn't let Rod and me walk away from the job. If we had abandoned that truck in a grave of melting snow, the callous incident would have haunted me the rest of my life.

I would not have been able to raise my own son with a clear conscience or teach him about accountability and integrity the way my father had taught me. Neither could I have taught him responsibility for his own actions if I had not been willing to accept responsibility for mine.

Dad's dedication to the ranch didn't end that last day. For the first week of January, he and I drove out to the country and followed the new manager driving the stock truck to the HO Bumps to feed cattle. Every couple of miles, we stopped by a bale of hay that had fallen out of the loose stack on the big truck. We loaded it into Dad's pickup and fed the few bales to the cattle on the way into town.

Things in life never seem to last. Our best horses die. Rain doesn't always fall. But the life lessons I learned from my family will endure in me as long as I breathe.

25.

Place-Names

"Wisdom sits in places," well-known anthropologist Keith Basso taught us during his research on the Western Apaches. It is a lesson we all learn in Wyoming if we live here long enough to establish our own kindred traditions.

The landscape is our totem. Its place-names are the genesis for family growth. Stories in the land portray intimate details of ancestral memories that connect us today with our cultural heritage. If we ignore those stories, our careless indifference will render the West mute.

When my brother and I were boys, our favorite neighborhood was the family ranch in the western Hanna Basin of Carbon County. With that land, Great-Grandfather Ike had bequeathed his descendants a deep-rooted legacy that made me beam with pride as a boy.

American Indians lived out there before us and were later driven from parts of Wyoming when immigrants arrived. I like to concentrate on things my family had in common with them.

Ike emigrated from Denmark in 1865, the year after Bismarck's Prussian army invaded his homeland. My mother's Scottish ancestors survived the Highland Clearances before shipping out to America for a fresh start. Disenfranchised families from many cultures saw the American West as a new place to call home, and families had come here from violent pasts for a very long time. Even Native Americans came from elsewhere over thirteen thousand years ago to occupy the land that would become known as Wyoming.

My father and I often discussed family place-names while riding through the country looking for sheep and cattle. We drove over the ramshackle bridge across Indian Creek, a permanent stream Ike had designated in honor of the first inhabitants on the ranch.

We hunted sage chicken on Bothwell Rim, named for a lonely neighbor with pet wolves before he was arrested for the lynching of James Averell and Ella Watson in 1889. Dad hired Vince and Galusha to build a windmill in Little Shoe Canyon near where his grandfather found a fragment of sun-shrunk footwear, lost by an old sheepherder the year Wyoming became a state.

Unique characteristics of so many places chronicled episodes of family history that were unrecorded in books, unlabeled on maps. Important stories threaded through the fabric of our generations by oral traditions, just like the Native Americans had done to preserve theirs. Rod and I had to learn place-names if we were going to find the locations where Dad gave us chores to perform.

Dad once sent Rod and me to gather horses in the lower Coal Creek pasture several miles from the ranch house. We had to ride horseback to the same spot from two different areas.

"I'll meet you on the north end of Pegleg Butte where Coyote Springs opens into the big playa next to the DO range," Rod said before we split up.

We hooked up half an hour later in a shallow swale smaller than Prexy's Pasture, a place too subtle to show on maps you buy at the store. But we knew right where to go. I felt so confident about my place on the familiar landscape, I believed I could find a needle in any haystack.

But the historical significance of place-names eluded me until 1986, two and a half years after my family had left the ranch. I drove to the country and walked toward the barn to visit the new manager. I had called him earlier to tell him I wanted to photograph an archaeological site on the south end of Bead Hill.

"Where's that?" he asked.

I described the location, and the man said, "Oh, we call that Long Ridge."

One hundred and ten years of landscape nomenclature disappeared when we left the ranch. The last guardian of our family geography was gone. My head slumped until my chin hit my chest.

Why hadn't we taken the time to write down more of the names? When I reached the barn, my boot scraped in the loose dirt next to the door, and a billowing cloud of corral dust conveyed the truth of the matter to me as an epiphany.

My family *had* written stories about places in ranch history. We used the slanting penmanship of fence lines scribbling their way across dunes, the sweeping cursive of cut hay in the meadow below the barn, and the well-placed punctuation of windmills and water holes over the range. The ink we used for the narrative came from the deep well of Miller blood that nourished our ancestors' lives.

Inhabitants who came before us had written their own stories that way too, in the grainy paragraphs of sediment under my feet. Older tales of our country were told with stone tools, cold fires, and the bones from animals that had fed hundreds of families for thousands of years. Stratified pages of landscape history were layered in the ground like leaves in a book lying flat on the shelf, written in different languages, awaiting translation.

The problem was not that important stories hadn't been written. The problem was that we hadn't yet learned the value of all that they said. Wisdom would continue to sit in places—until informed readers helped it stand.

26.

Family Talismans

I have been a professional archaeologist since 1974, even though I worked part-time as a cowboy for Dad between 1979 and 1983. Archaeologists are taught to interpret human behavior from patterns they observe in the material objects people leave behind when they move from place to place.

But inferences about human behavior are risky. The archaeological record is only an incomplete window into the past. We can never prove what happened years ago—we can only suggest plausible explanations.

In my collection of I Lazy D artifacts, I have a brown glass bottle from six that Rod had found eroding in a sand dune near the ranch house. The top of the neck, which once held a cork, was attached to the rest of the neck as a separate piece, most likely dating the bottle to the early 1900s, before the widespread use of automatic bottle-making machines. A century-old six-pack of beer.

"Who do you think left these?" Rod asked Dad while we were boxing up everything to move out of the ranch house.

Dad studied the bottle. "Probably Norm, Kirk's brother. He camped there for a time. He was a hard drinker too."

Soon after, Dad gave me an amber-colored bottle he had found years earlier in the ranch dump. "You boys played with it out there."

He laughed. A hole the size of a BB gun pellet opened into its side from when Rod and I practiced shooting targets as kids.

It's shaped like a tall log cabin, so Dad thought it once contained pancake syrup, but it turned out to be an American Life Bitters bottle manufactured before 1876. If Rod and I hadn't been such good shots, it would have premium value as a collectible today. But kids growing up in the country like us didn't think that far ahead.

My favorite bottle is a purple glass receptacle embossed with the words "SKABCURA SHEEPDIP" that once held a sulfur-based solution administered to sheep to rid them of scabies. Ike Miller probably purchased the medicine in the late 1800s when he owned large sheep herds.

I keep my Morgan silver dollar collection in a deep drawer of the rolltop desk I had inherited from Ike. Kirk had purchased some at the Rawlins National Bank where his father had once been president and gave them to his grandkids on their birthdays in 1964, one shiny dollar for each year of our age. Those thirteen coins I received started a collection I maintain today.

Westerners lived near the silver mines that had been dug into the Rocky Mountains for the ore they could melt and mint into coins. Bedrock minerals were solid and reliable—silver coins jingled in your pockets. The familiar echo of clashing Morgans reverberated in every bar, bank, brothel, and stockyard when Kirk was young.

Most of my artifacts are photographs Mom took. An old shoebox labeled "Betty and Frank" holds black-and-white pictures taken at the ranch when Rod and I were kids in the 1950s and 1960s.

In one photo, I'm three years old and on horseback, my left hand resting on the saddle horn, gripping the bridle reins. The gelding's head is out of the picture, but from the angle of his neck, I can tell he had turned to face the barn. His maneuver tightened the left rein and loosened the right, so it hung much lower, not a good riding posture considering Dad always admonished me to "ride with your reins even."

I couldn't have ridden far that day, probably just a few laps around the front corral. My bare feet didn't even reach the stirrups, and I concentrated more on the photographer than on my horse. But I tried to look like I knew what I was doing.

"Rod and Mark could ride horseback almost before they could walk," Dad told his friends.

Mom smiled when he spoke, as if she'd rather have emphasized pedestrian skills when we were kids.

Those early riding photos are old now, fading a bit as the images age. Scenes that once were unusually clear have become blurred amid weathered shades of gray.

My brother kept ranch artifacts too. He used Dad's bridle when riding on the I Lazy D, the one with matching conchos on the cheek straps that glistened at either side of the horse's head. Each sterling silver ornament was concave on the inside where a metal bar crossed from edge to edge to hold headstall leathers in place. The conchos were convex on the outside, inlaid with a golden "M" for Miller. They were the only monogrammed tack Dad ever owned, so they must have been valuable to him, probably a gift from his father.

Riding back to the ranch from the Indian Creek pasture one day, Rod opened the last gate into the ranch yard, exhausted from his trip. He led his horse through and noticed one of the conchos on Dad's bridle was missing. After putting his horse in the barn, he walked to the house to tell Dad.

"Better go back and find it," Dad said.

Rod mounted up and retraced his tracks for miles through the pasture he had just ridden, spending hours in search of a silver disk the size of a dollar with a golden "M" on one side.

Late in the afternoon, after he had ridden clear to the west end of the pasture, he found the concho lying on the ground by a gate near Saltiel Corral. His horse had rubbed it off earlier that morning when Rod closed the gate.

But we didn't always have that kind of luck.

I inherited Kirk's Railway pocket watch and wore it in my jeans all the time. One day, I rode horseback with a lady friend into the sand dunes where we dismounted for a romantic picnic lunch. The watch must have slipped from the chain and fallen into the sand when we were rolling around on the blanket. I didn't notice it missing until we were ready to leave. I searched for over an hour but didn't find it. After we churned up so much soft sand, the watch must have gotten buried deep in the dune. I felt sick about it. Such a careless mistake.

The family kept larger ranch artifacts in the hayloft, including a snow sled built by Ike's brother, Chris, well over a century ago. Kirk used to hook it behind his pickup and pull us grandkids over the snow in the lower meadow.

On one trip, he drove through the first turn too fast, causing me to let go of the wooden side panel, and I pushed my hand to the ground to keep from falling off. The metal runner blade caught the fingertips of my glove and jerked it off. The torn fabric still lay in the snow at the end of our ride—good thing the runner hadn't caught my fingers too.

My entire extended family enjoyed reminiscing over artifacts after we left the ranch. Certain items reminded them of happy times in their youth, each one telling a story.

Aunt Marggy loved to talk about the I Lazy D, especially in her later years. Warm and bubbly, she was the life of the party at so many family gatherings. For one of our Fourth of July celebrations, she dressed up as Lady Liberty and led a group of partygoers along the road at the boat club, holding her torch high.

Every conversation I had with her carried us back to the ranch and the time we all spent there together. During one visit, Marggy asked me to do her a favor.

"Bring me a rock," she said.

"I'd be happy to."

The following weekend, I drove to the ranch with Uncle George. We found a sandstone outcrop near the Halfway Corral that bristled with odd-shaped rocks and boulders heaped by nature upon one another.

"I'll cut some sagebrush too," George said. "It'll make her place smell like the country."

I gathered a flat piece of oxidized sandstone two feet across and slid it downslope from a low, fractured cliff of bedrock. *This one won't blow away*, I thought when I struggled to lift it.

Colorful colonies of thick lichen covered its weather-stained surface. Three layers of dying and dead lichen superimposed over one another. The colors of each darkened the farther away they distanced from life. The oldest layer at the bottom was fragile and black, touching the stone. The next was orange, on top of the black, brighter than the sandstone itself. The youngest colony was light green, barely toned with vanishing chemicals that had sustained it in its struggle for life.

The rock represented the I Lazy D, sturdy and solid, a layer of lichen for each family generation living out there. Ike's, gone the longest, was represented by dark lichen, poorly illuminated like distant memories of him, but it became the foundation for all those that followed. Kirk's generation grew on top of the first and brought vivid color to the I Lazy D. Aunt Marggy could still breathe life into the newest hue.

But what of the generations that followed? Rod and I were unrepresented on her stone. Our children were absent as well. Perhaps the ranch intended for us to develop roots elsewhere, to cling to rocks on some other landscape where the wind wouldn't blow us away.

27.

A Vanishing Way of Life

One morning, I sat with Dad at the breakfast table in my folks' Cheyenne apartment, drinking coal-black coffee. He and Mom had moved there several years after leaving the ranch. Like most days, Dad and I had been visiting about our time on the I Lazy D.

"Do you miss working there?" I asked him.

"No." He shook his head. "What's there to miss? Do you think I miss driving the stock truck to the RS Meadow and hauling hay all by myself? I had to take that truck over the roughest road on the ranch, load it half full of bales, and unload them at the top of the valley. Then I returned for the other half and filled the whole truck when I got back to the top."

"Why do it that way?"

"The road was too rocky to haul a full load. Would you miss something like that?"

I sat in stunned silence. Dad's blue-hazel eyes were soft when he spoke, his crow's feet creeping closer every year toward his temples. He took another sip.

Could he have spent all his life doing something he didn't miss?

"You were out there for sixty-four years. Don't you miss anything?"

Sitting back in his chair, he stared off into space and gave it more thought. Finally, he looked me in the eye and smiled. "I miss watching the cattle in the spring, standing in the meadow, hearing them fart and belch when they eat new grass."

It was a common scene, but one I had never paid much attention to. Cows knee deep in fresh grass, raising their mouths when they chewed. Wet leaves dangling in the slobber that dripped from the end of their snouts.

They would bend down and grab more forage between their lower teeth and palate, tearing away three bites before chewing a mouthful again. Wiry green grass ripped when they pulled, and dew drops fell from bent blades as the cows stepped through the meadow. Fat cattle eating grass at the foot of ID Ridge, farting and belching when they finished. I smiled too when I pictured the scene.

Several years ago, a dead pine tree fell over on the south face of the ridge above that meadow. It had stood there alone, an old trunk weather beaten by decades of windblown sand blasting across its gnarled bark. A dozen crooked limbs reached out to touch the sky and pointed toward every bearing on the compass, though not a living stem or needle remained. Silhouetted against the autumn sun, it resembled an eerie sentinel, always watching, ever alert.

I never tried to climb it out of respect for its age, but I did touch the coarse-textured bark. A faint, beckoning fragrance of pine nestled deep in a crack where the largest branch married the trunk. The wind across the ridgetop whined through nooks and crannies in its broken frame, like hollow voices of past country spirits whispering secrets to those willing to listen.

Everything about that old tree was dead when I first saw it, except for its message to me. An immortal symbol of rugged persistence on our ranch, something that stood in majesty over the land long after it expired.

About a decade after I became state archaeologist, I was invited to participate in a symposium on ranching culture at the University of Wyoming. Our panel discussion lamented the disappearing agricultural landscape, an issue important to all citizens since so much of the American West is public domain. The subject had particular relevance to ranching families—their future identity and generational legacy in the nation's history were at stake.

When it was my turn to speak, I talked about growing up on the I Lazy D and offered my thoughts on the public perception of the real and mythical West. Myths are simply traditional stories whose characters and events have imaginary or unverifiable existence. People may believe them, but they are based on uncritical thinking rather than on objective inquiry. They can become hopelessly intertwined with reality, often leading to an ambiguous picture of history and shaping public opinion.

"Take the legendary frontiersman Kit Carson," I said. "He set out to rescue a white woman captured by the Jicarilla Apaches in 1849. His search party caught up with the Indians too late to save the woman, but during his reconnaissance of the abandoned camp, he discovered a book he described as the first of its kind he had ever seen."

The book had been written about Kit Carson himself, most likely *Kit Carson: The Prince of the Gold Hunters*, written by Charles Averill and published that same year in Boston. Kit was portrayed on its pages as a great hero, a slayer of hundreds of Indians.

Carson bemoaned his failure to live up to his fictionalized reputation, so the legendary Carson began to dictate the behavior of the real Carson. These two disparate forces nurtured the myth created by an actual participant living in the West and the author and urban publisher living in the East. Their mutual influence on fact and fantasy intertwined into a convoluted legend that survives today.

"Western residents have long been criticized for perpetuating their own mythmaking," I said. "But the external forces that help conjure up those myths, like that Bostonian publishing house, have been ignored in the discourse for too long, and they can reach tens of thousands of curious souls."

External forces are present today in even greater magnitude than before. The nation's public continues to mold mythical images of the

West to suit their expectations, perpetuated more often by the art and entertainment industries than by direct personal observation.

Our family practiced quality ranch management for over a century, under the illusion of actual family ownership for half that time. But we were still lucky. My ancestors had built Miller Estate Company into a strong livestock operation, even though market vicissitudes created anxiety in some of our urban corporate owners who didn't participate in the day-to-day ranching operations.

We were not alone. More and more family ranches have been sold to faceless companies or anonymous financiers over the years, or they've been restructured into enterprises unfamiliar to those families who once worked them. Some family ranches have come full circle in the twentieth-century American West. Just as in the late nineteenth century, many Westerners today have placed too much of our agricultural legacy into the hands of absentee owners, people who never rode behind livestock or got bloody at branding time.

The time is largely past when two old ranchers could happily seal business deals with a handshake. Their mutual grip conjoined the blood, sweat, and tears of a shared rural life, and it's a trait nearly impossible to find today. You had to live the life they lived to truly understand that durable bond.

I realized when I spoke at the university that these changes in family ranch culture had burdened my soul for a very long time. My own rural heritage was slowly fading away in front of my eyes. And when too many family ranches are gone, only their artifacts will remain.

28.

Bloodline

In the years following our exit from the I Lazy D, I occasionally woke up in the dark, beads of sweat dripping from my brow, my pillow soaked. The nightmare never varied—I was still working at the ranch, but Mom and Dad were gone.

I would call them the next morning to check in. Mom always answered instead of Dad. She loved hearing from family members no matter what the circumstances. Her oxygen machine hummed in the background, processing the air she needed to breathe, pulsing it through serpentine tubes that led to her nose.

"How are you and the old man doing? I was just thinking about you and decided to call."

"We're fine. How's Josh?"

"Great."

She never complained about the labored breathing caused by too many years of smoking, but she always wanted to know about her grandkids. Betty Rose loved her family. She had always been the glue that held us together. In her children and their kids, she saw the unbridled opportunities of youth, the promise of their success that further validated her own existence.

In January 1997, the call about her illness came not from my dream, but from Mom herself.

"I have a cancer," she said.

"We'll be right there."

Leona, Josh, and I hopped into the car and hurried over from our home in Laramie.

Mom's cancer had invaded several vital organs. Dad told her that Rod and I could take her to the hospital or she could stay at home with all of us to watch over her. She decided to check in at United Medical Center for closer observation and then quickly deteriorated once she arrived.

I visited her room one morning when she was so weak she could barely keep her eyes open.

"Use this," a nurse told her, handing Mom an inhaler.

I took it from the nurse and placed it between Mom's cracked and peeling lips. "Breathe."

"It hurts too much."

"Do it anyway."

I pressed the aperture against her mouth and made her squeeze the instrument to force air into her lungs just to keep her alive.

She regained a little strength when one of her friends from Cheyenne walked in. Mom mumbled an introduction and told the friend my name. "Mark's getting a book published," she said.

I recently had some historical research accepted by a university press and hoped the book would be released while Mom was alive. But her exhausted body couldn't keep fighting. In four short days after admission, she died. She was seventy-two.

I called my cousin Bill to tell him and his sisters about Mom.

"The thing I remember about Betty Rose," Bill said, "is that she never forgot a birthday. She sent a card to Susan, Sandy, and me every year, long after we left the ranch."

Mom had spent her life knitting the fabric of family.

We held a service for her at St. Thomas Episcopal Church in Rawlins, the same church where my brother and I had served as acolytes decades earlier. He and I were asked to say a few words.

Rod mentioned the most recent lesson from Mom, that of courage under adversity coupled with unflagging generosity to family. I focused on how to navigate the correct path toward the purchase of a Boy Scout shirt and what Mom's lesson taught me about how to approach other important destinations in life.

Afterward, we stayed for a while talking to everyone.

"Hello, Mark."

"Rimrock! I never expected to see you again. Thanks for coming."

Lonnie Fisher had been a young teenager when he first worked on the ranch. He lived on the place for several years in the 1970s and 1980s, growing up as a hired hand. At the beginning, he often rode his horse on top of the highest ridge, poking along in sight of everyone else down below. He spent so much time on the skyline, we took to calling him Rimrock.

Rim grew into a top hand and was the only man to stay on at the ranch when my family left. We lost touch with him after that.

"Your mom and dad helped raise me," he said. "I owe them for that."

An hour later, we buried Mom's ashes in the town cemetery.

"Betty Rose never hurt anyone," Dad said over her grave. They had been married for forty-seven years, so he ought to know. "The husband is supposed to die first."

Years before Mom's death, she and Dad developed a routine of working newspaper crosswords printed in the *Wyoming Tribune Eagle* and the *Casper Star-Tribune*. Mom chose the *Eagle* puzzle, easiest to complete, while Dad worked the other. After she died, Dad worked both puzzles every morning, as if Mom were still sitting there.

"Crosswords stimulate my brain. Intellectual exercise," he told me one day when I was in Cheyenne for a visit.

After studying the next clue, he scribbled letters in small boxes with cramped penmanship caused by the grip of ruler-slapped fingers—a grade-school teacher's solution for his being left-handed. He laid down the pencil to flex his bony knuckles and rotate a stiffening wrist. Six squares were filled in: F-O-R-E-S-T.

Reaching across the puzzle, he scratched an itch on his sleeve-less right arm that rested on a miniature wool fleece spread out on the kitchen table. Soft morning sun shimmered through the window and washed over the white fabric, turning the wool golden. At seventy-seven, Frank had been away from the ranch for over twelve years. Now, his blue-collar body sat in the same chair every day of his life, the place he and I collaborated at times on difficult puzzles.

Dad tapped his newspaper. He glanced toward me through eyes that shone with fire fueled by the stockman's life he had led, eyes that glistened like his father's.

"How far can you walk into a forest, Mark?" He liked to challenge my brain during every conversation.

"I don't know." I was never sure how to answer his questions.

"Halfway, because once you reach the middle, you're beginning to walk out." He smiled and then read the next clue.

Not unlike the path each one of us walks through life.

Dad kept the same apartment after Mom died, working crossword puzzles and cryptograms and looking forward most evenings to a hot supper of Safeway tamales. He planted two boxes full of "pitiful petunias" in the spring, nurturing the full blossoms, culling bad stems, and watching the healthy plants grow.

He even dated twice but made a rookie mistake. He first went out to dinner with the woman living in the apartment above him, and a week later, he ate at a restaurant with his neighbor across the street. When he brought the second date back, the first one came out of her apartment upstairs and stood on the front porch staring at them.

"She saw us get out of the car, and I know they're friends. I doubt either one will go out with me again." Dad laughed.

We celebrated his seventy-ninth birthday in October 1998. By then, he was wearing his own oxygen hose, suffering from bronchitis aggravated by decades of smoking.

Although he quit smoking cold-turkey seventeen years earlier, cigarettes had already caused irreversible damage. Old age and illness tightened his joints, so he didn't go out anymore. His driver's license was about to expire, and when I asked him about it, he said he'd decided not to renew it. "I hardly drive. I don't want to be behind the wheel if I start to cough."

I thought back twenty years earlier when Dad got ticketed by a patrolman for letting his license lapse. "Let's renew it anyway. You never know when you might have to drive somewhere."

Dad finally agreed, and I took him downtown. He walked beside me into the license bureau with his portable oxygen tank strapped over his shoulder. After we explained our situation to the clerk at the counter, he led Dad and me to the visual exam station.

"Look in here, Mr. Miller. Tell me if you can see the colored numbers separate from their backgrounds."

Dad leaned against the eyepiece for five seconds and then pulled back. "Yes, I can." He started walking away.

"No, no, Mr. Miller! I need you to read the numbers aloud."

Dad completed the exam and I drove him home. He never used the new license, but we both had fun with the clerk.

Dad's health deteriorated that winter. I learned later that he had told his best friend, my godfather, who had driven up from Arizona in the fall, "This will be the last time we're together."

Dad never complained, so Rod and I were unaware of the seriousness of his condition. We knew he was weaker, but the pain he hid behind his ubiquitous smile was invisible to others around him. Whenever we asked him how he was, he always grinned and said, "I'm fine. Old age is just a progressively debilitating disorder, but I am imperceptibly better every day."

Rod and I visited him regularly to grocery shop, clean his place, and watch football. Dad would sit in his rocking chair in the corner of the living room, tethered to the oxygen machine by twenty feet of transparent hose draped over his ears and tucked under his nose.

His plastic lifeline slackened whenever he moved. He would take a loop in his hand when he walked to the kitchen, snapping his wrist to flip the line over the couch like he was dallying a rope around the snubbing post at the ranch.

The hose and oxygen machine anchored him, defined his movements, and limited the size of his world. If you wanted to find Dad when you visited, all you had to do was grab the hose and follow it through the apartment. He'd be at the other end of the line. A man who had grown up on a ranch of two hundred and fifty square miles now lived in the confines of six hundred square feet.

As state archaeologist, I attended many staff meetings in Cheyenne and often spent the night with Dad. One morning I came into the kitchen and he was brewing the coffee.

"Here's ten bucks," he said. "Why don't you drive to McDonald's and get some sausage and egg biscuits? Not muffins. I like the biscuits."

I returned with breakfast, surprised not to see newspapers next to Dad's coffee cup. "Where are your crossword puzzles?"

He shrugged. "I don't do them anymore." His eyes half closed.

I realized he was walking near the end of his forest. "You're the greatest father a guy could ever have. I love you, Dad."

Tears poured down my checks, the only time I remember crying in front of him. My body trembled when I leaned over toward him. His weathered hands grabbed mine and squeezed with diminishing strength.

"You're quite a son, Mark." His way of saying he felt the same.

By May 1999, Dad could no longer function independently. Rod and I called his doctor for an appointment, knowing full well Dad wanted to die quietly at home in his rocking chair, probably with his boots on. But when Rod and I were unable to care for him, our only recourse was to seek help from those better equipped.

We pulled into a parking lot and assisted Dad out of the car. He slowly straightened up and turned his head to see the doctor's office behind us. "I can't go in there," he said.

"Sure, you can," Rod said.

"I'll get a wheelchair," I said.

Dad stared at us with a laser-like gaze that burned through my face to the nape of my neck. His blue-hazel eyes, undimmed by the passing years, carried a single message to his offspring: *You two damn well better know what you're doing.*

His feeble body rocked back and forth when he bent toward the armrests on the wheelchair. I helped him sit down, hoping we had made the right choice. The doctor saw Dad briefly and then sent him to the hospital for his first visit since blood poisoning in his foot more than forty years earlier.

He was admitted about three in the afternoon on May 11 by an attractive young nurse who came to his room to prepare him for bed. She fussed with a tray full of bottles and a clipboard, laying them on the heat register. "We'll have to put you in this gown, Frank. I need to remove your pants."

"Fine," Dad said with a smile, reaching for her waist, "as long as I can take yours off too."

Doctors and nurses poked and prodded him with a dozen different needles, injecting chemicals, extracting blood. They salved his feet. They bent his fingers. They listened to his heart. Then they told us he had cancer.

Dad nearly froze the first night in his room. The single blanket they had given him was paper-thin, and the heater next to his bed never turned on, so I complained to the orderly the next morning.

His second night, a nurse brought him an extra blanket, but this time, the heater blew stifling hot air over his frail body. Oblivious to any discomfort, Dad lit up when I arrived to feed him the beef and potatoes they had brought him for supper.

"Hi, Mark," he said.

How could he recognize me from across the room through eyes now glazed over from so many drugs? He pulled the blankets up under his chin, holding their edges tight with both hands against the front of his unshaven neck. The skin around his white knuckles drew taut like the hide on a half-starved steer. He looked at me with his familiar grin.

I sat beside him and cut the roast beef on his plate into small pieces. Dad had cautioned me all my life, "Take small bites and eat slowly. Chew at least thirty-two times before you swallow."

I stabbed the first piece of beef with the hospital fork and placed it in his mouth, counting each movement of his jaw when he chewed. Then I gave him a spoonful of potatoes, followed by another piece of meat. He lay back exhausted before we made it halfway through the meal.

The man who had fed me on occasion when I was a baby couldn't lift his own fork. I raised another small slice of beef, barely touching his lips.

"No more," he said.

I put the fork down and moved the tray away from him to let him rest. "I'll see you tomorrow," I whispered in his ear.

He died in his sleep early the next morning, only thirty-six hours after admission. Rod and I went to the hospital to view his body. His watch, still buckled around his wrist, ticked off the minutes of time while we stood there. Dad's oxygen hose hung from a nearby hook, now abandoned.

The last family member who ever managed Miller Estate Company was gone.

29.

Carrying On

The day after Dad died, Uncle George and I drove out to the I Lazy D to gather a cupful of dirt from the big winter pasture. We continued on to the Sparks ranch in Colorado where Mom grew up and did the same there. I planned to bury the two urns containing Mom's and Dad's ashes beside each other in a single plot in Rawlins, after mixing the cups of ranch dirt together to form a base where their ashes would lie.

Out at the ranch that day, George and I noticed a dead cow lying on the side of the road, but we didn't have time to check it out. A few days later, back in Rawlins with George for Dad's funeral, we were eating breakfast with a couple of old friends. We all reminisced about Dad, our years on the ranch, and getting the cupful of dirt from the pasture.

"We saw that cow the day she died," one of my friends said.

"What happened?" I asked.

"We think she was shot. We checked her body with a metal detector. A loud beep sounded when we passed over her side. Probably a bullet in there."

"People hit cows with their cars all the time, but they seldom shoot them."

"We found a second cow across the county road from the first, where the turnoff heads to the old HO homestead. She'd been shot too."

They described the second cow as a wounded animal with a hungry young calf standing nearby. The cow lay on the ground, wheezing for air. Bubbles popped from her nostrils whenever she breathed, and her tongue lapped dirt from around her.

Her calf wanted to suck, but Mom no longer produced milk, and what remained in her udder had soured. The cow kicked at the sky each time she tried to rise, but her internal injuries were too severe. She lay back down, exhausted and dying of thirst.

"We contacted the ranch, and one of the cowboys came by. He left to get a rope so he could catch the calf before the cow died. We waited for hours, but he never showed up, so we went home. Then we came back out the next day."

During their second trip, my friends noticed that the calf had wandered away on his own, but the cow still lay in the same spot barely alive. Her hooves had dug deep furrows in the ground after days of trying to stand. The bubbles in her nose were flat now, and flies had arrived.

"Dad wouldn't have let an animal suffer like that," I said. "How can people be so heartless? If I had heard about it, I'd have driven out there and killed the cow myself."

"That's what we thought, so we got a hold of the sheriff. A deputy came out and shot her."

"You did the right thing." With his parent dead, that calf better know how to make it on his own.

After Dad's funeral service, I drove to Cheyenne to clean his apartment on Western Hills Boulevard. When I entered, the creak of unoiled hinges echoed through the empty home. I collapsed on the cushion of Dad's easy chair in a fit of unsettled emotion. My mind wandered back to that calf, roaming the winter pasture all alone. What would I do now with my mother and father gone?

The hollow silence of vacant space throbbed in my ears. My eyes darted around the empty living room, inert and shadowed, before settling on the end table next to Dad's chair, the one with a single drawer.

He always stored everything he needed in there—his crossword puzzle dictionary, half a dozen rubber balls to exercise his grip, his favorite foam rubber Bronco Brick to throw at the television when Denver missed a touchdown, and extra hoses for oxygen. The last time I opened it, about two weeks before he died, several days of unread mail was stuffed inside. Dad had packed it with the artifacts he needed for his daily routine. Rod and I called it his junk drawer.

I looked over at the end table, but indolence pressed me deeper into the chair. If I didn't move soon, I never would. Forcing myself to my feet, I reached for the junk drawer to begin cleaning there. It slid open, and I gasped, my eyes filling with tears.

Dad had removed everything except for two new objects: a small metal card stamped with his Social Security number and the World War II dog tags he had worn in the New Guinea jungle more than fifty years earlier. They were the only items required to process his veteran's life insurance policy, which he told me would cover his funeral expenses during one of our many conversations over crossword puzzles.

Before Rod and I even knew he was sick, Dad had converted his collection of artifacts useful in life to the first two objects I would need after his death. He never told us he had rearranged the drawer, never told us he was preparing to die. But this was exactly the type of thing he would do on his own without asking anyone for help.

Whenever Dad had something important to do, he did it, no matter how unpleasant it seemed. He died the same way, with stoic dignity.

I rubbed a metal dog tag between my fingers and felt the hole perforated for a neck chain. The opposite edge of the tag was grooved in one spot, and the flat surface had been stamped with Dad's name, his father's name, and the address of Dad's childhood home in Rawlins—the place his parents had waited for him to return from the war.

The whole family must have been anxious to see one another in

1945 after four years of ruthless fighting. There would be so much to talk about, so many things to do together, and old memories to recall.

I held Dad's last oxygen hose in my hands after I finished cleaning his apartment. The plastic was curled, lifeless, and cold. No air passed through any longer.

The shape reminded me of the way our ropes hung when tied to our saddles. I counted the plastic coils in my hand and then stretched the hose out and bent the nose piece into a loop like the end of a lasso.

How well had I really known Frank Miller? How much of him had molded into parts of me? His honor—I hoped I had inherited some of that. If I had, it took me decades to attain. Still, I doubt I managed it nearly as well as he did.

Rod was the stoic son. Josh had Dad's familiar smile. Mom and Dad were the resilient thread that bound our family tapestry together. How strong would that fabric be if it stretched too far from our roots? Would new winds tear through the weave and blow every fiber away?

As the surviving generation, Rod and I were now responsible for supporting the growth and development of our own offspring. But we lived in different places and moved many times. The backdrop of the ranch was no longer a teaching tool for Miller children.

I twirled Dad's hose, tossing the looped end down the hall of the empty apartment toward an imaginary horse circling in the round corral. For the first time in my life, I no longer had a secure place to tie off my end of the line.

30.

The Snubbing Post

The following summer, my high school friends met in Rawlins to celebrate our thirty-year class reunion. Cousin Bill and I decided to take a trip to the ranch before festivities began in town. We drove the same route Kirk had taken with us forty years earlier when he first told us the names his father had given to features on the landscape and bought us frosted root beers.

Bill and I reached the ranch yard and parked at the barn before walking over to the round corral where we had ridden so many Shetland ponies in the past. The snubbing post Dad had set in the middle of the corral in 1935 was gone.

"We weren't using it anymore," the manager's wife told us. "They wanted to throw it away, but I talked my husband into storing it in the barn. Thought I might set it in the front yard."

They had removed it within months after Dad died. The ground was smooth where it had stood and the dust settled.

"Why don't you keep it, Mark?" she said. "Better for your family to have it. It's in back of the barn past the stalls."

Bill and I walked through the old door under those ancient timbers harvested from the Freezeout Mountains and over to the rear pens where we often played as kids in the cool shade. The snubbing post lay on packed earth, resting after sixty-five years of service to the

I Lazy D, nearly the same age as Dad when we left the ranch. The post was cracked from old age, and a nail had been hammered into the wood where a nail shouldn't have been. When I was a boy, I often marveled at the significance of that post, a symbol of connection to the ranch, but now it lay like a corpse waiting for burial.

I noticed the familiar hole drilled clear through it that I had played with decades before. I would peer through it as a child and see in the near distance the dark horizontal poles forming the far interior side of the round corral. It reminded me of the viewing stations at historic sites where a visitor could look through an aperture pointed to a place on the landscape where some significant event had occurred.

"It's heavy," I said when Bill and I carried the post to the truck.

We finished touring the ranch and drove back to town for two days of reunion activities. The following week, I took the snubbing post to my home in Laramie.

Staring at it one morning, I remembered its significance in my youth, how it had helped tame young horses new to the ranch. Now, it endured as an inanimate piece of wood—no mystical powers surrounded it.

Artifacts and landscapes are deceptive. Neither the post nor the ranch itself had ever truly been the immutable core of my West. Each had been important to me at the time, but their significance drifted away over the long years of my absence.

No wrangler's rope wrapped around a piece of hard wood could ever match the tensile strength of my bloodline. The real snubbing post in my life always had been my family.

A couple of weeks later, I visited my brother at his new home on the Cañoncita Ranch in the Texas Panhandle. Guests were arriving for a house party just as Rod and I finished a horseback ride in Palo Duro Canyon, an unfamiliar landscape seven hundred miles from the ranch where he and I had grown up together.

An hour after dark and well into the festivities, I realized we had forgotten to take the horses and mule back to their pasture at the edge of the Llano Estacado, two miles away. Rod was busy entertaining our guests, so I offered to finish the job. I tightened the cinch on Big Bill, wrapped Eleven's reins around my saddle horn, and herded Preacher the mule toward the barn at the far edge of the property. I smiled, wrangling again, but this time in slow motion.

Preacher led the way, feeling his path with each step toward the pasture hidden out there in the dark. We followed a dim trail along the crumbly edge of rimrock beside the margin of the canyon. I was the visitor here, so I trusted navigation to the horses and mule who had lived in Texas their entire lives.

I hunkered down in my saddle as we walked between a three-hundred-foot cliff that disappeared straight down into the ravine on my right and the rest of Texas on my left, relieved to have such knowledgeable companions around me. I was reminded on that trip that the trails we take in life are less important than the travelers we ride with.

31.

Seduction of the Land

Early one evening in the new millennium, I went to bed at Uncle George's house in Rawlins, looking forward to a ranch trip the next morning to gather trunks of silver sagebrush. George fashioned sagebrush branches into pen and pencil sets that were in great demand. I had recently joined a writing group in Laramie that took its name from silver sage, prompting us to see if that particular species was as useful as others for making his pens.

We stopped at the large sand dune opposite the turnoff to the ranch house, the same dune where Kirk and his grandkids once built a willow fort. The margins of that parabolic landscape supported the largest stand of silver sage I knew of on the ranch. Shrubs grew waist high, anchoring portions of the stabilized dune wing against the wind. That day, a thin skiff of snow blanketed everything but the long leaves of silver sage around us. The dune surface shone smooth and white.

George needed a dense piece of sage to lathe into suitable pen parts, so we cut three different trunks to take back to town. He pulled on one large bush while I sawed through its base—measuring twice and cutting once—trying to free a sixteen-inch length from the dune. The wood snapped with a loud crack, and we stood to stretch muscles that had tightened in our backs.

Warm sun reflected off the snow, and the bright blue sky glistened with tiny ice crystals that danced in the air around us. No sound came from anywhere in the valley. Not even a breath of wind snuck through the brush. We stood there savoring the pure silence that only rural landscapes achieve. I loved the peace it always brought me.

Just then, a northern goshawk soared overhead, hunting for mice on top of the dune. A shrill wail shattered the quiet as the hawk glided past the slope where we stood. It swooped below the crest, rose again seconds later, flying into the clear sky over Indian Creek with a field mouse in its claws.

George and I stared at the scene. We had often witnessed that thin margin between life and death that exists in the country.

I grabbed the last of the sage. "Let's go to the Square Shooters for lunch."

Uncle George drove up ID Ridge, passing the nose of Firecracker Hill. When we got to town, we picked a table by the window just as a diesel truck roared past the diner. The constant hum of town life shook pictures nailed to the wall. A phone rang as we placed our order, and an armload of dishes crashed to the floor in the kitchen.

Three conversations interrupted each other at tables around us, the decibels rising as the lunch hour stretched past noon. Forced-air heat triggered an overworked fan whose mechanical rattle drowned most of the voices. Then a timer dinged on some hidden microwave just as silverware collided in the sink. A young girl crinkled a paper bag when she opened it for a meal ordered to go.

"He's a millionaire, ya know? I don't want to give him any more," I heard from an anonymous female behind me.

The man next to her said, "I want a chili burger . . ."

The end of his order was smothered by the sound of the lady at the counter ringing the cash register and telling someone else, "It comes to $2.99."

"Hi, guys," the owner smiled when she saw the most recent arrivals.

George and I grinned at each other after lunch, walking through those fragmented conversations toward the register to pay our tab.

Rawlins was a small town, but still much more densely populated than the sand dune under that hawk. My senses, so keenly tuned to the silence in the sage, had become disjointed by the incoherent pandemonium.

I had often asked Dad questions about ranching operations when he managed the I Lazy D, thinking his answers would help me become a better rancher too.

"When's the best week to begin haying? How do you know where to build a fence?"

He answered the same every time, regardless of the query. "You can't plan too far ahead. Do what nature lets you. Be flexible." Dad never tried to control nature, only to manage our careful participation in it.

Patterns in ranching behavior were more nuanced than I had expected. It was impossible to teach people this profession using textbooks and lectures. Dad had had to learn his trade by walking a lifetime in the boots of a stockman.

He learned to feel the earth for its moisture, smell rain before it arrived, and see plants interact as they grew. He would bite the grass to taste its freshness each spring. I even believed he could hear the heartbeat of well-managed range. If he had been with Uncle George and me cutting silver sage that morning, he would have heard the mouse grabbed by the hawk before I even saw it.

The din of another shapeless conversation rumbled above a throng of people gathered for the latest campus event during spring semester in Laramie. A new friend from my writing class stepped away from the rarefied edge of the crowd, almost floating to the far side of the room where she paused. She leaned forward and peered through the narrow window in the south wall of the atrium.

Sunlight invaded her hair until each fiber glistened and became incandescent. Her eyes sparkled in the soft rays when she stared into the sky and then grinned at whatever it was that she saw.

I often noticed her watching Wyoming this way, the pensive gaze of a curious onlooker, captivating me with her intimate curiosity. A southern woman, she had moved here twelve years earlier but still didn't feel an integral part of this place. An unsettled immigrant in a land of more permanent dwellers.

When she had broken away from the crowd, her eyes searched for some clue to let her know she belonged. Perhaps out there, beyond the wall, hid the reason she sought to call Wyoming her home.

Suddenly, the light through the window dimmed when a wandering strip of dark cloud blocked out part of the sun. My friend watched me approach, turning until her feminine profile reflected in the long glass pane at her side. The distance closed between us.

She smiled at me seductively and pointed to the cloud. "Mark, how would you describe that in your West?"

"Virga," I said.

She nodded.

Thin wisps of precipitation that drop from the sky in the spring but evaporate before reaching the ground. Moisture the western landscape needs to survive, though seldom seems to receive. Virga foreshadows new life then vanishes before expectations are met.

Standing next to my friend, I looked outside. "It's the rainfall that never lands."

"Of course." She looked past her reflection to the country she was trying to love. "It rains all the time where I come from."

I moved toward my seat in the small auditorium to await the upcoming event, though my mind remained at that window and the sunlit beauty of her intoxicating smile. Our conversation reminded me of a time when I was about thirty, almost the same age as my friend when she moved to Wyoming.

I was riding back to the ranch house on my brother's horse, a sorrel gelding named Bradley, after moving a few cattle into a pasture three miles from our barn. A dark cloud built in the sky and shaded out the sun. Its billowing shape expanded, as murky folds rolled with pent-up energy hidden in the deep recess of its core.

A distant rumble echoed around me, followed by an eerie silence.

The bottom of the opaque cloud thinned until a translucent sheet of gray fell away, as if the whole image had begun to melt.

Finally. We hadn't felt rain in a month.

Bradley walked directly beneath the distant blanket of mist coming down, his hooves landing with a hollow thud on the ground, kicking up ankle-high dust that peppered his fetlocks. Parched leaves of sage broke under his feet when he opened into a trot. I looked to the sky for the water we wanted, fooled by the short fingers of moisture above.

I untied my yellow slicker from the back of my saddle, hoping to need it this trip, and put it on without Bradley breaking his gait. A gray sheet of precipitation dripped in front of the blue sky and crept closer to the thirsty ground it hadn't touched in so long.

I pulled my ragged Stetson down over my ears and rode in that familiar, lonely space between rain and pasture, two strangers who are attracted to one another but too shy to connect.

Maybe they will meet this time . . . maybe today.

When moisture soaks into the ground, the rangeland transforms into a vivid world teeming with life. But neither the water nor the land can change things alone. Moisture filters through the earth to gather nutrients, collects in streams, and washes over rocks to purify itself before rising once more to the clouds.

Without this nourishment, the West can't survive. The country would languish, desiccate, and become a barren waste rather than the resilient landscape my family called home.

Virga rain was just like my new friend. They both needed to touch down and stay long enough to find nourishment in Wyoming. Would either of them be able to do that?

I had been riding that day in a semiarid pasture under the type of rain that can't finish what it starts, watching blades of brittle grass strain toward the sky. My horse and I were trapped in this limbo layer between two elements of the West that must unite to make it whole.

Powerless to change the course of nature, I removed my slicker and loped back to the barn, my hope vanished once more. The vapor of another broken promise disappeared when the rain never landed that day.

32.

Never Buy a Dead Horse

Dad has been gone for twenty-five years. Now, at seventy-two, I have spent more time away from the ranch than I ever spent on it. I didn't have the opportunity to raise Josh as a young cowboy out there as I had wanted, so I had to learn how to be a town father.

Today, my son amazes me with his intellect, integrity, and resolute compassion for all people, the latter trait clearly inherited from his grandmother. He is a successful senior manager for talent acquisition in a Fortune 300 company, operating out of Portland, Oregon. He and his wife have a wonderful home, great jobs, and a promising future.

Though some of my cousins still have Miller Estate Company shares, Josh is the only person with Miller for a last name who retains any stock in the ranch. He doesn't remember a thing about his short visits out there. One of my biggest personal regrets is that for the first time since 1881, a Miller parent has been unable to raise his son in the context of our livestock operation. I wish that burden had not fallen on my brother and me.

That is what I meant when I lectured on campus about the vanishing of traditional family ranching.

Even so, the seductive allure of the ranch landscape kept drawing me back for visits years after my parents passed away, and by then, it was my memories that haunted the mountains and valleys on the place. I reflected back on the obstacles I faced when I was ranching, smiled at feeding protein cake with Grandpa Kirk, frowned at losing that cow herd on Cheyenne Ridge, and bristled at the sight of countless rattlesnakes in the Haystacks.

I took Josh on a ranch tour when he was an adolescent, wanting to share my sacred landscape with him. Wind screamed though the Haystack canyons as we drove by, muting our conversation, blowing past our ruined windmills successive managers had abandoned.

Josh and I finished our trip at the remnants of Elephant Rock near Ice Cream's unmarked grave. A new county fence had been built through the middle of it, as if she had never lain there. The stone outcrop was soft and fragile now, more vulnerable than I remembered.

"What do you think of the I Lazy D? Pretty cool, huh?" I said as we got back into the pickup.

He turned on the radio and leaned back in his seat. "Yeah, it's neat. Can I have a piece of gum?"

Josh loved my folks, but he hadn't witnessed the interlace of four generations of Millers into this magical terrain. As time passed, Frank and Betty Rose's experiences continued to influence my own outlook on life, especially later when I served as the state archaeologist. Memories of their sharp instincts often helped guide me through important personal and professional decisions.

Shortly before I retired in 2014, a good friend from Cheyenne informed me that the legislature might adopt a bill giving my office access to millions of dollars to buy fossil specimens for display throughout Wyoming museums. Some advocates thought I should purchase certain fossils currently in the hands of private collectors, but I balked at the idea.

Amateur paleontologists had long searched Wyoming's sedimentary rocks for the ancient fossils they contained, and I understood their interest. But I disapproved of commercial collecting. Archaeologists had passed laws against such things in our field, and we worked with private landowners to protect archaeological sites on their property for the scientific value. The professional paleontological community had been working on similar, unfinished legislation in their own field.

"I'm an archaeologist, not a paleontologist. Talk with them," I told my friend. "We don't do dinosaurs."

"But one fossil is a prehistoric horse," he said.

He described a fully articulated skeleton the size of a large dog embedded in a gritty stone matrix someone had cut as a slab from the bedrock. The fossil was several million years old, and the asking price was three million dollars.

I argued against the purchase, pointing out that it would encourage profit seekers to recover valuable specimens without professional oversight. It was unfortunate that a scientific expedition hadn't found the skeleton instead and donated it to a public museum after their research.

Then I thought of Dad and the time he, Rod, and I had bought four head of saddle stock for the ranch. "I never paid more than eight hundred dollars for a horse in my life," I said. "If I paid three million for a dead one, my father would roll over in his grave."

Thankfully, the legislative bill didn't pass, and I retired without further incident.

A few summers ago, Rod and I drove out to the I Lazy D with our cousins Susan, Sandy, and Bill for a long overdue reunion of Kirk's grandkids, the first time in over fifty years we were together on the place. We visited several locations we had been with Grandpa Kirk in the early 1960s and took photos to compare then and now scenes.

All of us are much older, of course, and most of us have grandchildren of our own. We made our final stop that day at the salt lick campground on the saddle between Bradley Peak and the Seminoe Mountains, the same place Kirk took the five of us for the overnight camping trip more than half a century earlier.

The five old "grandkids" posed for a group photo ten feet beyond the small circle of fist-sized stones we had arranged back then for a campfire to warm our coffee and beanie-weanies. Those stones have long since cooled to the touch, and the windblown landscape has begun to consume them. They have joined countless other rangeland artifacts abandoned by previous inhabitants and scattered across the remote pastures of my youth.

The Miller family has become just one more layer in the long, cultural stratigraphy of the land, but there is a fitting epitaph to this story. While our footprints are buried in the dust of time, an eager, appreciative group of our state's residents inducted Frank E. Miller posthumously into the Wyoming Cowboy Hall of Fame in 2022, celebrating his lifetime service to the I Lazy D.

Dad's pristine HOF belt buckle hangs in my bedroom beneath the scratched ranch buckle he wore as manager. I sleep beneath those two priceless artifacts, even taking naps at midday. My hair is turning gray, at least what's left of it. I don't walk as quickly as I once did, and I would have a helluva time bucking seventy-pound hay bales onto a tractor-driven slip all day. I haven't ridden a horse in over twenty years.

As I look back, I'm filled with immense gratitude that my family chose to live on the ranch. They could have lived anywhere, but instead followed their passion of working the land that Ike Miller first fell in love with. Hidden within its ruggedly beautiful topography and pernicious weather lies the promise of durable family principles. Today, that sometimes paradise remains as much a part of me as the blood coursing through my veins.

Acknowledgments

I tried to be fair and judicious to the participants in this book, most of whom are long dead. All of them deserve to be remembered for their unique contribution to the I Lazy D. To everyone who rode for our brand, I am deeply grateful for your involvement in the fabric of my West. Any errors or omissions are my responsibility alone.

My brother, Rod, rode with me on countless ranching adventures. He graciously read early versions of my manuscript and suggested things to improve the clarity and imagery. His academic training in, and practical experience with, the English language greatly aided my storytelling. I trust him riding my back trail any day of the week.

Susan, Sandy, and Bill Shaffer are Rod's and my first cousins. We grew up together on the I Lazy D. They also experienced many of these events and remember them in their own way.

Uncle George Brox, Mom's brother-in-law, shared so many trips with me to the country I can't remember them all. George viewed rural Wyoming through the lens of a passionate sportsman, a keen naturalist, and a loving uncle. He passed away a few years ago, and I miss him beyond measure. He was one of my best friends.

Steve and his wife, Cindy Olson, lived at the ranch at the beginning of the new millennium. My gratitude to them for their warm hospitality and to Cindy for giving me the snubbing post Dad had set in the round corral when he was a teenager.

Andy Warren, Range Specialist with BLM, and Dr. Mike Smith, retired professor of Agriculture and Range Science at the University of Wyoming, graciously helped review my work on vegetation ecology. Andy did so decades before this manuscript was written, and Dr. Smith only recently. Both were active participants in the quest for accurate assessment of range condition in Carbon County.

Conversations with former I Lazy D cowboys helped me ensure greater accuracy in my recollections. Besides my brother and cousin Bill, Rob O'Connell, Dan Braig, Greg Brox, Gary Swanson, and Nels Spilski were particularly helpful. Thanks to you all.

Deb Davidson used to work at the wool warehouse in Rawlins, and she led me down memory lane about that operation. Thanks for the insights.

Dan Davidson of the Museum of Northwest Colorado in Craig shared his vast knowledge about Bob Meldrum. Dan is an excellent researcher, generous with his perspective, and passionate about Western history. He probably knows more about Meldrum than anyone else alive today.

I thank Alyson Hagy for her writing course, for her review of an early draft of the entire manuscript, and for more recent conversations about the writing craft.

I also appreciate the critiques of my fellow students back then. Alison Quaggin Harkin took the class with me and read the entire manuscript, offering keen insights. She is an excellent writer and a dear friend. RoseMarie London lectured once to our class about the publisher's perspective, a detailed presentation inspired by her New York City roots. Her acute interest in the West prompted me to take her out to the ranch for a quiet tour after the devastating World Trade Center attack shook us all to the bone. Her passion for writing helped inspire me to pursue the memoir path. Thanks, RoseMarie, for your comments on several of my stories, and for your enduring friendship.

About that same time, I joined RoseMarie's writing group called the

Silver Sagers. Other members included Chavawn Kelly, Jeffe Kennedy, Jonas Slonaker, Lynne Swearingen, and Julene Bair. We all viewed the rural West a bit differently, and the diverse comments I received from their readings of my work truly helped my portrayal of ranching.

Jody Berman, a professional editor in Boulder, Colorado, graciously reviewed my finished manuscript and offered valuable suggestions. She had helped me on an earlier project many years ago, and I was fortunate to collaborate with her then too. Jody is a gifted editor.

Sandra Jonas of Sandra Jonas Publishing exercised a yeoman's patience collaborating with an old cowboy trying to polish his memoir. Her professionalism shone throughout the process, giving me an excellent home for my story. She and Jill Tappert collaborated on the marketing plan for the book. Thanks to both.

My appreciation to the individuals who previewed the memoir and offered endorsements: C. J. Box, David Crow, Michael Gear and Kathleen O'Neal Gear, Candy Moulton, and Alyson Hagy.

Gratitude is also extended to Dalton Darnell and 310 Ranch Life for the cover photograph of Miller Estate Company's I Lazy D Ranch. Will Hudson, ranch manager in 2021, was particularly helpful in connecting us with the photographer.

I want to thank my son, Joshua, for being the man he has become. I regret he was unable to spend more time on the ranch while growing up, but maybe this memoir will convey to him how much the experience meant to me.

Barb, my partner since 2011, read multiple drafts of the manuscript, and tolerated my frequent frustrations while searching for the perfect word. She caught many grammatical errors, ambiguities, and overused similes. Her effort strengthened my story, but our personal relationship is my greatest reward.

Bibliography

Babcock, Charlotte. *Shot Down: Capital Crimes of Casper.* Glendo, WY: High Plains Press, 2000, 42–59.

Basso, Keith H. *Wisdom Sits in Places: Landscape and Language Among the Western Apache.* Albuquerque, NM: University of New Mexico Press, 1996.

Calef, Wesley. *Private Grazing and Public Lands: Studies of the Local Management of the Taylor Grazing Act.* Chicago: University of Chicago Press, 1960.

DuBois, Frank. Unpublished handwritten letter, November 22, 1982. Washington, DC: Office of the Secretary, United States Department of the Interior. On file with author, 1982.

Glenn, Don, and Everet Bainter. Unpublished typed letter to Dr. Fee Busby, University of Wyoming, Division of Range Management, February 1, 1983. Bureau of Land Management, District Office, Rawlins, United States Department of the Interior, 1983.

Gorzalka, Ann. *Wyoming Territorial Sheriffs.* Glendo, WY: High Plains Press, 1998.

King, Michael B. Movement and natural history of prairie rattlesnakes Crotalus viridis viridis, in Wyoming. Unpublished Master's Thesis, MS in Department of Zoology and Physiology, University of Wyoming, 1987.

Lukas, J. Anthony. *Big Trouble: A Murder in a Small Western Town Sets off a Struggle for the Soul of America*. New York: Simon & Schuster, 1997.

May, Herbert G., and Bruce M. Metzger, eds. *The Oxford Annotated Bible with the Apocrypha: Revised Standard Version*. New York: Oxford University Press, 1965.

Merewether, E. A. Geologic Map of the Wild Horse Mountain Quadrangle, Carbon County, Wyoming. Department of the Interior, United States Geological Survey, Washington, DC, 1971.

Meschter, Daniel Y. *Sweetwater Sunset: A History of the Lynching of James Averell and Ella Watson near Independence Rock Wyoming on July 20, 1889*. Wenatchee, WA: self-published, 1996.

Miller Estate Co. Minutes of the Board of Directors, August 10, 1983–November 9, 1983. Copy on file with the author.

Miller, Isaac C. Photocopy of handwritten manuscript, July 7, 1885, Rawlins, Wyoming. Submitted for publication to Bancroft Library, Wyoming Pioneers, Isaac C. Miller. Photographed for the University of Wyoming. In possession of the author.

Miller, Mark E., Rick Weathermon, and George W. Gill. "Investigating the Dune Murder in Carbon County Wyoming, circa 1880-1920." Paper presented at the 66th Annual Plains Anthropological Conference, October 1–4, 2008. Laramie, Wyoming.

Miller, Mark E. "Frank E. Miller in World War II New Guinea." *Annals of Wyoming*, 90 (3 and 4):43-51, 2018.

Miller, Mark E., and William E. Scoggin, eds. "Middle Plains Archaic Bison Hunting in South-Central Wyoming: Revisiting the Scoggin Site." *Plains Anthropologist*, Volume 62, Issue 244, Memoir 45, 2017.

Miller, Mark E. "Stock Raising and Winter Sheep Camps in South-Central Wyoming (1880–1957): An Ethnoarchaeological Example." *North American Archaeologist*, 39(1):51–77, 2018.

Mueller-Dombois, Dieter, and Heinz Ellenberg. *Aims and Methods of Vegetation Ecology*. New York: John Wiley & Sons, 1974.

Niland, John. *A History of Sheep Raising in the Great Divide Basin of Wyoming.* Cheyenne, WY: Lagumo Corp., 1994, 170.

Smith, Robert Leo. *Ecology and Field Biology.* Second Edition. New York, Harper & Row, Publishers, 1974.

Snokes, Arthur W., James R. Steidtman, and Sheila M. Roberts, eds. Geology of Wyoming: The Geological Survey of Wyoming, Memoir No. 5, Volume 1, 256–58. Laramie, WY: Wyoming State Geological Survey, 1993. Gary B. Glass, State Geologist.

Stoddart, Laurence A., Arthur D. Smith, and Thadis W. Box. *Range Management.* Third Edition. New York: McGraw-Hill, 1975.

Stubbendieck, J., Stephan L. Hatch, and Kathie J. Kjar. *North American Range Plants.* Second Edition. Lincoln, NE: University of Nebraska Press, 1982.

University of Wyoming. Cow-Calf Management Guide and Cattleman's Library. Cooperative Extension Service, Colorado, Idaho, Montana, Oregon, Utah, Washington, and Wyoming. Not Dated.

Watts, Peter. *A Dictionary of the Old West.* New York: Promontory Press, 1977.

White, Richard. *"It's Your Misfortune and None of My Own": A New History of the American West.* Norman, OK: University of Oklahoma Press, 1991, 616–17.

Wolf, James. R. *Guide to the Continental Divide Trail, Volume 3: Wyoming.* Washington, DC: Continental Divide Trail Society, 1980.

About the Author

Mark E. Miller spent his youth and early adulthood on a large ranching operation in Carbon County, Wyoming, started by his great-grandfather Isaac C. Miller in 1881. Mark lived around livestock for thirty-two years before he moved on to a full-time career in archaeology, receiving undergraduate and graduate degrees at the University of Wyoming and a PhD at the University of Colorado. He served as Wyoming State Archaeologist for three decades and today holds an adjunct professorship in the anthropology department at the University of Wyoming.

In 2003, Mark won a resident fellowship in the prestigious Ucross creative writing program located in northeastern Wyoming. He is the author of four books and monographs, as well as scores of scientific articles on the early history and prehistory of the state. His technical and creative works have appeared in the University Press of Colorado, University of South Dakota Press, University of Utah Press, High Plains Press, *Annals of Wyoming*, and the *Wyoming Archaeologist*, among others.

Mark lives along the Big Laramie River in Albany County, Wyoming.

Made in United States
Troutdale, OR
12/09/2024

26185581R10163